ARIS & PHILLIPS HISPANIC CLASSICS

LOPE DE VEGA

The Cleverest Girl in Madrid

La discreta enamorada

Translated by

Donald R. Larson

Edition, Notes and Introduction by

Donald R. Larson

and

Susan Paun de García

LIVERPOOL UNIVERSITY PRESS

First published 2022 by
Liverpool University Press
4 Cambridge Street
Liverpool
L69 7ZU

www.liverpooluniversitypress.co.uk

This paperback edition published 2024

British Library Cataloguing-in-Publication data
A British Library CIP record is available

ISBN 978-1-80085-597-7 (hardback)
ISBN 978-1-83553-712-1 (paperback)
eISBN 978-1-80085-553-3

Typeset by Tara Montane
Cover image: Photo courtesy of Anteayer Indumentaria (anteayer.es)

TABLE OF CONTENTS

ACKNOWLEDGEMENTS

It is a great pleasure to introduce this book by acknowledging the many contributions to it made by friends and colleagues in the profession, some of whom may be unaware of the nature and extent of their involvement. Given the impossibility of naming them all, we would nevertheless like to single out a few who played a particularly important role in the inception, construction, and development of the volume. In the sense that the book began with the writing of the translation of Lope's play, first mention should be given to the Association for Hispanic Classical Theater, whose annual meeting in El Paso in 2015 included a workshop on translation given by the masterful David Johnston. As explained in the Translator's Note included in the Introduction of this book, that workshop proved to be truly inspirational to the author of the translation of Lope's play found herein, who hastens to clarify that Professor Johnston has not as of this writing read *The Cleverest Girl in Madrid* and is thus in no way to be held responsible for any infelicities that it may contain. Support of a somewhat different nature came from the AHCT when in 2019 it saw fit to name *The Cleverest Girl* co-winner of the Franklin Smith translation prize.

Those who have read the translation and who made valuable suggestions for its improvement include Nena Couch, Don Dietz, Cathy Larson, Susan Paun de García, Paco Ramirez, Sharon Voros, and Jonathan Thacker. Professor Thacker is additionally to be given particular thanks for his interest in this bilingual edition from the beginning of its existence, and for his unwavering support during the various stages of its development. Obviously, in this context support does not mean approval of all the editorial decisions that went into the book's composition, nor agreement with all the opinions it expresses.

Instrumental in the translation's dissemination was a semi-public reading *cum* reception held in Cincinnati, Ohio in the summer of 2017. The happy event would not have happened without the creativity and exceptional organizational skills of Ted Wills, Gayle Linkletter, and Peggy Somoza. All are sincerely to be thanked.

Finally, we would like to express our gratitude to the exceptional staff at Liverpool University Press – notably Chloe Johnson, Tara Montane, and Patrick Brereton, who with unfailing competence, courtesy, and attentiveness saw this volume through the production process. We are profoundly in their debt.

DRL and SPG

INTRODUCTION

Life of Lope

Lope Félix de Vega Carpio, the author of *La discreta enamorada*, was born in Madrid toward the end of the year 1562.[1] Although he claimed in adulthood to have been descended from nobility, his family was actually quite ordinary. His father, Félix de Vega, was an embroiderer, and his mother, Francisca Fernández Flores, from what we can deduce, was a homemaker. Both parents were originally from the region of Santander in northern Spain, and had come to Madrid the year before Lope's birth in search of better opportunities at what was then the newly established home of the Spanish royal court.[2]

As a child, Lope was extraordinarily precocious. His friend and first biographer, Juan Pérez de Montalbán, asserted in his *Fama póstuma* of 1636 that he could read both Spanish and Latin by the time he was five, and he supposedly wrote his first full-length play when he was around twelve (Pedraza, *Lope de Vega* 28). As an adult he was equally prodigious. By the time of his death he had become one of the most prolific authors of all time, responsible for hundreds of plays, countless beautiful lyrical poems, and a great number of works in other genres. It is on these grounds, and perhaps as well for the incredible energy that he brought to all aspects of his life, that he became known to his contemporaries as *el monstruo de la naturaleza* [the prodigy of nature].[3]

Lope's early schooling was with the Jesuits in Madrid at what later

---

1   The actual date of Lope's birth is a matter of some dispute. See Pedraza Jiménez, *Lope de Vega*, pp. 25–26.

2   The most authoritative, complete biography of Lope is still that of Castro and Rennert. For a brief, reliable summary of the events of his life, see Pedraza Jiménez, *Lope de Vega*, pp. 23–56. And for a helpful overview of the sources currently available for a reconstruction or that life see the Introduction to Samson and Thacker.

3   Unless otherwise indicated, all translations into English in this Introduction are by the editors.

on became the Colegio Imperial. After completing his basic education there, he is understood to have enrolled at the close-by Universidad de Alcalá de Henares, where he apparently spent the next four years (1577–1581). It is not clear that he ever graduated, although in several writings he intimated that he did. He also maintained that he had participated in the military expedition sent by King Philip II of Spain in 1583 against Portuguese rebels on the island of Terceira in the Azores, then a property of the Spanish crown. Shortly after this he became involved in the first of a life-long series of romantic liaisons.

The object of his affection on this occasion was Elena Osorio. The daughter of the head of a theater company in Madrid, she was herself an actress. The affair was tempestuous from the beginning, and became heatedly acrimonious when Elena turned her attention to a rival suitor. The consequence of this rupture is that Lope composed and circulated scurrilous verses attacking Elena and her family. Lope denied authorship of the libelous pieces, but the evidence against him was strong, and in late 1587 he was arrested and hauled off to jail. While there, he was sentenced by the court to two years of banishment from the kingdom of Castile and an additional two years of banishment from the city of Madrid. Even that didn't stop his verbal onslaught, however, and before he could commence his punishment his sentence was increased to a total of eight years of banishment from Madrid.

After leaving Madrid, Lope was married by proxy to the first of his two wives, Doña Isabel de Urbina, a member of a distinguished Castilian family. The marriage took place in early May of 1588. Later that same month, Lope found himself in Lisbon, where he contracted to join the armada that was forming in preparation for an invasion of Philip's enemy, England. The disastrous fate of that mission is well known, but luckily for Lope the ship on which he had embarked seems never to have left the Portuguese-Spanish coast.

In 1589 Lope settled with Isabel in Valencia. The city was at that time the site of fervent theatrical activity into which Lope soon inserted himself with important consequences for his playwriting. Although Lope and his wife were happy in Valencia, and although while there he continued to write plays at considerable speed, he was anxious to return to his homeland. Thus, in 1590, his two years' banishment from Castile completed, if not his banishment from Madrid, Lope and Isabel moved to Toledo. It was there he met the Duke of Alba,[4] and two years later he entered the service of this great nobleman. In 1592, he and Isabel moved to Alba de Tormes, the location of the ducal court.

Once again, the two of them seem initially to have been happy in their new circumstances, but there were dark clouds on the horizon. First came the death of Antonia, the child they had conceived. Next came the death of Isabel herself, in the act of giving birth to their second daughter, Teodora. And shortly after, Teodora also died.

Deeply affected by these tragedies, and anxious to involve himself once again in the theatrical life of Madrid, Lope now began petitioning the court to reduce his sentence of banishment from the capital. In time Lope's endeavors were to prove successful, and in 1595 he once again took up residence in Madrid, which was to be his home for the rest of his life.

Over the next several years, Lope acquired several further aristocratic patrons, among them the Marquis of Malpica, the Marquis of Sarria, and, most consequentially, the Duke of Sessa. Never one to sit idly, he now divided his time between serving these distinguished benefactors and writing, primarily works for the theater, which at this point were earning him great fame, not to mention considerable sums of money. These materialized with greater and greater rapidity, as did relationships with a variety of women. In 1598 he married Juana de Guardo, the daughter of a wealthy wholesale butcher of Madrid. The marriage, which lasted until Juana's death in 1613, seems to have been primarily one of convenience, but nevertheless resulted in four children, not all of whom survived to adulthood. About the same time that he married Juana, or shortly thereafter, Lope met the beautiful actress Micaela de Luján, and promptly fell deeply in love. The affair lasted some ten years, and during that period she and Lope conceived four additional children, of whom one, Lope Félix, was to become a particular favorite of his father's.

---

4 Antonio Alvarez de Toledo y Beaumont, 5th Duke of Alba (1568–1639).

After Micaela, there were other mistresses and other illegitimate children. Among the former, whose names are remembered, is Jerónima de Burgos, like Micaela, an actress. It was during his affair with Jerónima that Lope began to experience pangs of guilt over the irregular life that he had been leading heretofore. Those feelings were exacerbated by his uneasiness over the fact that, in his position of secretary to the Duke of Sessa, he was being required to write love letters in the Duke's name to the women his patron was attempting to seduce, thus being reduced to the dishonorable role of go-between. Convinced eventually that his life needed amendment, a change, he believed, that would be ensured by entering the clergy, he undertook the necessary measures and was ordained a priest in 1614.

Lope's desire for conversion was undoubtedly sincere, for like many men of his time he was deeply religious, but as might be expected he found it difficult to mend his ways. Thus, almost immediately he embarked on a short-lived, but stormy, affair with still another actress, Lucía de Salcedo. Then, in 1616, he made the acquaintance of Marta de Nevares and began a loving relationship that was to last until the end of her life sixteen years later.

Marta was very different from the other women with whom Lope was involved. She was not an actress, and, in fact, had no relationship with the theater. Interested in all the arts, particularly literature, she served as the inspiration for some of Lope's best works in this period. Unhappily, the final years of Marta's life were very tragic. She went gradually blind, and then, to add to her misery, she began suffering bouts of debilitating madness. Growing weaker and weaker, she died in April of 1632.

Throughout all Marta's travails, Lope, in a way that we might not have anticipated, was constant in his support. At the same time, he also managed to continue working. His productivity slowed, but his powers remained undiminished, as shown by such works as the great dramatic tragedy *El castigo sin venganza* (1631), the genre-bending comedy *Las bizarrías de Belisa* (1634), and his prose masterpiece in dialogue, a fictionalized recounting of his affair with Elena Osorio, *La Dorotea* (1632). Unfortunately, his own final years were quite sad.

The daughter he had with Marta, Antonia Clara, abandoned him in 1634, to go off with a gentleman of the court. And in the same year, his beloved son Lope Félix died while on a military expedition to the island of Margarita in the Caribbean.

His own health by now seriously compromised, Lope lived for only one more year. His death came on the 27th of August, 1635. He was buried the next day in the church of San Sebastián in Madrid, and there was immediately a tremendous outpouring of grief that spread throughout the city and encompassed nine days of official obsequies. The aftermath of Lope's passing was thus of a piece with his life itself: wondrous, all-embracing, and deeply human.

Arte nuevo and the *Comedia nueva*
It is often said that Lope de Vega was the father of the *comedia nueva*, the highly original form of drama that emerged in Spain in the late sixteenth and early seventeenth centuries, and there is more than a degree of truth to the assertion. Without the example of Lope's plays, this new sort of *comedia* – the term in this context does not refer only to what we know as 'comedies', but is more generic, encompassing all plays of whatever type that adhere to a basic, established pattern – might never have existed, at least in the shape that it assumed. At the same time, it needs to be recognized that, in his role as progenitor, Lope was not creating in a vacuum. Like most playwrights, he was well acquainted with the works of many of his predecessors and contemporaries, and he absorbed from them those qualities and features that suited his purposes, discarded the rest, and molded the whole into an astonishing assembly of plays that appealed to members of the public, while at the same time often achieving great artistic distinction.

Exactly what were the influences upon Lope's drama has been a matter of some critical disagreement. He was manifestly aware of the works of the classical playwrights Plautus and Terence, and absorbed many of the conventions of their comedies into his own. It is also clear that he was very familiar with the performances given by the Italian theater companies that toured Spain in the last quarter of the sixteenth century, and that he allowed himself to be inspired by their energy and connection with the audience. Beyond such instances, however, and a few others, including Lope's indisputable indebtedness to Fernando de Rojas's great early Renaissance tragicomedy *La Celestina*, there is less scholarly consensus, in part because in many cases we cannot say with certainty that Lope actually knew the works and practices to which he was supposedly beholden. And in the case of plays by Lope's contemporaries, there is often an additional problem of chronology, centering on the matter of whether those pieces that bear a likeness to Lope's were composed earlier or later than his. In such circumstances, it would seem appropriate to exercise caution in identifying so-called 'sources'.[5]

That being said, there is a nexus that has been of particular interest to critics over the years, and it has to do with Lope and Valencia. As was pointed out earlier, after his service with the Armada Lope settled with his wife Isabel in that coastal city. Valencia was at the time a hotbed of theatrical activity that included a number of very good playwrights who later became well-known, among them Andrés Rey de Artieda (1544–1613), Cristóbal de Virués (1550–1609), Francisco Agustín Tárrega (*c*. 1554–1602), and Guillén de Castro (1569–1631). Over the years Lope evidently came to know many of these writers, and as it turns out, a number of their published works from the period strongly resemble some of his own early plays. It is unlikely that the correspondence was accidental, and thus the questions arise: who influenced whom; who was the teacher and who the disciples; who contributed what to the creation of the *comedia nueva*?[6]

Those aspects of Lope's output for which the critics have avidly sought antecedents and parallels, and which constitute the features by which the *comedia nueva* is known, are enumerated and characterized in his *Arte nuevo de hacer comedias en este tiempo* [New Art of Writing

---

5 For a discussion of possible sources of influence for *La discreta enamorada* see below in this Introduction.
6 On the Valencian playwrights, their relation to Lope, and their role in the creation of the *comedia nueva*, see Froldi and Weiger. Cf. Pedraza, *Lope de Vega*, p. 35.

Plays in These Times], a discourse in verse that was delivered to a literary academy of Madrid and published in 1609.[7] In this work Lope describes his theatrical practice, and defends it against the strictures of the critics of his day, who found it insufficiently 'classical'. The tone throughout fluctuates, wavering between the apologetic and the defiant, the serious and the ironic and playful. The basic intent seems to be two-fold; first, to demonstrate that Lope was well aware of the 'rules' of good dramaturgy that were advanced by his decriers, rules that were allegedly drawn from the *Poetics* of Aristotle, and that his recurrent deviation from them was purposeful; and second, to persuade his listeners and readers that his plays, and those of like-minded dramatists, were worthy of respect and esteem, and that, in fact, they represented a 'new art'.

In discussing relevant aspects of his dramatic corpus, Lope is careful not to present them as rigid counter-rules, but rather as recommendations to others looking for success on the stage. The ultimate arbiters of that success, he makes clear, are not the critics but the members of the audience. It is thus incumbent upon the aspiring playwright to take into account the tastes and the interests of the spectators. To secure the favorable judgment of this jury, what Lope calls the *vulgo*, he specifies a number of norms, some of which coincide with the dictates of the neo-Aristotelian critics, but many of which do not.

With regard to their form, Lope states that plays should consist of three acts, the first to introduce the action, the second to complicate it, and the third to resolve it, but not until the very end in order to maintain suspense. In accordance with Aristotle, he goes on to stress that the action ought to be 'unified', which is to say focused throughout the work on one story-line; if there is a secondary plot, it should in some fashion be related to the first. Lope also recommends that the time lapse of the play should be unified and cohesive in like manner, meaning that, insofar as possible, each of the three acts should have the span of one day or less. Flexibility in this regard, however, must be allowed for works of certain genres, particularly, Lope says,

---

7   On this important work, see, among a number of excellent studies, three in particular: Montesinos, Rozas, and the edition of García Santo-Tomás. Cf. Pedraza, *Lope de Vega*, pp. 270–71.

historical plays, which not infrequently display lapses of dozens, if not hundreds, of years. As for the third of the three so-called classical unities, unity of space, he seems to be less interested in that, although, as with time, he acknowledges that flexibility is necessary in plays based on history, legend, myth, and so on.

Plays of the *comedia nueva* are always written in polymetric verse, each work containing a variety of different meters. In general, dialogue is developed in eight-syllable or eleven-syllable lines – the maximum length that does not necessitate subdividing a line, and generally considered a length in tune with the natural musicality of the Spanish language. In the *Arte nuevo*, Lope discusses the matter in some detail, maintaining that specific verse forms should be employed in each scene or happening to reflect their particular nature. For reasons of esthetics and to indicate changes of emotion of the characters, playwrights used changes in the metric structure, which spectators of the time would have been able to recognize and would have understood when the action changed tone, cued by the poetic form.[8]

La discreta enamorada is written in verse forms that illustrate Lope's recommendations of what theater should be like in *Arte Nuevo de hacer comedias en este tiempo*:

> *Acomode los versos con prudencia*
> *a los sujetos de que va tratando.*
> *Las décimas son buenas para quejas;*
> *el soneto está bien en los que aguardan;*
> *las relaciones piden los romances,*
> *aunque en octavas lucen por extremo.*
> *Son los tercetos para cosas graves,*
> *y para las de amor, las redondillas.*

(lines 305–12)

> Tactfully suit your verse
> to the subjects being treated.
> *Décimas* are good for complaining;
> the sonnet is good for those who are waiting

---

8   For a metrical analysis of *La discreta enamorada* and explanations of the metrical forms used, see below in this Introduction.

in expectation; recitals of events ask for
romances, though they shine brilliantly in
octavas. Tercets are for grave affairs and
redondillas for affairs of love.

(Brewster 34–35)

Overall, Lope states, the language should generally not be convoluted and difficult to understand, but rather simple and straight-forward. He does allow for a certain amount of ambiguity, however, because it encourages the more intelligent members of the audience to pride themselves on their acuity. He also makes an exception for those occasions when characters adopt for dramatic purposes a more sententious manner of speaking.

On a related topic, Lope states that the register in which a character speaks ought to correlate to that character's station in life: kings should talk like kings, servants like servants and so on. Such correspondence should also be observed between the actions of the characters and their social roles. When present in a play, Lope argues, decorum of this sort functions to enhance the verisimilitude of the work, something that he says is expected by the public. Interestingly, although he maintains that decorous behavior is especially important for women characters, he countenances female to male cross-dressing from time to time because, he says, it is pleasing to the audience.

Verisimilitude is also the justification for the mixing of genres within an individual work, something that is not found in the majority of classical plays and that was anathema to the neo-classical critics. Thus in the *comedia nueva*, as in Shakespeare, comic scenes are often intercalated in works that are for the most part serious or even tragic, and scenes with dark, tragic overtones are frequently present in comedies. By the same token, characters representing very different walks of life are jostled together in the same work. Lope defends this blending on the grounds that it is both satisfying to the public and true to the world of nature, where 'variety' is of the essence. In this manner the stage holds up a mirror to reality.

Surprisingly, Lope has relatively little to say about subject matter in *the comedia nueva*. The best plots, he asserts, are those that have to do with honor, because they are the ones that have the most profound effect upon audiences. The nature of that effect is to inspire 'virtuous' actions, an observation that is doubtless unsettling to many contemporary readers and critics who have come to conceive of honor as a profoundly and exclusively negative value. Lope leaves no doubt, however, about what he means by virtuous. It is that honor, when properly put into practice, which is not always the case, rewards the good and punishes the bad. In doing so it functions as a basic system of justice.

Such, then, are the norms of successful playwriting as elucidated by Lope in the *Arte nuevo*. As we would expect, they reference defining features of his dramatic production. Those features are also characteristic of the vast majority of later Spanish seventeenth-century plays, which is to say that those plays were all in some degree modeled on his example. These are the works, along with Lope's and some of those of his immediate predecessors, that constitute the *comedia nueva*. Lope was not the single creator of that genre, but his contribution to its genesis was instrumental and decisive, and it constitutes an important part of his artistic legacy.

The Structure of Comedy

The plays presented on the stages of Spanish playhouses in the early part of the seventeenth century encompassed an astonishingly wide variety of dramatic categories. There were Biblical plays, theological plays, plays dealing with history, plays that relate the lives of saints, melodramas, tragedies, and several other types as well. Particularly prominent among these diverse kinds of theater were romantic comedies, the genre with which *La discreta enamorada* is associated, As Brian Corman has noted, such plays, sometimes called 'classical' comedies, have been a staple of theater-going for over two thousand years, giving them the distinction of constituting "the longest, most continuous generic tradition in Western literature" (3).

Romantic comedies have not only had a long and venerable life; they have also remained remarkably consistent in the happenings they dramatize, the character types they present, and even the jokes they tell. Their reliance on time-tested, conventional features, many of which descend from the Roman playwrights Plautus and Terence, who themselves borrowed freely from the so-called New Comedy of the earlier Greek dramatist Menander, has been seen by some critics as a weakness. The renowned British director, Peter Brook, has argued, on the contrary, that repetition is a strength: "The strongest comedy," he writes, "is rooted in archetypes, in mythology in basic recurrent situations; and inevitably it is deeply embedded in the social tradition" (70). To which we might add that a significant part of the interest that comedy has for many readers and spectators lies precisely in discovering how freshly and creatively authors can refashion the basic formulas they have inherited.

What the recurrent situations of romantic comedies construct is a love story. The plots of such stories display countless variations, but in their essence they are very much alike. Basically, they tell of the efforts of a young man – or as was frequent in the theater of Spain in the seventeenth century, a young woman[9] – to win the heart, and generally the hand as well, of that character's object of desire. In pursuance of that end, the young man or woman must overcome obstacles of some sort.

Some of these impediments are societal: for example, the demand that partners in love be of more or less equal means, standing, and age. Other blocks are personal: parental disapproval of the match, which exemplifies the proverbial generational conflict, is one; another is the threat posed by a rival who is vying for the attentions of the loved one. What is notable about *La discreta enamorada* is that the parents of Fenisa and Lucindo, the two young lovers, function as both kinds of blocking characters. They are, on one hand, typical disapproving elders, and on the other they are competitors to the romantic interest of each child. A triangle such as this, one in which the father is rival to the son for the love of the same woman, as is the case in Lope's play, has a particularly long theatrical history that stretches from the

---

9   On the brave, determined, intelligent, and sparky young women who so frequently serve as the protagonists of seventeenth century comedies, particularly those of Lope and Tirso de Molina, see, among others, Blue, *Spanish Comedy.*

Korianno of Pherecrates (known today only in fragments), to the *Casina* of Plautus, to Molière's *Miser*, and on to the present day. Such plays have been of particular interest to the critics, for they seem to suggest an intriguing psycho-sexual dynamic, a relationship that the Austrian psychiatrist, Ludwig Jekels, in his influential thoughts on comedy, has characterized as an inverted Oedipal situation.[10]

Whatever the nature or number of obstacles to be surmounted in a comedy, they must be overcome before the end of the play to allow the audience to experience the expected happy – or at least, suitable – dénouement. Fundamentally, then, comedies are, as Alexander Leggatt has noted, "'problem-solving' plays" (3). In most comedies the resolution of problems, the progress toward the happy ending, is accompanied by a good deal of laughter. That doesn't mean, of course, that the action is always risible or that the mood throughout is continuously light-hearted. As many critics have noted, works classified as comedies very frequently have in them moments of darkness, periods characterized by sadness, fear, hostility, and, not infrequently, cruelty. Thanks to both Sigmund Freud and Henri Bergson, we now recognize that even laughter often has a dark side, an aspect that is marked by impulses of antagonism and aggression. In romantic comedies, such as *La discreta enamorada*, those feelings, shared both by other plays and members of the audience, are more often than not directed toward the principal blocking characters.

As Northrop Frye and others have observed, the action of the typical classical comedy outlines a pattern comprised of three phases, or movements, centering on the relation of characters to their social context.[11] In the first of these, society is dominated by its senior members, who impose – or attempt to impose – a structure based on traditional values and beliefs. This phase is seen as stable and outwardly harmonious, but also harsh, stifling, and oppressive, and the mood it conjures up is dark and bleak. The second phase represents an overturning of the previous one. Rules are disregarded,

---

10   See Jekels, 'On the Psychology of Comedy'.
11   See Frye, 'Mythos of Spring' and 'The Triumph of Time'. See also Segal, *Roman Laughter*, pp. 99–136.

order is replaced by disorder, and identities are unsettled and often misperceived. Here, the mood is open, but mystified and confusing. The third phase seems in some regards to signify a return to the first, for order and stability are restored, and society is once again functioning normally, as exemplified by the marriage of the young lovers. We feel that things are now as they should be, but we also sense that they are somehow different from what they were at the beginning.

The three movements of comedy sketched by Frye have much in common, as he and others have remarked, with the recognized phases of ancient seasonal festivals.[12] Such festivals traced a development from deprivation and sterility, through a period of transition marked by license and misrule, deceit and misunderstanding, to resolution in the rebirth of life and joy. What both comedy and seasonal rituals – from which some have argued it descends[13] – importantly share is a drive toward freedom and reframed identity, an urge that provides, in the words of the Austrian psychoanalyst Ernst Kris, a "holiday from the superego" (185).

The same drive, encompassing the same three phases, characterizes the Christian calendar which, although it inverts somewhat the order of the phases, culminates in a celebration of regeneration and renewal with the observance of Easter. Particularly relevant in this context is the Christian season of Carnival, a time when, as Mikhail Bakhtin has written at length,[14] imperatives are forgotten, conventions are flouted, hierarchy is shaken, insults and invective are exchanged, normal societal and gender roles are cast aside, copious amounts of

---

12   On ancient fertility rites and seasonal festivals, see *The Golden Bough*, the classic work of Sir James Fraser. For the relation of comedy to ancient seasonal festivals, see Segal, *Roman Laughter*, pp. 98–136; Barber; and Cornford.

13   See, in particular, Cornford.

14   See, among other pieces, 'Carnival and Carnivalesque' and *Rabelais and His World*. For the practices of Carnival in Spain, see, particularly, Caro Baroja and Gilmore, but also Ruiz, pp. 121–62. Whereas earlier theorists of Carnival tended to see it as ultimately solidifying the status quo by functioning as a 'safety valve' through which anti-authoritarian tendencies could be vented, several more recent writers, including Bristol and Burke, have regarded it as containing the potential for significant social subversion. Presumably, the question will continue to be debated.

food and drink are consumed, sex is winked at, and in general the world is turned upside down. Indeed, so widely recognized now are the parallels between Carnival and romantic comedy, and other forms of comedy as well, that it has become a critical commonplace to characterize the genre's basic nature as carnivalesque, providing a space where the liberties assumed by the characters are enjoyed vicariously by members of the public. The pleasure they derive, free from remorse and consequences, has been aptly characterized by Erich Segal as a kind of "orgy in the mind" (*Death* 9).

The Characters of Comedy

Like the conventional plots they accompany, the character types encountered in classical comedy have been remarkably enduring. Making their initial appearance in many cases in the Greek plays of Menander (*c.* 342–290 BCE), they were brought to new life in the later Latin comedies of Plautus (*c.* 254–184 BCE) and Terence (*c.* 195–150 BCE), from which they made their way to European Renaissance theater, and eventually to modern films and television sit-coms; there they remain to the present day, alive and kicking. Among the prototypes there are a number that over the years have been especially prominent. Pride of place in this cohort is the young man madly in love, the hero of the play, about whom we have already spoken. The object of the young man's desire is a young woman who may be of the same social group as the young man, or she may be of a lower class, which inevitably complicates the relationship. In Roman comedy often a *meretrix*, or prostitute, in later times the adored one, was elevated to the more decorous role of courtesan, as we see in *La discreta enamorada*.

Notable among the remaining stereotypical characters is the *senex durus*, or harsh old man; he is sometimes the father of the hero – as in *La discreta enamorada* – and sometimes the father of the young man's paramour. Whichever the case, his basic function is to oppose the relationship developing between the young lovers. His obstructing efforts are typically of no avail, however, because they are countered by the actions of the hero's sidekick, frequently called the *servus fallax*.

In ancient days often a slave, by the late Middle Ages the *servus*, as the term indicates, is a servant, recognized both for his loyalty and craftiness, and frequently his sharp wit as well, for which reason in Spanish Golden Age theater he is called the *gracioso*. Finally, in this enumeration of conventional characters, it is important to mention the *miles gloriosus*. Known in English as 'braggart soldier', he is often the hero's rival in love, and is typified by his windy and exaggerated recounting of his military exploits. Interestingly, in Lope's comedy he is enacted by the character who also takes the role of the *senex*, the Captain, which helps to explain the latter's frequent peremptory outbursts.[15]

That character types exploited in ancient Roman comedies should occupy an ever-increasing presence on the stages of early modern Spain is not difficult to explain. The plays of Plautus and Terence were read – and occasionally performed – in Latin, in Spanish universities from the early 1500s. Further familiarity with those comic archetypes was acquired when, in the mid-1500s, travelling troupes of entertainers from Italy began to perform in a number of European countries, primarily France, England, and Spain. In the latter, the most important of these itinerant companies was that of Alberto Naselli, known as Zan Ganassa, which toured extensively throughout Iberia in the late 1500s and early 1600s. Over time, it acquired huge popularity with both audiences and dramatists, and in the process exercised extraordinary influence over the development of Spanish theater in the late sixteenth century.

The shows that the company of Ganassa and other Italian troupes presented in Spain were chiefly of the genre known as *Commedia dell'arte*, a mode of playing typified by improvisation upon basic situations, rather than adherence to fixed scripts, by a stress upon physicality in the action, by humor that inclined toward slap-stick, and perhaps most notably, by the fact that most of the characters appeared on stage in masks. The dramatic function of such masks

---

15   On the role of Roman models in the shaping of characterizations in the Spanish *comedia nueva* see Rothberg, 'Algo más sobre Plauto, Terencio, y Lope' and D'Antuono, 'Lope de Vega y la Commedia dell'arte'.

was to indicate to the audience the stock types that the actors wearing them represented, many of which were akin to the conventional roles of Roman comedy.

One of these types was Zanni, a character of the lower class, typically a servant, who was known for his coarseness, but also for his cleverness. Another type was Arlecchino, also a servant, but one who was characterized as being rather simple, and perpetually hungry. Spanish *graciosos*, including Hernando in *La discreta enamorada*, would seem to be an amalgam of these two stock figures. Still another character was Pantalone, a rich and cranky merchant of the *senex* sort, who imagined himself a great lover, and thus did all he could to keep the young lovers apart. Rounding out this list of types was Il Capitano, the *miles gloriosus*, or braggart soldier, who was often said to be Spanish. As mentioned, we see him in *La discreta enamorada*, where he is amalgamated with the figure of Pantalone, who plays the role of *senex*.[16]

The *Comedia de capa y espada*
The romantic comedies that were particularly popular with audiences in Spain in the early modern period are those that are known as *comedias de capa y espada*, so called because of the manner in which their leading male characters were typically attired, which is to say with cloak and sword. The term was already in use in the seventeenth century, as shown by a characterization found in the *Theatro de los theatros* by the dramatist and theoretician Francisco Bances Candamo, composed in three versions between 1689 and 1694. Describing these comedies, Bances writes:

> *Las [comedias] de capa y espada son aquéllas cuios personages son sólo Caualleros particulares, como Don Juan, u Don Diego, etcétera, y los lances se reducen a duelos, a celos, a esconderse el galán, a taparse la Dama, y, en fin, a aquellos sucesos más caseros de un galanteo* (33).

> [Cloak and sword plays are those whose characters are individual gentlemen like Don Juan or Don Diego, etc., and the action typically has to do with duels, jealousy, a hero who conceals himself, a lady

---

16   On the Italian *commedia dell'arte* troupes that toured Spain in the second half of the 16th C and their influence upon Spanish drama see Arróniz and Shergold.

who covers her face; in short all those everyday events that make-up a courtship.]

As Bruce Wardropper has observed, Bances's definition, although brief and limited, does point to important elements of the genre ('Comedia española' 194–95). The plots of the plays, fast-moving and complicated, are packed with strong emotions and exciting and confusing events. As for the stories they tell, they have to do with courtship and love, and they spin their tales not with fabulous happenings and fantastical details as in some other comedies of the period, but in a way that is no-nonsense and familiar. With a little imagination, members of the audience could easily project themselves into the lives and adventures of the characters.

Fleshing out Bances's description of the *comedias de capa y espada*, it is reasonable to begin with the matter of their temporal and spatial settings. The location of the action varies: sometimes it is Spain, sometimes another country; sometimes a large city, sometimes a small town or village. As for the temporal span of *comedias de capa y espada*, it is typically about two days, sometimes a bit more, sometimes a bit less. According to the precepts of neo-classical theory, concision of this nature produced on stage a sense of verisimilitude, but as Ignacio Arellano has argued persuasively (*Convención y recepción* 37–69), in the case of *comedias de capa y espada* the effect was – and is – more likely the opposite: not an impression of realism, but one of amazement and wonder. More than anything, this feeling has to do with the nature of the stories told, narratives that are extraordinarily fast-moving, crammed with incidents and intrigues, twisting now this way and then that, constantly pressing ahead. How, we ask ourselves, is it possible for people to experience so many different happenings, so many contradictory emotions, in such a short period of time? The answer is, of course, they can't, but that doesn't impair our enjoyment of the presentation. What we take away afterward is the speed of the performance, the vitality and energy, the bustle and animation, the humor and the craziness. In short, for three hours or so, we have been swept away.

In their treatment of both their spatial and temporal settings, *comedias de capa y espada* tend to avoid sizeable jumps and gaps, displaying instead continuity and concentration. Their form is 'closed', to use the term favored by modern theorists, or 'united', to employ the expression found in earlier neo-classical criticism (Pfister 249–57). Plays are typically grounded in the specific topography of the place in which they are set, inducing in spectators in the playhouses a warm feeling of connectedness and belonging, a feeling heightened by multiple references in the plays to specific streets, plazas and paseos.

The comedia urbana

Constituting an identifiable subset of *comedias de capa y espada*, one that *La discreta enamorada* typifies, are those that Jesús Gómez (25) and others have denominated *comedias urbanas*. Works of this group are heirs to the tradition of earlier, pre-Lope theater, such as the plays of Torres Naharro and others, derived ultimately from *La Celestina*. Unlike the plays of a related genre called *comedias palatinas*, which characteristically transpire in a romanticized past and aristocratic ambience, *comedias urbanas* unfold their action in the present moment and in an upper-middle class environment. The location of their action, as their name indicates, is a recognized metropolitan area. Some works are placed in Seville; others in Valencia, or Toledo. By far the most favored space, however, is Madrid, the city in which many of these plays had their first performances.

La discreta enamorada has much in common with earlier *comedias urbanas*, in that it is set in contemporary Madrid, populated by non-noble characters, with a plot centering on a love intrigue that is not promiscuous, venal, or pecuniary. In such plays, as Bruce Wardropper has written:

> The hero and the heroine are a gentleman and a lady of the gentry class, who are spasmodically in love with one another, although at times they may think themselves to be in love with someone else. At any given moment one member of this couple is sure that they "are meant for each other," and so is consumed by jealousy whenever the other meanders from the straight path of their "true love". So sure is this temporarily jilted lady or gentleman of the predestined nature of their love that he

(or she) schemes ruthlessly to re-entrap the errant partner. Since their love is predestined – Lope regards love as a "correspondence of stars" – events bring the lovers to see the error of allowing their affections to wander. They are eventually reunited forever in their love (and, coincidentally, in marriage).

'Urban Comedy' 49–50

Another essential characteristic of *comedias urbanas*, namely a parallel "contrived amorous relationship" between the servants of the lady and the gentleman, "predestined not by the stars but by their servitude to a master and a mistress, and by a seldom-broken law governing Lope's paradigm" (50), is notably lacking in *La discreta enamorada*, but other plot complications characteristic of the genre noted by Wardropper are indeed present: "Flirtation poses as true love; a duel or a street brawl threatens to eliminate the hero; role-change or transvestism creates misunderstandings; the already prevalent jealousy is compounded by acts deliberately calculated to make one partner or the other more jealous" (50).

Themes
With regard to the themes of the *comedias de capa y espada*, there is general agreement that there are two that stand above all others. They are, first, love, and the sub-themes that characteristically accompany it: jealousy, deception, role-playing, marriage, and so on; and second, honor.

Love
Love is the primal force in *comedias de capa y espada*. It is the motivation behind the actions of virtually all the characters of the various works. However, this force is subordinated to beliefs and institutions that sustain the social and institutional order of the time. Essentially, true love always leads to the social stability maintained by marriage, and the plays usually end in one or more marriages to restore the order that has been disturbed.

Tellingly, love in these works characteristically strikes each of the young lovers with great rapidity, as suddenly as a bolt from the sky, or as the poets had it, an arrow from Cupid's bow. Sometimes love is triggered by what the lover has read or heard. Most often, however, it stems from what has been seen, as seems to be the case with Fenisa's love for Lucindo in *La discreta enamorada* (see below). Hence the stress in this work, and in innumerable others, upon beauty and physical attractiveness. At the same time, love is often said to be blind, in the sense that it cannot be rationalized or explained. It is sometimes equated with madness, and frequently compared to sickness and fire. Once kindled, it is irresistible; it easily overpowers the force of the will, and demands to be fulfilled. The gratification sought undeniably includes physical pleasure, but the ultimate objective, as in the majority of romantic comedies, is betrothal and conjugal union.[17]

In their single-minded pursuit of their desire, the young lovers very often resort to actions that can be considered amoral, if not immoral. Frequently these efforts are undertaken to thwart the marital plans held out for them by their parents. What the latter typically wish for their children is a match that offers social or economic benefits to the family, and to achieve their wishes they are prepared to exert considerable pressure. What the romantic protagonists want, on the other hand, is the liberty to marry the person of their own choice, and the freedom to enjoy their youth and beauty. Thus, their lapses into deceit, trickery, and misrepresentation. These deeds are not condoned in the plays in which they are displayed, but they are forgiven. After all, the old adage teaches that *'los yerros por amores, dignos son de perdonar'* [transgressions for love are worthy of forgiveness].[18]

It is interesting to note that the normal patriarchal social rule that children obey their parents is subverted in *La discreta enamorada*, effectively turned on its head, with the marriages at the end accomplished according to the wishes of the children and not the parents because, as Lucindo notes at the end of the play, it is better for like to marry like, for the young lovers to wed one another and for

---

17   On love in the *comedias de capa y espada*, see, among others, Serrano Poncela and Cañas.
18   See Templin's study.

their parents to wed each other. The upside-down relationships have
been undermined by Fenisa's schemes, righted with the assistance of
the servant and *gracioso*, Hernando. This 'generation gap', as Everett
Hesse observes, completely dominates the action, with the essential
irony that "the 'oldsters' who should be wiser than the 'youngsters'
turn out to be the boobies who are outwitted at every move" (11).

What is most arresting, perhaps, about the performance of love in
the *comedias de capa y espada* is the down-to-earth quality of the
portrayal. Love is not depicted as something aspirational, spiritual,
Platonic, but as a powerful, natural urge, felt by all human beings. No
doubt surprising to some is the fact that it is represented, particularly
in works of the late sixteenth and early seventeenth centuries,
including Lope's early comedies, in ways that are unabashedly erotic
and sensual, and on occasion decidedly risqué.[19] Thus, what is desired
by the lovers, or would-be lovers, is not contemplation and adoration,
as in medieval courtly love, but possession and physical pleasure. The
point is made very clear in *La discreta enamorada* when, at different
moments in the action, not just Fenisa and Lucindo, but Belisa and the
Captain as well, all express how thrilled they feel at the prospect of
spending the upcoming night with the object of their yearning.

Jealousy

In the *comedias de capa y espada* love is habitually accompanied
by feelings of jealousy. Jealousy comes in many shapes and forms,
but in romantic comedies it is typically embedded in a relationship
of triangular desire: character A (the lover) learns, or suspects,
that character B (the loved one) has transferred his or her affection
and sexual favors to character C (the rival). Sometimes the jealous
feelings of the lover are fixed on the loved one, sometimes on the
rival, and often on both. Whatever the case, the lover who is subject
to the condition suffers wracking torments, from which there seems
to be no escape.

---

19   Arellano, *Convención y recepción* (pp. 83–98) has important pages on the
matter. In the coarse portrayal of love in these early plays he sees the influence of
the classic playwrights.

Thus, in *La discreta enamorada* so many triangles are formed and fed by jealousy that it would seem that everyone is jealous of everyone else. When Gerarda pretends to prefer Doristeo over Lucindo, her aim is to make the latter even more besotted. She is paid in kind when Lucindo taunts her with attentions to 'Estefanía'. Gerarda is jealous of Fenisa, who in turn is jealous of Gerarda. The Captain is jealous of his son's youth and gallant mien; Belisa is jealous of the Captain's attention to her daughter. A non-existent triangle is created through confusion when Lucindo finds his father on Gerarda's street and misunderstands the ensuing conversation, believing that his father intends to marry the courtesan. The Captain, in turn, thinks that Lucindo is talking about Fenisa when he describes Gerarda as a woman of many partners. It is overheated episodes like these that inspire much of the dramatic interest of Lope's play, and indeed of comedy in general. As Karl Vossler has written, "*El suplemento de los celos es lo que hace apto para la escena y dramático [el] amor. Donde no hay rivalidad, se paraliza*" (299). [The admixture of jealousy is what makes love dramatic and stageworthy. Where there is no rivalry it is lifeless.][20]

Jealousy can lead to deception in the form of hidden or false identity, such as Hernando's cross-dressing as 'Estefanía' at Lucindo's behest in the Prado in order to provoke jealousy in Gerarda. Later, Hernando again assumes a disguise, pretending to be Lucindo courting Belisa in a delightful parody of courtly language. Gerarda assumes a false

---

20   In his provocative study of the emotion in Lope's (actually Cervantes's) time, Steven Wagschal characterizes Lope's use of jealousy in *La discreta enamorada* as employing "many of the commonplaces associated elsewhere with jealousy: revenge, suspiciousness, doubt, blindness, voyeurism, and suffering". Adopting a contrarian point of view, Wagschal regards jealousy in this play as essentially base: "However, these [commonplaces] seem to have passed beyond what can be designated by the term *topoi*, and should rather be called clichés. Slippery and dirty, while having the quality of the itch associated with pepper and the mildly irritating bite of the mosquito, jealousy is demeaned to its lowest, most trivial essence in this comedy that also debases the power of love, while portraying characters worse than ourselves who are successful in their endeavors and climbing in social status" (pp. 90–91).

identity (as 'Estefanía') in a malicious attempt to convince Fenisa that Lucindo is her lover who has abandoned her, putting her life in danger of death at the hand of her 'husband' Doristeo. The idea behind the hoax is to convince Fenisa that Lucindo is faithless and base, so she will cut off relations with him. For a while, her plan succeeds in deceiving both Belisa and Fenisa, who feel duped by the gallant until Hernando clears things up. But once again, in the final act, Gerarda assumes male garb in order to go out at night unaccompanied to spy on Fenisa and Lucindo.

Throughout the play, misunderstandings add fuel to the plot. In the Prado scene, when asked the name of the 'lady' he escorts, Lucindo pulls out of the air the name 'Estefanía', which happens to be the name of Doristeo's sister. Convinced that it is indeed his sibling that Lucindo is referencing, Doristeo then jumps to the conclusion that the family honor is at stake and resolves to avenge it.

The catalogue of Fenisa's schemes and deceptions is the backbone of the work's plot. Her claims that Lucindo is stalking her are in reality instructions for him on how they can communicate and meet. As Lucindo's future mother, she asks that he be summoned so that she might give him her maternal blessing, in reality an excuse to meet and, through a feigned fall, even embrace.

Throughout the play Fenisa relies heavily on notes [*papeles*]. In one instance, she tells Belisa that she wants to go over a list of gowns that the Captain will buy for her, when in reality she wants to read a letter that Lucindo has written to her. Later, she will again deceive her mother with a letter from Lucindo, making her believe that in it Lucindo declares a desire to marry Belisa, part of a scheme to prevent the Captain from sending Lucindo to Portugal.

A key misunderstanding that brings on the climax of the plot occurs when Doristeo reveals to the Captain that his son is in love with Fenisa, provoking the rage of the former and at the same time resentment of the latter.

While most of the schemes serve to prolong the story, the last one brings things to a close. But Fenisa's final deception is to convince the Captain that he should come to her chamber at night when, in reality, she sends him to Belisa's bedroom and she welcomes Lucindo to hers. The situation is compromising, and forces the respective couples into marriage to save their honor, which, of course, is the happy 'proper' pairing of like with like.[21]

Honor

Like love, honor in the *comedias de capa y espada*, and in Spanish Golden Age theater in general, has multiple faces. In the case of honor, there are two in particular, one of which looks outward, the other inward. The first of these is often called 'external honor', but is also known by a number of other names, among which is 'public honor'. This aspect, basically the same thing as reputation, deals with the evaluation formed by other members of one's honor group and the manner in which they treat one in accordance with that evaluation. The second of the two aspects is usually termed 'interior' or 'internal honor', and, as the expressions suggest, it has to do with one's evaluation of *oneself*. Some relate it to an innate awareness of right and wrong; others speak of conscience, or inner principles. It is not sufficient merely to have principles, however; one must be prepared to act on them, without consideration of how the actions are viewed by other people. One must be, in other words, a selfless exemplar of what would today be called 'virtue'.[22]

In addition to the distinction between external and internal honor, there is another that should be mentioned, having do with the basis upon which public honor is accorded. It is the difference between what the philosopher Kwame Anthony Appiah has termed 'recognition', on the one hand, and 'appraisal', on the other (12–19).[23] In the case of the former, honor comes from what one *is*. It might stem, for example,

---

21   For a full synopsis of *La discreta enamorada*, see below in this Introduction.

22   For illuminating general studies of the concept of honor see Appiah, Bowman, Pitt-Rivers, and Stewart. For well-balanced examinations of honor in Golden Age Spain in particular, see, among others, Defourneaux (especially pp. 28–45); Bennassar ('Honor and Violence'); and Taylor. For a study of honor in Lope, see Larson, *Honor.*

23   These two categories are roughly the same as what Gustavo Correa calls 'vertical honor' and 'horizontal honor'. See his 'Doble aspecto'.

from the individual's occupying a social, military or governmental position of importance, like the Captain, who is treated with great deference by Finardo and Doristeo at the end of Act 2 in *La discreta enamorada*. It could also come from a person's having inherited a title of nobility. Or it could simply mean that one is a member of a 'good' family, such as the family of Belisa, a matter that is looked into by both the Captain and Doristeo when they contemplate marriage with her daughter. The grander one's distinction, the higher one's rank in the social order, the greater the degree of honor accorded.

In contrast to 'recognition' honor, 'appraisal' honor comes not from what one *is*, but from what one *does*, how one acts as judged by societal norms for one's gender, class, and occupation. In early modern Spanish theater, and in Spanish society of the time in general, the standards for men and women were very different. Men, particularly those of the upper classes, were supposed to be truthful, loyal, strong, brave, generous, and tireless in the protection of the safety and integrity of the family: a group of qualities that were derived from the old chivalric ideals and often subsumed in the general category of *hombría*, or 'manliness'. Women were expected to be obedient, decorous, charitable, and above all, chaste. These female qualities also fell into a general category, which in this case was called *vergüenza*, which may be roughly translated as 'modesty'. Those who failed to meet the norms of society, and their lapses were common knowledge, were subject to shame and opprobrium and other forms of disrespect from the members of their honor community. Thus, it was often averred that to be accorded honor was life's greatest reward, and to be tarred with dishonor its worst punishment.

One of the complications of the so-called Spanish honor code is that individuals could be dishonored not just because of what they themselves did, but because of what others did *to* them without suffering reprisal. If a man allowed another man to cheat him, or lie to him, or act disloyally toward him, and failed to exact retribution of some kind, he was judged to be lacking in *hombría*, and thereby defamed in the eyes of society. This explains the anger of Doristeo and Finardo in the scene just referenced at the end of Act 2 in *La discreta enamorada*, when they presume that Lucindo has tried to deceive them about the object of his affection, and go off in search of him to demand satisfaction.

A more serious situation occurs when one male knows, or has cause to suspect, that another male has behaved in a sexually predatory fashion toward a female member of his family – daughter, sister, or wife – for whom he is responsible and charged with protecting. With his masculine honor placed in jeopardy, the 'offended' male supposedly has no choice but to exact vengeance, which sometimes extends to the 'unchaste' woman as well. As we have seen in *La discreta enamorada*, Doristeo leaps to the conclusion that Lucindo is dishonestly pursuing his sister, and immediately vows to take revenge.

In the theater of the Spanish Golden Age, the two dimensions of honor – external and internal – do not necessarily correlate. Characters can have a great deal of external honor, without possessing much in the way of internal honor; and the reverse is also true. The explanation of the inconsistency is that they rest on different sets of qualities. Patience and forgiveness may be important aspects of internal honor, but they are basically irrelevant to external honor. Avenging slights and insults are perhaps requisites of external honor, but extraneous to internal honor. As Ignacio Arellano has pointed out, the disjunction between the two kinds of honor, both in society and on the stage, became increasingly strong as the seventeenth century wore on. Also evolving were attitudes toward the various aspects of external honor which, after the death of Calderón, became increasingly parodic and satirical (*Convención y recepción* 51–59; 'Generalización' 114–28).

The fall of external honor into disrepute and disregard at the end of the seventeenth century in Spain was observable in many other European countries as well. That rejection continued in the following centuries, to the point that, as Bowman has shown, it is today regarded as useless and irrelevant among large swaths of the population in a number of Western cultures. There are, of course, valid reasons for this. As time went on, honor became more and more obsessed with punctiliousness and redress of even the most trivial slights, and its rigidities and not infrequent cruelties became ever more manifest.

But it should be remembered that in earlier times, it was recognized for its positive aspects. In places where the institution of law was weak or non-existent, it functioned as an instrument of basic justice. At the same time, it served to affirm and reinforce those values that respective honor communities considered necessary for peaceable existence. It was widely upheld because, as the British historian Keith Thomas has written, "[h]onour thus functioned as a social discipline, encouraging all members of society to perform their allotted social role by holding out the incentive of collective approbation and the deterrent of disgrace" (177).

The World of the Play: Contexts

When we enter the world of *La discreta enamorada*, we are in Madrid at the beginning of the seventeenth century. These were the first years of the reign of King Philip III – he had succeeded Philip II on the throne in 1598 – and during the period of transition from father to son Madrid was undergoing a huge growth spurt, one that rendered it virtually unrecognizable to those who had not been there since it was the small, provincial town of half a century earlier. Its enormous expansion, from a population of about 30,000 inhabitants in the mid-1500s to one of approximately 65,000 in 1600,[24] was the result of the decision taken by Philip II in 1561 to make the town the permanent seat of his court and de facto capital of Spain. Prior to that moment, the court had been peripatetic, moving from place to place in order to reinforce monarchical authority and discharge justice throughout the land. As time went on, that arrangement grew ever more problematic, and the need for an enduring home for the government more obvious. Why Madrid was the chosen site is not entirely clear, but one reason, it seems evident, is that it was in the exact geographic center of Spain.

As we would expect, much of Madrid's rapid increase in population in the final years of the sixteenth century was composed of people who had come to fill positions at court.[25] Another large group of new

---

24 The figures are from Gelabert, p. 207. Other authorities give somewhat different numbers. See, for example, Elliott, pp. 277–79.
25 On Madrid in the time of Philip III and Philip IV, its demographic make-up,

arrivals was made up of those who did not work directly for the king and his ministers, but who were needed to support those individuals: servants, cooks, bakers, tailors, coachmen, guards, and so on. Still others were provisioners and shopkeepers who supplied the goods upon which the others depended. Finally, there were members of various aristocratic families, who flocked to Madrid from the provinces in order to increase their influence and visibility there, bringing their own retinues with them.

Another factor in the vast expansion of Madrid as the century turned had to do with economic conditions in the country. As the colonies of the New World rose to self-sufficiency, the market for goods produced in Iberia shrank, leading to the closing of factories in many towns of the motherland and a consequent massive loss of jobs. At the same time, many of those who worked the land also found their existential security gravely imperiled. The taxes they paid, always oppressive, were now being raised ever higher. On top of that came a series of natural disasters: severe drought, followed by excessive rainfall, followed by drought once again. The inevitable result of these calamities was a cycle of devastating crop failures, which led in turn to mass famine, particularly in the years 1599–1600. Finally, to compound the misery of the countryside, there occurred a number of outbreaks of plague. The aftermath of these combined blows in small towns and rural areas of Spain was a flood of migrants to the cities and larger towns of Spain, especially Madrid, where it was assumed there was a greater chance of survival.

The consequences of Madrid's unprecedented growth in the final years of the sixteenth century were both positive and negative. On the one hand, it was turning into a bustling, lively capital with numerous places of diversion and social intercourse, such as theaters, markets, *paseos*, cafés, and so on. This side of its life is very much on display in the dramatic works that take place there. On the other hand, the city was badly overcrowded, housing was inadequate, jobs were scarce,

---

its architectural and topographic features, its social, political and economic life, and so on, see, among others, Brown and Elliott, pp. 1–30; Ringrose; Deleito y Piñuela; and the various essays in Feros and Gelabert.

poverty was rampant, streets were dirty, and sanitation was wanting. This aspect of its life was much less present on stage, partly, no doubt, because people typically went to the theater to be entertained, not to be confronted with the troubles of daily existence, and partly because the vast majority of the characters of plays of urban setting were of the upper classes, and thus not as affected by those problems as characters of the working class. Still, it is interesting to note that even the *damas* and *caballeros* of such plays refer on frequent occasions to money, as if they, too, were aware that one's well-being and pecuniary condition could be precarious.[26] Their concerns pale in comparison to those of their servants, the *graciosos*, who live in a constant state of deprivation, and who are not timid about expressing their unhappiness over their penury.

Also largely missing from Spanish plays of the time was any indication that the country was suffering not only economic dislocation but severe loss of prestige and respect in the area of foreign affairs. Throughout most of the sixteenth century Spain was the dominant European power. It was continuously expanding its influence and the territory it controlled, both through victories on the battlefield and through diplomatic and marital arrangements. That all changed in the final decades of the century, however, as the country began to suffer military setbacks – think of the defeat of the 'Invincible Armada' in 1588 – and a concomitant financial breakdown, signaled by several declarations of royal bankruptcy. The evidence of this unwelcome turn of events is found in the various treaties of peace signed with traditional enemies, such as England and France, around the turn of the century. Few of these circumstances are even mentioned in the theater, and when foreign events are alluded to – in *La discreta enamorada* Spain's war against the rebels in Flanders is briefly referenced – it is to suggest that everything is fine.[27]

Modern historians agree that Spain was in 'crisis' during the reign

---

26 See Bass; Greer, '(Self) Representation'; Blue, 'Diverse Economy'; and Arellano, *Convención y recepción*, pp. 98–102.

27 On the treatment of military campaigns in Spanish theater of the early modern period, see Loftis.

of Philip III and the final years of the reign of Philip II, and that crisis was acknowledged by numerous writers of the day, even if only hinted at in the theater.[28] Those most engaged in the problems of the time were known as *arbitristas*, and in their works they proposed a great variety of solutions to those problems. Their answers invariably incorporated the need for changes, but the changes advocated were rarely systemic in nature. As the distinguished scholar J. H. Elliott has written:

> Modern society, thinking in terms of structure, sees the solution to its problems in terms of structural change. Seventeenth-century society, thinking in terms of organisms, was concerned with restoring health, not with transforming structures. It would purge, and bleed, and if necessary amputate, to get the constitution back to a harmonious balance [...]. But the hierarchical order of society was regarded as fixed and immutable. (256)

That society is best structured as a hierarchy was not a notion unique to early modern Spain. Ranked ordering of social life has been characteristic of many cultures around the world since they first began to emerge. What is somewhat unusual about the case of Spain is how deeply the concept was entrenched in the thinking of the time, and how resolutely it was monitored.

As in many places, the summit of the terrestrial hierarchy was the king, who was regarded as divinely anointed. Below him came the *grandes* of the realm, the highest rank of the nobility, and below them were other nobles upon whom a title had been bestowed. Further down were *hidalgos*, noblemen who had no title, and after them members of the high bourgeoisie, warranted to be called *caballeros*. Then were ranked a large group of professionals – lawyers, doctors, professors and so on – and various classifications of shopkeepers. Next were the servants, laborers of diverse sorts, and the peasants. And lastly came

---

28   The number of studies dealing with the crises of Spain in this period is daunting. Among brief, but authoritative, general treatments see Elliott, pp. 213–86; Kamen, *Spain: 1469–1714*, pp. 242–75; Lynch, pp. 1–228; and Thomson, pp. 135–88. Excellent overviews from a social and economic point of view include Bennassar, *La España del siglo de oro*; and Casey and Ruiz.

those who had no income and no prestige: vagabonds, beggars, and other outcasts.

As would be expected in the early modern period, this hierarchical organization of society was bonded to the assumptions and structures of patriarchy. Males controlled the levers of the government and the institutions and teachings of the church. They were the inheritors of property, and titles were passed down through male lineage. Males also established the rules upon which relations between men and women were to be conducted. Within the family, the eldest male exercised control over the behavior of other members, or attempted to, and assumed the right to determine whom his children would marry. In short, one's status in the world depended not only upon one's place in the social order, but upon one's gender as well.

As early as classical Greece, there was a gendered division between the world of politics – the public sphere, belonging to adult males – and the world of family – the private sphere, belonging to women and children. The female of the species was considered inferior to the male, in mind and body, a concept that continued to dominate in medieval philosophy and society until Humanists brought it into question.

Could a woman be virtuous? Could she perform noteworthy deeds? Was she even, strictly speaking, of the same human species as men? These questions were debated over four centuries, in French, German, Italian, Spanish, and English, by authors male and female, among Catholics, Protestants, and Jews, in ponderous volumes and breezy pamphlets. The whole literary genre has been called the 'querelle des femmes', the 'woman question' (King and Rabil, xix).

Feminists maintained that this public-private division underpins the patriarchal system, and thereby marginalizes and subjugates women.[29] Others contended that the division and consequent different parts played by men and women in their respective spheres respond to the broader needs of the society in general.

The stress upon social hierarchy in early modern Spain was aligned with another trend which has been called the 'theatricalization of

---

29　See Kerber, Vickery, Landes, and Gal.

life'.[30] Referring to the importance afforded theatrical activity and theatrical thinking of the time, the term encompasses a number of different phenomena. One of these concerns was the craze for play-going that materialized in the final years of the sixteenth century and continued all throughout the following century. Another involved the stress upon spectacle in public events, not just court processions and pageants in Madrid and other large cities, but also civic and religious ceremonies and observances throughout the land. Most relevant in the present context, however, was the revival at the time of the age-old topos of *theatrum mundi*.

This concept, which postulates that the world is a kind of theater and life a kind of performance, has its roots, as the eminent classicist Ernst Robert Curtius has written, in Plato and the Cynic philosophers (138–44). In the texts of such medieval scholars as John of Salisbury, the notion was further elaborated, acquiring in the process a specifically theocratic orientation. According to this way of thinking, the earthly orders enumerated above were divinely constituted on the model of the orders of the heavens.[31] Members of each of the echelons were charged with particular duties and responsibilities, and in the eyes of God all echelons were of equal worth. Thus, one was expected to accept one's lot without complaint, knowing that at the end of worldly existence salvation or damnation depended not on earthly rank but only on how well or how badly one had performed one's given role. To resist or seek to modify one's role was wrong. To break rank was unacceptable and a threat to the smooth functioning of society. To aspire to upward mobility was an offense to the divine scheme of things.

In the early modern period in Spain, the religious trappings of the view that life is akin to a play had been largely discarded, although they remain in a number of pieces including the well-known *auto sacramental* of Calderón de la Barca, *El gran teatro del mundo*. The

---

30   See, for example, Fischer-Lichte, pp. 80–82. Orozco Díaz remains an indispensable study.
31   See Rico, *El pequeño mundo*.

metaphorical concept remains, but now it is essentially secularized.[32] The appropriate playing of the various roles that constitute the hierarchical order is seen, as before, as vitally important to social stability, but those roles are no longer held to be divinely ordained, which doesn't mean that they may be freely and autonomously chosen. Rather, they are largely determined – and enforced – by society itself.

Role-Playing and Disguise

The roles available to the members of the two sexes in early modern Spain, both in real life and on the stage, were limited, and the appropriate playing of those roles placed severe constraints upon the individual. Both men and women were oppressed by the perceived obligation to satisfy society's injunctions in matters of the heart, and women in addition suffered from their lack of freedom and choice in many particulars of daily living. Both in real life and upon the stage it was not easy to resolve the difficulties that occurred when individual needs and wants came into conflict with social obligations. In such oppressive situations, a strategy that was sometimes employed to achieve greater personal fulfillment is what Jonathan Thacker in *Role-Play and the World as Stage in the* Comedia, has called "anti-social play-acting" (17). Sometimes this disruptive behavior involves temporarily discarding one's prescribed role in favor of another that is more appealing and rewarding. Another form occurs when the character appears to be acting in accordance with the model of his or her role, but is in reality following a different script entirely. On the stage it is often this deviant conduct that paves the way to a happy ending.

In *La discreta enamorada*, at some point each character plays a role that is at variance or in conflict with what is considered the norm, in terms of empowerment, actions, and qualities. In other contexts servants and members of the female sex present themselves as passive and submissive. Here, on the contrary, the manservant and

---

32   On the evolution of the commonplace of the Great Theater of the World, see Warnke, Skrine, and Vilanova.

especially the lady get the better of the other characters.[33] Elsewhere, action turns around women; they are the prizes to be sought by the men. In this play, the title character is a contradiction of the norm, as Thacker observes: "[t]he central female figure is intriguing in herself, enticingly transgressive, but also representative of the freedom to act that the forces of patriarchy and social conservatism would curtail" (*Companion* 164).

In the hierarchical society of early modern Spain, 'honorable' women of a certain social standing were restricted to internal or closed spaces – their own homes or those of close friends or perhaps the inside of a coach. An exception would be attendance at mass, a public event requiring travel from home to church, but never alone. 'Virtuous' females, as mentioned in the earlier discussion of honor, were supposed to play the role of worthy, contained, and modest maidens, keeping to the interior female space. On the rare occasion when they might venture out – to attend mass, as does Fenisa in the opening scene of *La discreta enamorada* – women would have a chaperone or companion, in Fenisa's case, her own mother. They would be expected to lower their eyes and not gesture with their hands to demonstrate their modesty. Belisa reprimands her daughter for straying from this norm. In defense of her actions and attitudes, Fenisa ticks off items on a veritable check list of rules and standards that lovers often violate; she vehemently denies participation in clandestine courtship, consisting of secret visits, gifts, and messages from a suitor, sometimes from him directly, sometimes through a third party. While until now Fenisa has kept to the norms in her actions, she reveals that her thoughts are otherwise, becoming increasingly preoccupied with the very actions of which she claims innocence. As the play progresses, Fenisa maintains the appearance of dutiful daughter and chaste fiancée, but behind the façade she creates and directs a clever script of stratagems so as to thwart parental control and convert both her mother, Belisa, and her suitor, the Captain, into unwitting pawns.

For her part, Belisa maintains the appearance and posture of an

---

33   This calls to mind another Lope play, *Mujeres y criados.*

upright widow proud of her own virtuous past, dedicated to protecting the honor of her daughter. We see, however, that this posture is at odds with, on the one hand, the account of her own sister that as a young girl of about the same age as her daughter, Belisa was obsessed with the idea of getting married. And on the other hand, her suspicions that the Captain is interested in marrying her reveal a vanity behind her assumed role as widow and mother. Although she wears the socially prescribed widow's weeds that declare her disinterest in other men and pretends that her interest in the Captain is strictly financial, she is quick to check her appearance upon hearing of his visit, frivolously concerned with her clothes, hair, and makeup. And it is her vanity that allows her to be convinced that Lucindo wants to marry her; in the balcony courtship scene, she plays the role of young lover, offering favors to 'Lucindo' as she would be expected to do.

In contrast, 'loose' women would exercise their considerable freedom of movement in the company of men unrelated to them by blood or marriage. Gerarda, openly flouting any pretense at modesty and virtue, pretends to be in control of herself and her suitors, completely immune to love. She plays the role of the huntress, preying on lovers for financial gain, spurring their interest in her through jealousy, proud of her detachment from the snares of love. But when Lucindo loses interest in her, she falls into her own trap.

As does Fenisa, Gerarda creates a script casting herself as 'Estefanía', a married woman, in love with Lucindo and pursued by a jealous husband, played by Doristeo, who will kill her if he can. The ruse is designed to satisfy Doristeo's suspicions about Lucindo towards his sister Estefanía, but mostly her own suspicions about the relationship between Lucindo and Fenisa.

Along with Hernando, Gerarda is one of two characters in the play who use costume as essential to their role-playing. As a courtesan, her dress displays her status as a 'woman of love'. But when she comes to Fenisa in the third act, she comes as a properly veiled married woman, not a courtesan, although accused of adultery by her enraged 'husband'. Gerarda pulls out all the stops in telling her tale to Fenisa, creating a back story of a wealthy family and an arranged marriage that is so unhappy as to have brought her to the brink of suicide more than once. Then she fell in love with a gallant lieutenant, with whom she had an affair until her husband's watchful and jealous eye turned the lover's attention to another, Fenisa.

The story, which could well be a synopsis of a *comedia* or *novela corta*, convinces Fenisa that Lucindo has been in effect playing a role, pretending to be her unmarried suitor with honorable intentions. Gerarda congratulates herself on a successful performance whose purpose was to discover the truth about Lucindo's relationship and prevent his marriage to Fenisa.

Gerarda later abandons this role and adopts another, dressed as a man to allow her freedom of movement to spy on Lucindo's nighttime venture to climb Fenisa's garden wall. She declares her true identity and her supposed love for Doristeo to the man she assumes is Lucindo; however, instead of Lucindo she finds herself with Doristeo, who recognizes her voice.

Her final play, or ploy, is to get all of the remaining characters out of Belisa's house and onto the street, faking a fire to bring this about. The result is a revelation of the true state of affairs and Gerarda's return to her original role as courtesan.

The men in *La discreta enamorada* also maintain socially accepted and expected roles as lovers, suitors, and servants, and adopt fictitious roles to further their pursuits. As stressed earlier, males would be expected to maintain the honor of their own family circle, but at the same time were supposed to engage in amorous behavior that could threaten the honor of others. Lucindo plays the role of young roué, casting himself as a besotted rival for the affections of Gerarda, a role he abandons all too readily when he learns of Fenisa's interest in him. But before that, he also writes, directs, and acts in a script that will provide a crucial plot complication: Estefanía. In order to provoke jealousy in the courtesan, Lucindo invents a lover and picks a name out of the air. He enlists Hernando's participation in the ploy, casting his servant as his new love interest. Hernando, for his part, musters his courage and dresses for the role, the darkness of the night in the Prado aiding his performance. He is again called upon to play a costumed role when, disguised in the clothes of his master, he courts Belisa at her window, ad libbing a dialogue that would surely belie his true identity if the widow were less vain and less inclined to believe that she is truly being sweet-talked by a man young enough to be her son.

It is appropriate to conclude that much of the pleasure *La discreta enamorada* and other *comedias de capa y espada* give to the audience derives from watching the different characters toy with their roles, creating, as Thacker notes in his essential study, a play within a play within a play, and roles within roles within roles: i.e., actor A assumes the part of character B, who has been given the part of C in the social hierarchy, but casts that aside to take on the identity of character D. The effect is that of a Hall of Mirrors in the FunHouse of an amusement park, a place that is known for inducing in those who enter a state of giddiness and laughter.

Life in Madrid

As discussed above, the story of *La discreta enamorada* transports us to Madrid, the newly established capital of Spain, and the time is the early seventeenth century. Befitting a plot that revolves around deception, much of the action takes place at night and in public places – the street or the Prado – where characters meet, fall in love, dispute their honor, and seek their fortune.[34] Interior private scenes are set in the houses of the principal characters: Gerarda, whose address is not disclosed, and both Belisa and the Captain, who are neighbors on the Calle de los Jardines.[35]

The beginning of the second act takes place in the Prado. Known today as the Paseo del Prado, running from Plaza de Cibeles to Plaza

---

34   Uriarte details the time and location of each scene (pp. XV–XIX).

35   There seem to be two streets with this name at the time of the play, either of which could be what Lope had in mind. The first Calle de los Jardines is a small street in the barrio de Sol, in the center of Madrid. Nineteenth-century historian Antonio Capmany notes that the houses of the ambassadors to Venice and France, as well as that of the famous Caballero de Gracia, owner of the land on which all three were built, had spacious gardens, which gave the street its name (p. 236). The second Calle de los Jardines is now called Marqués de Cubas. It was originally called Jardines because the gardens of several palaces overlooked the street (Madripedia).

de Neptuno, the Prado de San Jerónimo[36] was a favorite place for social interactions and exhibition of wealth that the upper classes enjoyed. The Prado de San Jerónimo took its name from a monastery constructed by the Catholic Monarchs near Recoletos. Three rows of poplars formed two broad avenues, with various small fountains and a small pavilion for music where the fountain of Neptune is located today.[37] The combination of shade from the trees and the cool mists from the fountains made the Prado de San Jerónimo a favorite place to visit in the summer. Strolls were common during the day, and after dark, it gave place to trysts, suppers, and serenades. French historian Marcelin Defourneaux describes a typical evening there:

> The Prado [...] was frequented by high society on starry summer evenings and often late into the night. The ladies drove in their carriages and the gentlemen were mounted on their fine horses. It was understood that, if the women were not already escorted by a mounted attendant, any gentleman could engage them in conversation through the window of their carriage. Intrigues developed fast and were helped on by the darkness and by the fact that the women were incognito. They hid their faces with mantillas which they might lift deliberately on occasion. But this anonymity could lead to confusion and it tended to favour the enterprise of 'professional ladies', who, more and more, haunted the lanes and groves. (70–71)

Courtship Customs
La discreta enamorada presents us with a view of courtship customs of the time as reflected in the literature of the Renaissance. Lovers are smitten by love at first sight, by a devastating passion, as is the

---

36   For illustrations of the Prado in the time of the play, see Boix. See also Deleito y Piñuela, *Sólo Madrid es corte*.

37   In fact, one of the chief attractions of the Prado were the fountains, five of which, according to sixteenth-century writer López de Hoyos, were of singular artistry, sumptuous construction and particular design, all of granite. Four of the fountains had round basins; the fifth and final fountain in the form of a drinking trough or tank had two spouts, one from the head of a dolphin and the other from the head of a serpent. All were remarkable for the sound of the water in the basins (Deleito y Piñuela, *Sólo Madrid*, pp. 117–18).

case of Fenisa's love for Lucindo. Usually, lovers had to make use of an intermediary (a 'Celestina' or procuress) in order to speak to one another, a practice Fenisa vehemently denies having used. Even so, in the first encounter between Lucindo and Fenisa, she uses a handkerchief as a means of attracting his attention, making the article a sort of go-between. From that point on, the young lovers' parents become unwitting intermediaries.

If an unmarried woman ventured outside the home, she was accompanied, like Fenisa in the first scene, escorted by her mother, Belisa. The young woman would be expected to keep her eyes lowered so as not to permit any chance of love at first sight. Nevertheless, lovers might find an occasion to speak to one another, pass notes or exchange glances in church. And it was possible to arrange a meeting at the barred window of the woman's own house. This custom is used by Lope in the first scene of the third act to present a moment of confusion, deceit, and misunderstanding.

The local settings and customs reflect notable differences in restriction and movement of genders and social strata. The first characters we meet in *La discreta enamorada* are mother and daughter, coming out of church,[38] where they have heard a 'Jubileo' or jubilee mass.[39] They are courted at their balconies later in the play, but do not appear either in a carriage or in the Prado, as does the courtesan Gerarda. Clearly, there are differences between what 'proper' women and 'loose' women can do.

---

38 Given the location of their house on the Calle de los Jardines, the church could possibly be San Ginés or San Sebastián. Due north of the Plaza Mayor, San Ginés is one of Madrid's oldest churches, dating from the 14th century, and has been central to Madrid life for centuries. Lope de Vega was married there. The Saint Sebastian Church or Iglesia de San Sebastián is a 16th-century church in central Madrid, located on Atocha street. Famous authors buried there include: Miguel de Cervantes (1616), Lope de Vega (1635), and Juan Ruiz de Alarcón (1639).

39 According to Herbert Thurston in the *Catholic Encyclopedia*, a Jubilee is a celebration of a special anniversary (especially the 25th, 50th or 60th) of some event, such as the succession of a king or queen. During a Jubilee year (*Año jubilar* or *Año santo*), Catholics can obtain a plenary indulgence through confession, repentance, and the accomplishment of certain religious acts, such as regular attendance at mass.

In *Hombre pobre todo es trazas*, Calderón's character Don Diego summarizes the options for lovers to meet: *misa, reja, coche y Prado* [the church, the balcony, the carriage, the Prado]:

Ya sé, que tengo de ser	I know I must be
Argos la noche y el día.	Argos night and day.
Por la mañana estaré	In the morning I will be
En la iglesia á que acudís,	in the church you attend;
Por la tarde, si salís,	in the afternoon, if you go out,
En la carrera os veré,	I will see you in the street;
Al anochecer iré	in the evening I will go
Al Prado, al coche arrimado,	to the Prado, close to your carriage;
Luego en la calle embozado.	then in the street, behind my cloak.
Ved, si advierte bien mi amor	See how well my love observes
Horas de calle Mayor,	the hours of the High Street,
Misa, reja, coche y Prado.	mass, balcony, carriage, Prado.

(Act 1, scene iv)[40]

The Church

The atmosphere of the mass was not always one of devotion or piety.[41] The Council of Trent (1545–1563) proposed reforms to remedy 'abuses', and towards the end of the sixteenth century, bishops insisted that worshipers observe silence during the mass, and that non-religious activities (dances, farces, plays) not be held within the church. The Council also reaffirmed obligatory attendance at mass on Sundays and the numerous feast days throughout the year, although exceptions were made for economic or even personal reasons. Nevertheless, the faithful attended mass to do business, to make connections, and to court or woo. Ladies, their faces veiled, could maintain frivolous conversations during the mass with other ladies or with gallants and dandies, who took great pains to look their best in church. The presence of celebrities could boost attendance as well. Crowds came to the 'misa de las Marías' in the Iglesia de Jesús to see the actresses María Calderón, María de Córdoba, and María Riquelme.

---

40   Cited in Roca de Togores, p. 375.
41   See Deleito y Piñuela, *Sólo Madrid* and Kamen, *Cambio cultural*. See also Fernández Luzón.

The balcony

When in 1561 Philip II made Madrid the capital of the kingdom, the resulting increase in population and the concomitant construction boom gave particular importance to the balcony as an important feature of urban life, especially in the houses of the more powerful, where the exterior facades served as an indication of the social position and affluence of the owner. Because taxes were assessed on the basis of the number of windows and balconies opening onto the street, a greater number of them indicated wealth. Besides the practical function of supplying light and air to the interior rooms, balconies became essential liminal elements in social life, permitting the residents, especially women, to connect with what was happening in the street without leaving the confinement of the private space. Balconies were a place from which they could witness public events and engage in private, although often clandestine, conversations. As Bass and Wunder[42] observe (in reference to changes in Sevillian civil architecture), the barred windows and balconies became associated with sexuality and honor:

> Prior to 1492, domestic architecture, following Islamic custom, had supported the tradition of female enclosure; almost all Sevillian homes had interior patios with windows facing the inside providing light and ventilation for the rooms around them. During the construction boom of the 1500s, Sevillians began building new homes (and retrofitting old ones) with windows and balconies facing the streets. Decorative iron bars, painted black or green, fronted the newly fashionable windows. Not surprisingly, these barred windows bridging the public and the private – and thus undoing centuries of tradition – became closely associated with female sexuality and male honor in Golden Age art and literature. (118)

The carriage

Literature of the time gives us good insight into the use and abuse of carriages. While some writers decried the traffic congestion and the ostentation of carriages as manifestations of vanity, others found the carriage to be a useful prop for courtship. In the *Entremés famoso*

---

42   See also Lucas Domingo.

del Triunfo de los coches (1611?) by Gabriel de Barrionuevo, Doña
Hipólita launches into lengthy praise of carriages, comparing them
to gallant lovers who know how to keep a secret. In the Prado, she
observes, a carriage can serve the same function as the balcony ['*si
vamos al Prado nos sirve de balcón*'] (58).

Costume and attire

In the tradition of Western dress, the primary function of a garment,
as Anne Hollander observes, "is to contribute to the making of a self-
conscious individual image" (xiv). As many scholars have noted, dress
in the early modern world was indicative of one's social identity, with
strict expectations according to gender, class, and social function.
The frequency of sumptuary laws restricting certain expensive and
ostentatious types and qualities of garb to strata of society that could
afford them would seem to indicate aspirations of social mobility on the
one hand, and the possibility of deceptive appearances on the other. It
goes without saying, as Donald R. Larson writes, "if the use of clothes
to produce a false impression took place in Spanish seventeenth-
century society with some frequency, it occurred with much greater
frequency still on the stage, which has been characterized by Marjorie
Garber as a 'privileged site of transgression'" ('Clothes Encounters'
19).

However, Larson continues, we must "distinguish between the
transgressions of the players and those of the characters they were
enacting" (19). Just as characters and actions on the stage would not
necessarily offer a realistic portrait of life, costumes on the stage
would not be faithful representations of normal attire.[43] Instead,
they functioned as a signal to the public, communicating clearly and
quickly the social status, occupation, or profession of the character.
As well, costumes could convey whether characters were at home,
in the street, or on the road, and whether the action was taking place
in daytime or nighttime.[44] For example, a richly adorned dress might
indicate that the characters are in a palace, whereas a colored cape

---

43   See Madroñal's glossary for descriptions of individual pieces of clothing.
44   See Díez Borque, 'Aproximación semiológica'.

would indicate that the action is taking place in the street (Ruano and Allen 313). Feathers adorning a soldier's uniform might also convey insight into his vanity or pride (Arellano, 'El vestuario' 87).

Women's clothing
During the Renaissance, exterior beauty was considered to be an indication of inner goodness, the face to be the reflection of the soul. Therefore, a woman would strive to conform her exterior appearance (dress, makeup) to an ideal. Rules of hygiene and cosmetics would require women to avoid water, an element associated with mutability and considered pernicious to one's health, instead making liberal use of powders to whiten the skin and rouge to render the cheeks and lips closer to the ideal, and fragrances to disguise the odor of the unwashed body. Note that Belisa checks her makeup before the Captain enters, and Gerarda mentions *pastillas* (lozenges) to sweeten her breath. Perfumes such as rose water or orange blossom water were used in abundance.

Modes of dress would clearly reflect the differentiation between public and private spheres. A woman of noble status in the seventeenth century would dress more richly in public than at home, her dress representing not only her station but also her fortune. The basic dress worn in public was the gown (*saya*) consisting of bodice and skirt (*saya entera*), which was worn over a farthingale (*verdugado*) to give the dress a rigid effect; its shape varied according to the fashion, but was always designed to hide the feminine body, considered a source of temptation. The farthingale was a status symbol, and its use required practice, as was the case of the *chapín*, a sort of platform overshoe that elevated the wearer with its six or seven layers of cork soles. *Chapines* were heavy and uncomfortable, so walking – in reality, sliding – in them was an effort that kept women from moving quickly, or much at all. In order to cover the feet, as required by codes of decency, skirts would need to be lengthened accordingly. Again, as part of the effort to 'contain' women, the bodice of the dress would consist of a corset (*corpiño*) of layers of wood or bone. Below, a woman might wear a richly worked underskirt (*faldellín*), visible when entering or leaving a coach, as another signal of her status and wealth. The overskirt could be drawn up in such a way as to form deep pockets (*faltriqueras*) on the side. The outfit would be completed by a great starched ruff (*lechuguilla* or *gorguera*) that kept the head erect. The lady would carry a handkerchief decorated with a lace border, as Fenisa does in Act 1.

In private and at home, this mode of dress would be impractical and unnecessary. A woman would not wear a *saya entera*; instead, she would wear a separate bodice (*jubón*) over a blouse and an over-skirt (*basquiña*). This two-piece outfit was more comfortable and therefore gave a woman greater freedom of movement.

However, when she undertook to leave her home, a woman would need to be covered by a voluminous cloak (*manto*). Depending on her status and her purpose in venturing into the public sphere, her face could be covered (*tapada*) except for the left eye, an ambiguous gesture that hides the identity of the person wearing it, therefore granting the wearer mobility and independence, while making her both 'alluring and deeply unsettling'. We can imagine that when he appears as a woman at the beginning of Act 2, Hernando would take advantage of the impossibility of recognizing the identity – or gender – of the *tapada*, "a clearly recognizable social type: seductive, defiant, and disruptive of the social order" (Bass and Wunder 99). While Hartzenbusch suggests that Belisa and Fenisa make their first entrance *tapadas*, it is probably more likely that Belisa would have followed the opinion of the Spanish humanist Juan Luis Vives: "let women's faces be free of veils, but [instead] veiled with modesty."[45] This is in contrast to the advice of León Pinelo in his treatise on the veil: "*si saliere, ha de ser como una casa portátil, cercada, cerrada y cubierta*" (2:240–41) [If she were to go out, it must be as if she were in a portable house, walled up, enclosed and covered]. Given the formidable power of one beautiful eye peeking out, *tapadas* could incite, call out, and attract ("*incitan, llaman y atraen*" 2:332). Note that, after the initial scene when Belisa and Fenisa are on the street outside a church in which they have just heard mass, these women

---

45   Cited in Bass and Wunder, p. 105.

never leave the house until it is supposedly on fire and occupants must evacuate. Fenisa uses her wits, not her cloak, to elude the confinement of her mother and outwit the Captain's vigilance, inciting, calling, and attracting Lucindo (although it must be repeated that it is Hernando who can read the messages of love in Fenisa's unveiled – honest and forthright – eyes).

The veil (also called *toca*) was a frequent device in *comedias*, as were the *volante* (a costly veil worn beneath a hat, used for travel), and the mask, all permitting a 'dangerous' means of disguise and flirtation, despite several royal edicts that attempted to abolish the custom. Although the personal identity of the wearer might be hidden, the rich materials used would indicate her social identity.

Women over the age of forty would not be subject to the same rules and standards of feminine beauty as younger women. The mature bodies and heads of widows, housewives (*amas*), lay religious women (*beatas*) or chaperones (*dueñas*), would be covered in plain, unadorned dresses or the black woolen nun-like habit (*saya monjil*) praised by Hernando when, pretending to be Lucindo, he courts Belisa in Act 3.

Men's clothing

The dialogue in *La discreta enamorada* does not reveal as much about male costume, with the notable exception of the Captain, whose gala uniform signals his vanity and desire to make an impression as a gallant, albeit old-fashioned, suitor: "*Sale BERNARDO viejo, muy galán con su gorra de plumas, espada y daga, en fin, como capitán a lo antiguo.*" [Captain Bernardo enters. He is elderly, and very gallant, with a plumed hat, sword, and dagger, like a captain of the old style.] (Stage direction before line 461).

For other characters, the cape plays a crucial role. It provides Hernando a disguise on two occasions. In the first instance in Act 2, in the Prado, Hernando fashions his cape into a skirt so that when he covers his head with a mantle, he can pass for a woman, thus hoping to provoke jealousy in Gerarda, for whose benefit the charade is performed. In the second instance, in Act 3, beneath Belisa's balcony, Hernando wears Lucindo's gold-embroidered cape and a broad-brimmed hat to hide his face, causing the widow to mistake the gallant's clothing for his person.

Corrales

The site of the first known performances of *La discreta enamorada* was Salamanca's Corral de Comedias, one of dozens of such *corrales* that sprang up all over Spain in the final years of the sixteenth century and the beginning years of the seventeenth century, the majority of them in large cities like Madrid, Seville, and Valencia, some in smaller cities like Salamanca, and some in villages of as few as 3,000 inhabitants. Open to all who could afford the price of admission, and hence classified as public theaters, they were places where the *vulgo*, the popular audiences, had the final word on what was worth seeing. Many of these *corrales*, as their name suggests, had their origin in temporary performance places that were set up in the patios, or yards, that were located in or adjacent to existing buildings. As time went on, and the need for more enduring and accommodating venues became apparent, improvised stages were replaced by permanent, purpose-built theaters, each of which, like all performance spaces, 'framed' the performances held on their stages in specific ways.

The concept of framing, originally developed in the mid twentieth century in the field of behavior sociology, eventually migrated to other disciplines as well, including the semiotic study of theater. Prominent among its applications there is the physical setting in which the performance event takes place. Typically that environment is taken to include, at a minimum, three different frames. The first of these is the placement of the performance site, normally a theater, within the urban fabric. The second is the nature of the space within the theater where the spectators see and hear the performance. And the third is the nature of the space within the theater where the members of the company create the performance. Each of these interlocking frames is encoded with messages, and thus they shape and condition not only the kinds of performances that take place within them, but also the way in which audiences interpret them.[46]

---

46   For a general study of framing see the works of Goffman, particularly, *Frame*

Public theaters of Spain in the early modern period were found, for the most part, in the heart of the community. In Madrid, for example, the two *corrales* of the time, the Corral de la Cruz and the Corral del Príncipe, were located just a few short blocks from the Puerta del Sol, long considered the focal point of the metropolis. The neighborhood in which they were set was socially mixed, encompassing the homes not just of laborers, shopkeepers, artists and writers, but also those of members of the highest aristocracy. Just as important, it was close to structures that represented power and authority, including municipal buildings in the Puerta del Sol and the nearby Plaza de la Villa, while a short distance from these stood the Alcázar, the principal residence of the royal family and the seat of monarchical government during Lope de Vega's lifetime. The literal and cultural placement of the *corrales* of Madrid, sites of the majority of first performances of the plays that comprise the *comedia nueva*, thus tended to favor the creation, production, and reception of works that, while not without vehement critiques and subversive gestures on occasion, were of basically conservative orientation, tending, for the most part, to confirm existing social, political, and religious beliefs and institutions.

The two public theaters of Madrid were not the first such theaters constructed in Spain in the last decades of the sixteenth century, but they were the most important, and their architecture eventually furnished the model for many other *corrales* throughout the country, including the Corral de Salamanca.[47] The size of these theaters varied considerably, but the layout and features of the public space and performance space tended to be quite similar. Each of these interior areas, like the outside, exterior context, were rich in symbolism.

The public space of a typical *corral* consisted of an enclosed patio, usually quadrangular in shape, the far end of which abutted the stage of the theater, at the rear of which was erected the structure called

---

Analysis. On the concept of physical framing in the study of theater, see, among others, Bennett; Carlson, *Places of Performance*; Greer, 'A Tale of Three Cities'; and McAuley.

47   On the *corrales* of Madrid, see, among others, Davis and Varey; Díez Borque, *Teatros del Siglo de Oro*; and Ruano de la Haza and Allen.

'the *vestuario*'. The remaining sides of the enclosure were formed by three walls that contained viewing areas for the spectators, two of these along the lateral flanks of the courtyard, and the third, directly opposite the stage, connecting the other two. The lateral walls in many cases belonged to existing buildings, while the third wall, which fronted on the street, was often purpose-built. The larger part of the patio was devoted to an open space, normally not roofed over.[48] During performances the rear portion of this area was occupied by *mosqueteros*, or groundlings, who watched the entire spectacle while standing. Exclusively male, and characteristically of the poorer classes, they paid a minimal amount to attend. Relatively better-off male spectators could, if they so wished, pay an additional sum and sit on benches located either directly in front of the stage, or on steps, called *gradas*, which lined the patio on both sides.

Above the *gradas* on the lateral sides of the *corral*, were the higher and more expensive levels of viewing: *aposentos*, *desvanes*, and *tertulias*. *Aposentos*, which were more or less equivalent to boxes in modern theaters, were typically repurposed from windows and balconies of residences that existed in the buildings that overlooked the patio. *Desvanes* and *tertulias* – the latter reserved for members of the clergy and intellectual professions – were especially constructed and positioned both against the side walls and the street wall of the theater. Also found in the latter were boxes for dignitaries and authority figures, and a place called the *cazuela*, or stew pot, that was set aside for unaccompanied women. The price of admission to these diverse sectors of the public space varied as widely as might be expected, with that of *aposentos* – often let out for entire theatrical seasons – being much the most expensive, and that of the *cazuela* being the least.

---

48   Many corrales had an awning that protected the audience from the sun, but not from rain. "The Cruz opened in rudimentary form on 29 November 1579, and survived, with modifications, until 1736, when it was replaced by a *coliseo* (proscenium theatre). [...] The yard was roofed in 1703" (Davis, 'Cruz').
"The Príncipe opened on 21 September 1583 (on a site now occupied by the Teatro Español) and lasted, albeit much modified, for over 160 years, being replaced by a *coliseo* (proscenium theatre) in 1744. [...] The yard was roofed in 1713" (Davis, 'Príncipe').

What one may conclude from the foregoing is that the area inside early modern *corrales* that was the province of the spectators was both inclusive and hierarchical. All those who had sufficient funds were able to attend performances, thereby creating a feeling of oneness and community. At the same time, the place where a person sat or stood was spatially marked, signaling that individual's position in society, and in so doing generating a feeling of differentiation and ranked order. Generally speaking, and in contrast to what occurs in modern theaters where the opposite is usually true, the higher one's social position, the higher one's viewing point in the *corral*. The organization of life inside the theater thus reflected the organization of life without. All were members of one society, but within that society some were superior to others.[49]

The same impression of hierarchy that was created by the public areas of *corrales* was generated as well by the presentational space, the area reserved for the actors and other members of the theatrical company. Dominating that space was the stage, in essence a simple platform that was raised about a meter and a half above the level of the ground. The dimensions of the stage varied from *corral* to *corral*. In the Corral del Príncipe,[50] the best known of all the *corrales*, it measured 28½ Castilian feet wide and 16 feet deep. The dimensions of most provincial stages were presumably smaller. Unlike the majority of modern stages, those of *corrales* had no proscenium arch and no front curtain. Such an arrangement was doubtless conducive to a feeling of intimacy and of strong connection with the audience.

Below the stage there was a pit, unseen by the audience, which served as a dressing area for male actors, and from which, through the use of trapdoors, they could, when their role so required, emerge onto the stage, as if arising from the netherworld. More prominent, however, was a structure at the rear of the platform called the *vestuario*.

---

49   On the symbolism of spaces in early modern Spanish corrales, see Díez Borque, *Teatro y sociedad.*
50   See illustrations of the Corral del Príncipe by Manuel Canseco, which include the facade, the view from the stage, both north and south (lateral) views, and the view from the *cazuela*: <http://aix1.uottawa.ca/~jmruano/Corral.html>.

In the Corral del Príncipe, it consisted of three corridors, one at stage level, the other two above, each of which was divided by supporting poles into three recesses. All of the recesses were normally hidden from audience view by curtains, making them available for use by female actors as dressing-rooms, as indicated by the term *vestuario*. They could also be utilized, however, as performance spaces when the curtains were parted.

Counting the pit, there were four levels of playing area in the Corral del Príncipe which could be used scenically and dramatically: the pit, the stage itself, along with the corridor at its rear, and the two upper corridors, or galleries, located above the stage. In addition to these, there was a fifth level, located under the overhanging stage roof and hence invisible to the public, which contained the various 'machines' utilized in performance. The four playable levels existed in a kind of hierarchy, and each of them was rich in figurative suggestions. Characters that appeared from the pit were typically connected with the diabolic and with the underworld. Those that stood and moved on the stage itself were customarily understood to be representative of ordinary human existence, with all of its virtues and flaws. In contrast, characters who appeared in one of the recesses of the first corridor above the stage were assumed to possess, at least for the moment, superiority of some sort, social, ethical, or political. And finally, as we might expect, figures who represented the divine order, such as angels and martyrs in religious plays, would emerge in one of the recesses of the second corridor above the stage, no doubt to the delight and wonderment of the members of the audience.

In addition to its ability to express metaphorically different orders of hierarchy, the vertical dimension of the stages of *corrales* was well suited to creating visual images that supported the tensions and divergences that abound in Spanish Golden Age plays. These include such basic oppositions as power vs. subjugation, knowledge vs. ignorance, truth vs. deceit, reality vs. illusion, indoors vs. outdoors (which often carries suggestions of female vs. male), old age vs. youth, concealment vs. revelation, and, of course, the fierce conflict that occurs over and over in this theater, love vs. honor.

But it would be wrong to give the impression that the configuration of the stages of *corrales* only furthered thematic usages. It had numerous practical applications as well. For example, the many recesses found at the rear of the stage could be used to provide places for the characters to hide, or for them to have private conversations. They served as well to suggest the multiple sites of action that are found in many Golden Age plays. At the same time, the relative emptiness of the stage when the curtains covering the recesses were closed worked well when the setting of scenes was purposely indeterminate. That bareness, along with the reduced dimensions of the platform, permitted the actors to make swift entrances and exits and to move rapidly from one part of the platform to another. It also allowed the supporting crew to quickly place and remove whatever simple items of scenery that were called for by the events of the play, which were normally very few. Both of these features functioned to create a feeling of speed and energy during the performance, holding the attention of the members of the public and pulling them into the show.

Date of Composition and First Performances

Like the great majority of the hundreds of works that Lope de Vega wrote for the theater, *La discreta enamorada* cannot be dated with absolute precision. In their monumental *Cronología de las comedias de Lope de Vega*, S. Griswold Morley and Courtney Bruerton conjecture (311), primarily on the basis of an analysis of the metrical forms employed in the play, that it was written between 1606 and 1608, probably in 1606. That the play cannot, in fact, have been written later than 1606, and most likely in that year or just before, has more recently been established by a previously overlooked document that attests to performances of the work in the city of Salamanca on the 25th of October and the 1st of November of that year.[51] Whether they

---

51 The document referenced is titled *Diario de un estudiante en Salamanca*. Published in 1977, it is the diary of an Italian gentleman, Girolamo da Sommaia, who studied at the University of Salamanca in the early 1600s. An avid theater-goer, da Sommaia includes in his diary a detailed listing of all the many performances he attended while in Salamanca, as well as others that he had not seen but of which he was aware. Among them are the performances of *La discreta enamorada* in 1606.

were the very first anywhere cannot be affirmed with certainty, but it seems reasonable to assume that, if not the earliest, they were very close in time to whatever enactments may have preceded them.

Although the Corral de Salamanca, the site of the first-known performances of *La discreta enamorada*, has long disappeared, we are in possession of a fair amount of information about the theater, thanks to the survival of a number of documents pertaining, principally, to various renovations of the theater, chiefly those of 1604 and those of 1607. The records indicate that it was constructed in the patio of what was early on the Hospital de la Santísima Trinidad, and that it is quite possible that it was already in existence by the mid-1580s.[52] Somewhat later, the hospital itself moved to a different location in Salamanca. The building that was its prior home remained, however, situated on the Plaza San Román, across from the Convento de Santa Clara. The *corral* thus stood at the core of the city, in a diversified quarter in which were found both government offices and the residences of families that represented various social classes, including the upper nobility. Like that of the *corrales* of Madrid, then, the placement of the Corral de Salamanca speaks to the importance of the theater to the economy of the city, as well as to its critical role in the civic and cultural life of the metropolis.

Reading *La discreta enamorada*

La discreta enamorada is a story of love, rivalry, jealousy, and disguise, of the triumph of true (and proper) love over lust and financial interest. Triangles abound and love objects shift, now through deceit,[53] now through clever intrigue, until each is afforded a proper partner. Full of plot twists and complications, it is set in a world of deceptive appearances populated by engaging characters, especially the young women, Fenisa and Gerarda, who are intelligent, astute, and in charge.

See Domínguez Búrdalo; see also Ferrer Valls.

52   On the history of the Corral de Salamanca, its placement within the city, and its features and properties, see Martínez Aguilar as well as Rodríguez G. de Ceballos and Nieto González.

53   For a discussion of types of deceit, see Roso Díaz.

They manipulate their suitors with their charms and their schemes. Fenisa, in love from the start, is both tender and fierce, unashamed to hold her head high, prepared to fight for her own happiness.

Two households, one composed of a mother and her daughter, the other of a father and his son, will eventually combine, although not in the way that the parents originally desire. Captain Bernardo wants a young wife, namely his neighbor Belisa's daughter, Fenisa, who is in love with his son, Lucindo, but the youth is infatuated with the courtesan Gerarda. Gerarda puts power above love and plays her suitors against each other, creating a rivalry between Doristeo and Lucindo, who thinks he is in love, but is tutored in the reality of things by his servant. Hernando is quick to see that Fenisa is in love with his master and not with the Captain, despite having agreed to marry him. Fenisa's mother, Belisa, accepts the proposal in shock, having mistakenly assumed that the Captain would solicit her hand and not her daughter's.

The Title: Meanings of Discreción

Fenisa's clever stratagems to attain her goal of marriage give rise to the play's title, *La discreta enamorada*, which presents us with a contradiction of terms. *Enamorar* [to enamor] would seem at odds with *discreción*. The *Diccionario de Autoridades* (1732) defines the former as exciting, attracting, and moving desire and affection, in terms of appetite and surrendering one's will to desire.[54] This essentially means surrendering control, falling in love. This is passion, infatuation, not true love.

Closer to Lope's time, Covarrubias's dictionary of 1611 defines the various forms of *enamorar*, *enamorarse*, and *enamorado* in terms of losing control, love being a force that imprisons and captures the will of the 'victim'. Significantly, the female noun *enamorada* is a term that is always taken negatively, ranging from a woman in love to a lover. This shouldn't be confused with someone who is truly in love, for the effect of true love is positive (as is the case in Lope's *La dama*

---

54   "*[E]namorar: excitar, atraher y mover el deseo y afecto, para que uno apetezca, se incline y aficione a estimar y querer a otro. Vale también solicitar a otro, procurando se rinda su voluntad y deseos amorosos.*"

boba). Love provides the justification for Fenisa's actions; she didn't
know how to declare her love to Lucindo, so love sparked her clever
inventions.

Discreción[55] is discretion, prudence, sense, moderation, or caution,
all of which require control. As Nancy D'Antuono observes, Fenisa is
singular because she is discreet before she is in love:

> She is separate and distinct from other *enamoradas* because Fenisa has
> already achieved that *discreción* ordinarily seen as an effect of love,
> rather than as a prerequisite. Within the play itself, Fenisa's discretion
> sets her apart from the two other *enamoradas*, Gerarda, the courtesan
> (Lucindo's former lover), and Fenisa's mother, Belisa (although the
> latter might better be termed *enamoradiza*). The lack of judiciousness
> and circumspection on the part of Gerarda and Belisa points up their
> *necedad* and, by contrast, serves to amplify the portrait of Fenisa as
> *discreta*. (*Discreción* 31)

Everett Hesse suggests three meanings for 'discreción':

> "The first is prudence, wise judgment in words and deeds. The second
> involves a certain sense of modesty (of which Fenisa has only the
> required minimum). The third, featured most strongly in this play, is
> the ingenuity to outwit opponents, encompassing such terms as *enredo*,
> *traza*, *invención* and *industria*, although without this last term's often
> negative connotations." (10)

Sources and Inspirations

As was often the case in his early plays,[56] Lope found inspiration for
the plot of *La discreta enamorada* in an Italian source, concretely
in Giovanni Boccaccio's *Decameron*, a collection of one hundred
novellas whose themes revolve around an insistence on the human
ability to overcome or even exploit fate or fortune. For *La discreta
enamorada*, Lope turned to the third novella of the third day: A married
woman devises a plan to use her confessor, a friar, as an unknowing
go-between to arrange her affair with an attractive young man without
either her husband or the friar knowing.

---

55   For a discussion of the various meanings implied in 'discreción' see Bates.
56   See Arellano, 'El modelo temprano de la comedia urbana de Lope'.

Scholars agree that Lope's treatment is "not a servile imitation but, rather, a selecting of those elements which would prove most fruitful for Lope's conception of the *Arte nuevo de hacer comedias*" (D'Antuono, *La CHiSPA*: 72–73).[57]

Although there are common elements in Lope's treatment of Boccaccio's tale, from particulars of the setting (a marble fountain) to features of the plot, differences abound. Lope adds complications with sub-plots as well as a *gracioso* to craft his play 'in the Spanish style'. Lope situates the characters in Madrid, where they live, go to church, and socialize. His clever protagonist is a young girl with matrimonial, not carnal, designs.[58] The emphasis on 'discretion', in its various senses, in combination with 'in love', represents a new element that distinguishes Lope's treatment of the theme.

Additionally, in "its comic vitality, its sparkling dialogue, and its swift forward thrust of the action", D'Antuono finds a possible debt to the *commedia dell'arte* and possibly even a reference to Italian actors, Francesco Andreini (Capitano Spavento) and his wife, Isabella, *prima donna* of the troupe [I Gelosi].[59]

For his part, Felipe Pedraza suggests that Lope has written an

---

57 Myron Peyton discusses how Lope amplifies his source. Victor Dixon sustains that Lope's source was not Boccaccio's *Decameron* but rather Leonardo Salviati's 'moral' version, so popular that it had fourteen editions, eight of which were published before 1602 (pp. 186–87). Muñoz Sánchez concurs with Dixon. García Lorenzo maintains that there is very little of Boccaccio's story in Lope's play, citing it as an example of how critics pass along prior opinions: "De todas maneras, nosotros seguimos pensando que muy poco, poquísimo, hay del cuento de Boccaccio en *La discreta enamorada* y estimamos que esto es un excelente testimonio de esas opiniones que pasan de unos a otros estudiosos sin los replanteamientos adecuados e incluso a pesar de algunas dudas que tímidamente se expresan" (p. 124 n. 4).

58 It is interesting to note that Lope includes a somewhat lascivious widow: Belisa.

59 "Could not the Italian acting couple and the roles they immortalized have suggested the characterization of the corresponding roles in *La discreta enamorada* […]? Isabella died in France on 11 June 1605, and shortly thereafter Francesco retired from the stage. Lope's play was written between 1606 and 1608. Had Lope intended to honor their memory in *La discreta enamorada*? I believe so" (*Spanish Golden Age Theatre*, p. 243).

ingenious comic version of the mythological story of Phaedra (Fenisa), who ensnares her husband's son Hippolytus (Lucindo), frustrating the aspirations of a *"ridículo pero bondadoso y entrañable"* [ridiculous but kindly and loveable] Theseus (Captain Bernardo) ('Fedra cómica', 120).

Jesús Gómez has found an unspoken presence and echoes of *La Celestina* (Fernando de Rojas, 1499) in the play.[60] In the first act, Fenisa protests that no 'celestinesque' go-betweens have visited her and so Belisa can have no complaints. Instead of moralizing, as is Rojas's intent, Lope draws on references to *La Celestina* for comic effect, as well as using it as a resource for theatrical characters: the courtesan, the passive gallant, and the fair damsel determined to marry her lover. A crucial point of difference, however, is between the professional procuress (*alcahueta*) and the go-between (*tercera*). Fenisa does not need the former; instead she functions as her own go-between (Gómez 34–35).

Another echo of *La Celestina* is the notion of love at first sight.[61] As Matthew Stroud observes:

> There are few motifs more ubiquitous in Renaissance and Baroque poetry than those that link falling in love to the eyes. Based at least in part on Theophrastus, [...] this notion of love describes a process by which one is captivated by looking at the object of desire, prompting an exchange of humors or spirits. If the love is returned, both lovers feel complete and satisfied, but if the object of desire does not reciprocate, one feels empty because one has given one's soul to another while receiving nothing in return. (61)

Indeed, it is remarkable how many times characters in *La discreta enamorada* speak of eyes. In the first scene of the play, Belisa lectures her daughter on the necessity of keeping her eyes lowered, both as a sign

---

60 *"...además de utilizarla como posible repertorio de recursos y de caracteres teatrales, es el valor cómico y risible que descubre en ella y que desarrolla en la mayoría de las comedias estudiadas"* (p. 5). [...besides using it as a possible repertoire of theatrical resources and characters, is the comic value discovered in it and that he develops in the majority of the plays studied].
61 See Miaja de la Peña.

of modesty and as a means of preventing the effects of a man's gaze, more specifically the concept of 'morirse de ojo'. In his introduction to Lope's *El caballero de Olmedo*, a work often connected by critics to *La Celestina*, Francisco Rico explains that '*aojar*' means to harm or even kill by means of the evil eye (23); alternatively, it can mean to enamor ('enamorar'). Whether for harm or for good, love enters through the eyes, bewitching at first sight.

Of particular interest for *La discreta enamorada* is Juan Luis Vives's *De institutione feminae Christianae* (The Education of a Christian Woman), written in 1523 ostensibly for the education of Mary, the daughter of King Henry VIII and Queen Katherine of Aragon, and commissioned by the queen herself. In it, Vives discusses the education of unmarried women, as well as wives and widows, while also addressing "the social status of women in general, the church's doctrine on the sacrament of matrimony, and the moral instruction of womankind" (13). Referring to the eyes as portals of danger, Vives counsels vigilance: "As far as you can, close your eyes and ears, which give entrance to the machinations the devil makes use of in his assaults upon us" (82). He admonishes unmarried women to keep to the private sphere: "An unmarried young woman should rarely appear in public, since she has no business there and her most precious possession, chastity, is placed in jeopardy. Not only should she be accompanied by her mother when she issues from her house, but even when she is staying quietly at home, and this is enjoined upon mothers as well" (110). Returning to the eyes, he observes: "She will keep her eyes cast down, and will raise them but rarely and with modesty and decorum. She will not stare at anyone intently or in an unbecoming manner" (128).

Vives observes that love is an overpowering force: "It is in your power to let love in, but once you have let it in, you no longer belong to yourself, but to it. [...] When once love has crept into [women's] hearts, they embrace and cherish it as something sweet and pleasant, unaware that a deadly and terrible pestilence is hidden beneath those external blandishments" (146–47). Hernando warns Lucindo of the traps and snares of courtesans; Vives employs similar images of trapping or luring, but in reference to men luring women: "In this way they deceive unwary girls, covering over the yawning chasms of evil with their veneer of goodness, as the fowler hides the birdlime under food and the fisherman places bait on the hook" (150). While Vives praises virgins bountifully, he is severe in his condemnation of go-betweens, whom he describes as "basilisks or *katoblepae* that transmit a deadly poison from their eyes and annihilate you with a single glance" (111).

In *La discreta enamorada*, eyes are powerful communicators, windows to the heart and soul, revealing not only love but also jealousy, and glances are described as arrows or poison. Both the eyes and the tongue can convey true feelings, but they can also deceive (*"Falsos ojos, falsa lengua"*).

Conversely, the act of seeing can be synonymous with understanding, reasoning (*"No hay vista en hombre celoso / todo le parece mal;"* ["A jealous man is blind to all; / Everything seems worthless to him." lines 173–74]). A lack of perception is conveyed as blindness or confusion; the Captain suspects that Lucindo is trying to trick him into thinking ill of Fenisa,

Como el que con los espejos	Like the fellow with a mirror
puestos al sol, da en los ojos	Who uses it to reflect sun
al que viene desde lejos,	In the eyes of someone coming,
quiere el necio darme enojos	The fool hopes to aggravate me
con estos vanos consejos.	With his unproved, baseless warnings.

(lines 891–95)

Synopsis
Act 1

Fenisa, a shrewd and beautiful young woman is secretly in love with the handsome and dashing Lucindo. Unfortunately, Lucindo is in thrall to the courtesan, Gerarda, who tries to make him jealous by flirting with another gallant, Doristeo. One day Fenisa does manage to catch the attention of Lucindo by dropping her handkerchief in front of him on the street. Lucindo is intrigued, but insists to his servant, Hernando, that he is still in love with Gerarda.

Shortly after, Captain Bernardo, Lucindo's father, pays a call on Fenisa and her mother, Belisa. Belisa thinks that he has come to ask for her hand in marriage. His purpose, however, is to propose to Fenisa. Fenisa tentatively accepts his offer, believing that it will enable her to make contact with Lucindo.

Gerarda, sensing that Lucindo's interest in her may be wavering, informs him that she will be going to the Prado that evening with Doristeo. Knowing what she is up to, Lucindo decides to fight fire with fire, and tells her that he will be there also, accompanied by a certain 'Estefanía'. When Hernando asks his master later who Estefanía is, Lucindo replies that it will be Hernando himself, dressed as a woman.

Act 2

Lucindo and Hernando / Estefanía happen upon Gerarda and Doristeo in the Prado. Gerarda is taken in by the ruse Lucindo has planned and, wild with jealousy, begins to attack the cross-dressed servant. Somewhat the worse for wear, Hernando flees.

Shortly after, Lucindo and Hernando go to the house of Fenisa, where the two young people profess their love for each other. Fenisa tells Lucindo that she has devised a ruse so that the two of them can speak again. In essence, it is that she will tell the Captain that she wishes Lucindo to come to her so that she can give her future 'son' the blessing of his new 'stepmother'.

The following day finds Gerarda speaking with Doristeo. The courtesan admits to Doristeo that she is in love with Lucindo, and tells him that she has learned that the 'woman' who was in the Prado the previous evening is named 'Estefanía'. Doristeo is stunned, for that is the name of his sister. Convinced that his honor has been lost, he vows revenge on Lucindo.

The scene now shifts to the house of Belisa and Fenisa, where the two are conversing with the Captain. The Captain sends for his son so that he can receive the blessing of Fenisa. Lucindo arrives and receives the blessing, which is filled with double meanings. The Captain becomes angry and orders his son out of the house. Before Lucindo goes, however, he tells Fenisa that his suspicious father intends to send him to Portugal. Fenisa quickly comes up with a new stratagem. She will tell her mother that Lucindo wishes to marry her, Belisa, certain that Belisa will do all she can to prevent Lucindo from leaving Madrid.

In the final scene of Act 2 we are back on the street. Lucindo and Hernando are conversing when Doristeo and Finardo happen along. Finardo attempts to challenge Lucindo to a duel, telling him that he knows that Lucindo has designs on his sister, Estefanía. Lucindo responds that he doesn't know any Estefanía, and that his real love is Fenisa. Shortly after, Doristeo repeats what he has just heard to the Captain, who has happened along. Enraged, the Captain swears vengeance on his son, and storms off.

Act 3

Once again it is night and Lucindo and Hernando are outside the house of Belisa. Lucindo tells his servant about Fenisa's stratagem. Fenisa has convinced her mother that Lucindo will make love to her that evening at her window; it won't be Lucindo, however, but Hernando, disguised as his master. Soon, Hernando is wooing the delighted Belisa at her window, while Lucindo converses with Fenisa at hers. He tells her that he will come by for her the next day so the two of them can elope.

Now another intrigue is hatched. Both Gerarda and Doristeo wish to find out the truth about 'Estefanía', so pretending to be wife and husband, they will burst into the house of Fenisa and Belisa, he threatening to kill his 'adulterous' spouse, and she desperately seeking refuge.

Once inside the house, Gerarda draws Fenisa aside. Identifying herself as Estefanía, she tells Fenisa that her 'husband' has learned that she is in love with another man, who has returned her affection, and that the man's name is Lucindo. Taken in, Fenisa tells Gerarda/ Estefanía angrily that although she herself was once in love with Lucindo, she now gives him up.

Gerarda leaves and Lucindo enters. He has come to take her away and is flabbergasted when Fenisa receives him icily. She has learned, she says, that he is in love with someone named 'Estefanía'. When he protests that that is not so, she refuses to believe him, saying that she is now going to marry his father. Lucindo leaves and Hernando enters and explains to Fenisa how she has been misled. Soon after, he finds his master in the street and convinces him that Fenisa does truly love him, and that she has one final trick up her sleeve. She will invite the Captain to come to her room that evening, but arrange things so that he will unwittingly end up in the room of her mother, while she waits for Lucindo in her own.

The final scene takes place that evening. Doristeo, Finardo, and Gerarda all end up in front of the house of Belisa. They watch in astonishment as three different men – the Captain, Lucindo, and Hernando – sneak into the house, one by one. Determined to flush out the malefactors who are causing such scandal, they begin to shout, "fire, fire." Within moments five figures – the Captain, Belisa, Lucindo, Fenisa, and Hernando – emerge from the house. The Captain, somewhat sheepishly, explains that he is now married to Belisa, presumably by private vow, and Lucindo says that he is now married to Fenisa. The young lovers beg their parents for forgiveness for having deceived them, which is granted, and the play draws happily to a close.

Characters

Fenisa

Commenting on the general absence of mothers in the *comedia nueva*, Menéndez Pelayo suggests that the *dama* character, raised without maternal guidance, is drawn – at least by Calderón – as "*arrojada, valiente y medio varonil [... y] carece de cierta delicadeza y ternura, que sólo se aprende al lado de la madre*" [daring, brave, and half manly…lacking a certain delicacy and tenderness that is only learned at a mother's side] (*Calderón* 343). Following this logic, as a result of her mother's tutelage and care, Fenisa should in fact be delicate and tender, not at all daring or brave; but quite the opposite is true. Fenisa, the title character of the play, is in love with Lucindo and uses all her audacity, cleverness, and determination to achieve her desire: marriage.

From the first scene of the play, it is clear that Fenisa disagrees with her mother as to the proper comportment of young women. As David Gitlitz has observed, Fenisa's opinion could be interpreted variously, leading to diverging staging of the character at the starting point of the play; on the one hand, she could be played coolly, providing "the easiest transition into the clever, industrious and essentially positive, discreet Fenisa of later in the play." On the other hand, she could also be played as petulant, rebellious, even "intellectually aggressive" (57–58).

Everett Hesse summarizes the hurdles she must overcome as threefold: "first, to engage the affection of Lucindo whose heart now belongs to Gerarda, second, to bring together her mother and the widower, and third, to prevent a marriage between her mother and Lucindo which Fenisa herself had suggested as a diversionary stratagem, but which backfired at the last moment" (3).

Jonathan Thacker suggests that she is "manipulative in that she manages to act as dutiful daughter and fiancée at the same time as being a predatory lover" (*Role-Play* 115). She "does know exactly what she wants, possesses great social poise, and needs no encouragement to set about fulfilling her desires" (132). She uses the Captain, "the chief patriarchal representative as an agent in his own downfall" (134). She does not have a servant who participates in the intrigues, which means that Fenisa cannot rely on her maid to help her carry out her plan. It's all on her and her 'discreción'.

David Gitlitz observes variations of discretion in Fenisa's capabilities of perception: "If in these scenes in Act 2 we play Lucindo's love talk as not yet sincere, we call into question Fenisa's *discreción* insofar as it means wisdom in judging people's character. Yet Fenisa may well be at one and the same time discreet in her use of ingenious stratagems and indiscreet in her initial misjudgment of Lucindo's sincerity or her later misjudgment of his readiness to break faith with her" (62–63).

Belisa

Belisa, Fenisa's widowed mother,[62] is essentially a comic figure; her lessons of modesty and restraint are ironic, since she herself is obsessed with the prospect of marriage, first to the Captain and then to his son. Her panoply of flaws, imperfections, and foibles makes her easily duped or manipulated. She plays the role of the dutiful mother, casting herself as a model for her daughter to imitate. However, in contrast to her daughter, she is neither discreet nor discriminating. Instead, she is vain and presumptuous, a defect that has been seen to be the center of the play's comedy, and she is often the butt of the joke (Rothberg, 'El agente cómico' 76; A. Williamsen 170). Her vanity allows her to believe first that Captain Bernardo is in love with her, and later that his son, Lucindo, has fallen captive to her charms.

The contrast between what she says and what she does is another source of comedy. She urges her daughter to marry for money, but she herself fancies that she can marry for love. Fenisa, aware of her mother's foibles and fantasies, manipulates her mother in her attempt to attain her goal of marriage to Lucindo.

As Amy Williamsen points out, Belisa is not presented as wicked; nor is her vanity so exaggerated as to make her a mere caricature. Her vanity, a very human flaw, renders her susceptible to the trap that Fenisa lays for her:

> Vanity, combined with credulity, leads her to believe that Fenisa's story is true, that [Lucindo], the Capitán's son, really desires her. At the end of the play, Belisa realizes how she has been manipulated by her own daughter, but she does not react in anger; rather, she accepts the situation gracefully. After all, the situation brought about by Fenisa's

---

62 For an overview of mothers in *comedias*, see Caballero. In his study of mothers, Templin ('Mother', p. 22 nn. 8 and 9) counts 159 mothers in Lope (145 if we discard plays with less than certain attribution) in the thirteen volumes of the RAE editions. Pertinent to this play is what he terms the widow type, a ridiculous, unloving, indifferent woman without veneration or gratitude, "combin[ing] hypocrisy and giddiness" (of the *viudita de azar* with traits of a Celestina (p. 223); they range from promoters of their daughters to rivals. Templin lists two main plots of conflict between mother and daughter: 1) marriage for money (mother's wish) and marriage for love (daughter's wish) and 2) rivalry, involving the infatuated mother.

plotting is precisely the one that Belisa had wanted from the beginning. She has married the Capitán and Fenisa has found a suitable young husband. Everything ends in a satisfactory manner for Belisa; however, she herself did nothing to ensure her future − she was merely a pawn in her daughter's game. (170)

Although Rudolph Schevill deemed Belisa as little more than a *dueña* (18), Vern Williamsen finds her to be anything but a stereotypical mother: "More than any of the other women, she is subjected to rapid changes in the direction of her fortune, to which she reacts as the adaptable lady she is" (135).

Gerarda

Gerarda, a courtesan, forms with Doristeo the second young couple of the play. Lucindo is in love with her at the start of the play, but she is somewhat capricious, not willing to submit to any man. She enjoys making Lucindo jealous, but when she thinks he is courting another woman, it is she who is consumed with envy.

According to Carmen Hsu, the courtesan was:

…an integral part of coetaneous urban life. Her freedom of movement was evident and her identification with Madrid, the royal court city, elevated her. Within the open space that urbanization brought along, the courtesan provided a staple of elegant living. She carried with herself an insignia of social importance, culture, refinement, and sentimental companionship. (147)

The object of male rivalry, the courtesan's chief task was to make herself fascinating, and her suitors' was to conform to the established ritual of courtship. She worked hard to play the role, integral to which was its mutability and uncertainty. "A courtesan remains as a courtesan only so long as she can foil attempts to pin her down. This uncertainty misleads, keeps her on the right side of laws, and makes her sexy. Courtesans are the cleverest manipulators of careful self-representation" (Hsu 171).

As Arellano notes, courtesans are frequent characters in Lope's early *comedias urbanas* (*Convención y recepción* 146n3). A far cry from the typical models in Roman comedy (the scheming trickster or the enamored courtesan), Lope's courtesans are not generalized or mocked, as in the *Romancero general*, "but instead, they are now given speaking roles and are individuals rendered in both traditional and nontraditional ways. They provide models for more complex characters" (Hsu 149).

In the case of Gerarda, we find a character who is to a degree both emotionally and psychologically complex. A 'lady of love', Gerarda is beautiful, sassy, flirty, and provocative, not subject to anyone's control, neither that of a partner nor that of the society in which she moves and prospers. She has no formal or legal connection to any man, which is the essence of her freedom, allowing her to pursue her own plans and determine and control her own future.

Her most consistent trait is one that she shares with Fenisa: *ingenio*, cleverness and guile, even mendacity, in order to get what she wants. The difference between the two characters is the ultimate desired result. While Fenisa's stratagems are to secure a legitimate end – matrimony – Gerarda initially has no matrimonial goals. She does evince a somewhat cynical feigning of love, which seems to be linked to material gain. Although we have no evidence that Lucindo is a ready supply of treasure, her machinations to retain his connection to her seem less driven by love than by lucre. Indeed, Hernando refers to her in images of predation: a spider trying to lure prey into her web or an angler trying to hook her fortune and future. Her motivation is not love but greed. Her generosity lies in the number of suitors among whom she distributes her favors, their numbers, according to Lucindo, reaching twenty (*"que es mujer que a veinte trata."* line 877).

However, when push comes to shove, if matrimony is the only way to continue her relationship with her lover, then that becomes her goal. Despite the 'delicadeza' with which Lope depicts Gerarda's dubious morality, Rothberg sees her as shameless, *'desvergonzada'* ('El agente cómico' 87). She lies not only to the men she hopes to ensnare but also to her rival, Fenisa, playing the role of victim, unlucky in love and abandoned by Lucindo, seemingly in a plot to force him to marry her. In the end, she is relegated to her role as courtesan, essentially paired with Doristeo, who, in the last act, seems to have lost interest in her.

'Estefanía'

Vern Williamsen calls 'Estefanía' a "problematic" woman "whose existence depends on those who assume her role" (131) and who "assumes as many characters as she has inventors" (132). For Lucindo, she is an instrument to provoke jealousy in Gerarda. For Hernando, she is a role he assumes in the service of his master. For Doristeo, Estefanía is a sister he believes to have been dishonored by Lucindo. For Gerarda, she is a means to an end: to discover the true state of affairs between Lucindo and Fenisa and, she hopes, a means to break them up. For Fenisa, when she gives credence to Gerarda's 'Estefanía', she is heartbreaking proof that Lucindo has deceived her. In sum, "Estefanía lives in a metatheatrical sense, and the complexities of her character as she is devised by the various actors in the play – our only source of knowledge about her – finally become too self-contradictory, and the illusion disappears as easily as it was created" (V. Williamsen 133).

Captain Bernardo

Captain Bernardo, wealthy widower and retired military officer, is almost a caricature, an amalgam of the boastful soldier (*miles gloriosus*) and the typical *Comedia* father, repository of authority and order. Despite his years and social status, he behaves like a jealous young lover, and his boasting contributes to his being a comic foil. Chronicler of his own merits, in a lengthy monologue he boasts of his accomplishments on the field of battle and the resulting honors and riches, as well as connections to the highest level of nobility (His godparents are the Duke and Duchess of Alba).[63] His rank of Captain would have been designated by the King.

From his references to Palermo and Flanders, we can infer that he was part of one of the twelve companies of the Tercio Viejo de Sicilia, founded in 1536 by Charles V.[64] The Captain reveals that he

---

63   Fernando Álvarez de Toledo y Pimentel, 3rd Duke of Alba (29 October 1507–11 December 1582), known as the Grand Duke of Alba, was an adviser of King Charles I of Spain (Charles V, Holy Roman Emperor), and his successor, Philip II of Spain,

64   See 'Regimiento de Infantería'.

was born in 1560, which would make him forty-six when the play was performed in Salamanca. He would have been able to join the army at some point during the time (between 1571 and 1588) when the Third of Sicily fought in Flanders against the Duke of Orange.

The Captain notes his desirable physical attributes, advising Fenisa that he is younger than he looks. Although undeniably too old for Fenisa, he asserts that he's still attractive and in good shape, and promises to compensate his excessive age with gifts and gallantry. Despite believing himself to be a handsome catch, it is significant that Fenisa tells him that he should pay attention to his hair and beard before they marry, indicating that his appearance is not as youthful as he might think. (Perhaps as well this would make him more easily mistaken for his son in the last scene.) Nevertheless, he is conscious of the fact that he will suffer in comparison to his rival, his son Lucindo, and so determines to get the young man out of the picture, exiling him to Portugal. The plan, although not particularly clever, would be effective were it not for Fenisa's cunning maneuvers.

The Captain's lack of imagination and his interpretation of appearances as reality allow him to become his own worst enemy, serving as an unwitting aide to the schemes of Fenisa to commune with Lucindo. The dramatic irony of the Captain's bluster is more ridiculous to the audience and less threatening to the young lovers; unlike him, we see behind Fenisa's curtain and are witness to the play/ charade in progress.

Lucindo

Lucindo, the gallant of the play, is the unmarried son of Captain Bernardo. While he is the principal male role, his actions are dictated by Fenisa. Although he is at times passionate and daring, Fenisa is nevertheless always in charge. Lucindo is the object of both Gerarda's and Fenisa's attention, although one has to wonder why any woman would be attracted to such a shallow, fickle youth. His relationship with Gerarda is one of dependence on her whims; he suffers from the affronts and games of the courtesan, designed to heighten his jealousy. This is a relationship based on passion, not love, although at the beginning of the play, Lucindo doesn't seem to understand the difference between lust and love, believing himself to be *enamorado*. Gitlitz describes him as a "ridiculous dandy, or an aggressive young tough, much taken with himself" (59).

In contrast to Fenisa, Lucindo is not discreet. It takes his servant, Hernando, to open his eyes, to set him straight, and to help him interpret Fenisa's coded messages, but not before Lucindo dreams up a way to make Gerarda jealous in return; his plan is to have Hernando dress as a woman and accompany him to the Prado, where Lucindo can parade 'Estefanía' in front of the courtesan. The plan works due to darkness, allowing the disguise to take the desired effect, but it is not well thought out. The name he has chosen at random will create a conflict of honor with another of Gerarda's suitors, Doristeo, who thinks that Lucindo is threatening the honor of his sister, Estefanía. (Interestingly, this is one of the few instances of a character's honor resulting in threatened swordplay.)

Hernando

Although Lucindo is the leading male character, it is Hernando, his servant,[65] who has the greatest dramatic weight. Hernando, not Lucindo, discovers Fenisa's clever plan and rescues Lucindo from the most complicated situations. He can play out deceptions to a happy end thanks to his cleverness in thought and work, which surprise his master. His counsel and advice show him to be wiser.

Hernando embodies many of the elements of the typical *gracioso*, both in terms of dialogue and action. Like most *graciosos*, he uses colloquial, even vulgar turns of phrase, in contrast with the language of his master. Many of the words and expressions he uses are not transparent to the modern reader (*mosquetazo, martelo, moscatel, macacao, pandorga, canteleta*), and his allusions to proverbs, jokes, and stories are equally in need of explanatory notes ("*emprender a Irlanda*", "*todos duermen en Madrid, / hasta el Viejo Arias Gonzalo*", "*la doncella Teodor*"), as well as allusions to proverbs (viz. *Solón de Atenas*: flies in spider web).

---

65   NB: no female servant attends to Fenisa or Belisa; although Beatriz is mentioned in dialogue, she never appears on stage.

Typically *graciosos* talk about food and hunger, as does Hernando when he 'courts' Belisa and asks her to make *menudo* for him.

Luciano García Lorenzo finds two sides to this character: one serious (common sense and clarity of vision in advice, especially in contrast with the blindness of Lucindo) and one comic (124). Despite his humble, even vulgar qualities, Hernando is discreet, a perceptive observer, clearly seeing how Gerarda treats Lucindo like a puppet, how she manipulates him through jealousy. He perceives that the Captain is looking to marry, although he is not sure if it is to the mother or the daughter. He recognizes, even deciphers, Fenisa's coded messages and pushes Lucindo into action, guiding him, teaching him about life and how to live it. His advice, his lessons about love and jealousy, sometimes approximate sermons, as in Act 1, when he warns Lucindo of the dangers of "*mujeres libres*".

Notwithstanding his humble status, Hernando manages to convey a sense of dignity even when his actions are involved in ridiculous, carnivalesque roleplaying situations invented by Lucindo: disguised as 'Estefanía' in the Prado, or pretending to be Lucindo courting Belisa in the street outside her window. He is neither a coward nor a braggart, but a faithful servant with more perspicacity, experience, and maturity than his master whom he counsels with wit, intelligence, and loyalty. In fact, Hernando, while not *enamorado*, is certainly *discreto*, and as such is able to recognize Fenisa's *discreción* while Lucindo is blind to what is going on around him. He is Lucindo's rudder and moral compass, and until Fenisa takes over, he dominates his master.

Doristeo

Doristeo, a gentleman, begins the play in love with Gerarda. The second gallant, he is involved in the intrigues of the plot, but never to his own advantage. He is manipulated throughout, first as a passive pawn in Gerarda's schemes to make Lucindo jealous, and then as an active player in her plot to take Lucindo away from Fenisa. The honor of his family is put to the test when he believes that his sister is involved with Lucindo, the author of the Hernando/'Estefanía' farce.

Belisa's husband
Belisa is a widow, and so her husband is obviously not a character
who appears on stage. Nevertheless, in a conversation between
mother and daughter in Act 1, Belisa reveals that she did not marry
for love. If that is so, Fenisa asks, why was she so jealous of her
husband? The widow's reply points both to the unscrupulous behavior
of an adulterous husband, who gives away the family patrimony to
his lover, and to the response of a wronged wife protective of her
children's future. For the majority of women, married life was not
a proverbial bed of roses. In 1589, a priest observed that "it is a
disgrace to see how openly and unashamedly so many adulteries are
committed" (Kamen, *Golden Age Spain* 78).

While moralists might rail against adultery, the attitude of the society
was more tolerant of men in the commission of this sin, effectively
practicing a double standard of behavior. Young women were sheltered
and shielded, but young men were expected to have lovers, both before
and during matrimony. Some accounts reported that youths of twelve or
fourteen years kept mistresses to whom they devoted time and treasure
(Deleito y Piñuela, *La mala vida* 25–29). Keeping a mistress became a
social requirement for men of a certain class, and for some the standard
was to have a wife, keep a mistress, and engage a lover of a higher
social rank than the mistress. It is no surprise that writers of the time like
Antonio de Brunel sustain that the enormous sums men spent on their
'women' was the real cause of Spain's bankruptcy (Deleito y Piñuela,
La mala vida 27).

Metrical Analysis
Act 1

Baja los ojos al suelo	1	Redondillas
Belisa, el ser vecino –que en efeto,	497	Tercetos
A mi hija, capitán	546	Redondillas
Yo no sabía que era vuestro hijo	666	Versos sueltos
Aún no sale aquel galán.	711	Quintillas
¿Estaste aquí todavía?	991	Romance in a-a

Act 2

Notable frescura.	1109	Redondillas
Cuando tan hermosa os miro,	1129	Villancico
Dijeron que llevarían	1140	Redondillas
¡Qué mal se cura amor con invenciones!	1204	Soneto
¿Vengo bien?	1218	Redondillas
Tan consolado vienes, que presumo	1422	Versos sueltos
¡Ah, caballero!	1434	Redondillas
¿Para qué es tanto desdén,	1582	Quintillas
Hacedme aqueste placer,	1657	Redondillas
Una palabra, madre de mis ojos.	1761	Versos sueltos
¿Hay desdicha semejante?	1782	Redondillas
No tengo mal ninguno, por tu vida.	1818	Versos sueltos
Milagro, Fenisa, fue	1868	Quintillas
¿Que todo eso ha pasado?	1913	Octavas reales
Pues no te admires; que peor le tienes.	1937	Versos sueltos
Hablando está con su padre.	1960	Romance in o-a
¿Dónde va aquél?	2028	Octavas reales

Act 3

¿Que mi padre les contó	2076	Redondillas
Sosiega el pecho celoso;	2332	Quintillas
Si supiera vuestro intento,	2382	Redondillas
¡Favor, señores! Socorredme presto,	2446	Versos sueltos
Yo soy, gallarda señora,	2473	Romance in a-a
¿Que Lucindo os quiere bien?	2557	Redondillas
Salga del alma aquel violento rayo	2621	Soneto
Con la determinación,	2635	Quintillas
¿Es mi Fenisa?	2850	Versos sueltos
Arrepintiose.	2884	Redondillas
Yo no sé si le llame desengaño	2948	Octavas reales
Ya puedes volverte a casa.	2972	Redondillas
Di, Lucindo, ¿a un padre noble	3056	Romance in a-a

REDONDILLAS are stanzas of four lines of eight syllables each, generally rhyming the first and fourth lines. Prized for its agility, the re*dondilla* is one of the most frequently used forms in Baroque poetry, fundamental for dialogue, short exchanges, and for moments of tension and physical dynamism (duels, escapes, etc.). And most importantly, as Lope recommended, it is used for love scenes [*"Y para las [cosas] de amor las redondillas"*].

QUINTILLAS are stanzas of five lines, generally of eight syllables with consonant rhyme, combined at the poet's will, but with three limitations: no line should be '*suelto*' or unrhymed; the same consonantal rhyme should not be used for more than two lines in a row; and the last two lines cannot form a couplet. This leaves basically five combinations: *aabba, aabab, abaab, abbab, ababa*. This verse form is used often to characterize a range of emotions, from high to low. Lope used the traditional *quintillas* of the *Cancionero* with innovations taken from Italian poetry introduced by Boscán and Garcilaso.

ROMANCES are a series of eight-syllable lines of indeterminate extension, with assonant rhyme. It is the most characteristic and frequent poetic form of the Spanish language. In elite poetry, the *romance* is often easily divided into groups of four lines or 'sub-stanzas'. In his *Arte Nuevo*, Lope recommended the use of *romances* to tell stories: *"Las relaciones piden los romances."*

TERCETOS are three-line stanzas, generally eleven syllables each, with a consonant rhyme scheme of ABA BCB CDC, etc. They generally end in a quartetto to avoid free verses (*versos sueltos*) (YZYZ). They are used for matters of importance, such as legal deliberations, compromising situations, machinations of intrigue, emotional states, etc. Since they give a measured rhythm to the dialogue, Lope recommended that they be used for serious matters: *"Son los tercetos para cosas graves."*

OCTAVAS REALES are stanzas of eight lines of eleven syllables each in alternating consonant rhyme except for the last two, which form a couplet (ABABABCC). They are used for solemn occasions, in descriptive lyrical dialogues, maintaining a serious and elevated tone. In *Arte Nuevo*, Lope de Vega observed that they were useful to highlight narration. "*...en octavas lucen [las relaciones] por extremo.*" [recitals of events ... shine brilliantly in octavas.]

SONETO. The sonnet is composed of fourteen lines, generally of eleven syllables each, distributed in two quartets and two tercets, although the form admits many variations. The rhyme scheme of the quartets is usually *ABBA ABBA* with the tercets generally in *CDE CDE*. In Golden Age theater, it is recommended for soliloquies and transitions, communicating a thought or emotion in a form that seems to pause the action temporarily. Lope recommended the sonnet for those who wait or hope, especially in love: "*El soneto está bien en los que aguardan.*"

Songs and ballads
Within the polymetry of his plays, Lope characteristically integrated songs into his dramatic texts, in most cases from two to four.[66] Some were popular in origin, as was the song he weaves into Act 1 of *La discreta enamorada*. The four eight-syllable lines of the song (rhyming in *abab*) are not sung but instead are interspersed in Fenisa's dialogue (lines 557, 565, 573, 581) as she realizes her dreams of marrying Lucindo are dashed by his father's proposal to her.

Soñaba yo que tenía	I dreamt that my heart
alegre mi corazón.	was happy.
Mas, a la fe, madre mía,	But truly, dear mother,
que los sueños sueños son.[67]	dreams are only dreams.

For today's reader this passage might evoke *La vida es sueño*, but Calderón's play was written in 1635, almost thirty years after *La discreta enamorada*. The trope of life as a dream was well known and widely used during the Baroque, as was the topic of life as theater.

---

66 For a study of the function of songs in Lope's plays, see Gustavo Umpierre. See also Alín and Barrio Alonso.

67 See Alín and Barrio Alonso. See also Olmedo, p. 207; Pedro de Padilla, *Thesoro de varias poesías* (Madrid 1580) folio 466, cited by Ziomek, 212 n. 9; and Frenk, numbers 268 and 875.

Gemma Burgos Segarra,[68] following Rudolph Schevill, observes the use of the phrase in a *villancico* by Ruiz de Alarcón and in Cervantes's *La Galatea*, as well as in various other works by Lope: *Adonis y Venus*, *Audiencias del rey don Pedro*, *El desprecio agradecido*, and *Belardo el furioso*.

Villancico

In the second act, when Gerarda's musicians offer a serenade in the Prado, Lope inserts a song that Diez de Revenga (117, 118) describes as gallantry wrapped in traditional formulae, using sighs as an element of love. The form might be a traditional *villancico*, consisting of several stanzas (*coplas*) framed by a refrain (*estribillo*) at the beginning and end, giving an overall *ABA* structure. Given that this particular song does not appear in popular songbooks published before the date of the play, it would seem that Lope is the author of the lyrics (Alín and Barrio Alonso 291). While the song did not become popular in the years following the play, it should be noted that Joaquín Turina included it in his *Homenaje a Lope de Vega*, Op. 90 (1924).

'La de Lope': Suspiro por mí el deseo. (Villancico)

Cuando tan hermosa os miro,	When I see you so lovely,
de amor suspiro,	I sigh from love,
y cuando no os veo,	and when I don't see you
suspira por mí el deseo.	desire sighs for me.
Cuando mis ojos os ven,	When my eyes see you,
van a gozar tanto bien,	they will enjoy so much good,
mas como por su desdén	but, because of their disdain
de los vuestros me retiro,	I withdraw from yours,
de amor suspiro,	I sigh from love,
y cuando no os veo,	and when I don't see you,
suspiro por mi deseo.	I sigh for my desire.

---

68   Note to line 581 in the digital edition.

Our Edition

There is no known autograph manuscript of *La discreta enamorada*. As a consequence, we essentially follow Don Cruickshank's suggestions for editing early printed versions. *La discreta enamorada* does not appear in any of the twenty-five *partes* published between 1604 and 1647. We turned to the first known printed version, contained in the *Parte tercera de comedias de los mejores ingenios de España* (Madrid: Melchor Sánchez, 1653).[69] Despite its many errors, we have followed it as closely as possible, correcting obvious lapses and errors while noting significant variations in endnotes, referenced by the line number in which they occur.

In the 1853 edition of the Biblioteca de Autores Españoles (Vol. 24), Hartzenbusch corrects many of the errors in the 1653 edition, but takes liberties with the text, adding many unnecessary stage directions in a desire to clarify movement and position of characters. To a great extent, these additions were continued in subsequent editions. While in a few instances his suggestions are present in the translation, we have not incorporated them into our own edition of the Spanish text, which we have kept as faithful as possible to the first published edition. We have chosen to note asides only when they appear in the 1653 edition. Similarly, we have not indicated the person to whom a character is speaking unless it is noted in the 1653 edition. When we have adopted a reading or correction from another edition, we place it in brackets [] to indicate that it does not appear in the 1653 edition. To avoid redundancy, we have not included explanations for terms in Spanish when the English translation on the facing page provides them.

When significant textual variants are noted, we refer to them by the line number in which they occur. In several instances, the rhyme scheme indicates that one or more lines of verse are missing from the 1653 text. In some instances, other editors have added text to complete the rhyme scheme and we have noted both the addition and the source. In other

---

69 In his *tesina*, Uriarte mentions a *suelta* that he located and consulted in the British Museum. Evidently it consists of the play torn from the *Parte tercera*, bearing the identical page numbers (59–108) as the anthologized version.

instances, no suggestions have been made to complete the stanza; we have not added any text but instead have indicated the missing line by a series of periods [...........]. Additions or modernizations to the text that do not require notes appear in brackets [ ]. Similarly, explanatory notes provide clarification of passages in both the Spanish and the English text that might not be readily comprehended by the modern reader, specifically historical, linguistic, mythological, or literary allusions. They are also noted by line numbers.

Modern rules of accentuation are used throughout, including enclitic pronouns. We have mostly modernized spelling when those changes do not alter syllable count in a line. Such changes are: b → v (*buelbo* → *vuelvo*, *esclaba* → *eclava*); ç → z (*alça* → *alza*, *lienço* → *lienzo*, *moço* → *mozo*); g → j (*muger* → *mujer*, *sugeto* → *sujeto*, *ageno* → *ajeno*); (h) → h [supression of "h"] (*aviendo* → *habiendo*, *ay* → *hay*); i → j (*Iubileo* → *Jubileo*); o → u (mormurar → murmurar); q → c (*quando* → *cuando*); s → x (*estremos* → *extremos*); *sino* → *si no*; ss → s (*processo* → *proceso*); u → b (*auéis* → *habéis*, *auer* → *haber*); v → u (*vn* → *un*); *v.m.* → *vuestra merced*; x → j (*baxa* → *baja*); y → hi (*yelo* → *hielo*); y → i (*cegays* → *cegáis*); z → c (*Luzindo* → *Lucindo*, *zelos* → *celos*).

In several cases, we maintain archaic usage, especially but not exclusively when it affects the meter or rhyme: *agora* (ahora); *ansí* (así); *deso* (de eso); *desto* (de esto); *entrábades* (entrabas); *esotra* (esa otra); *fuérades* (fuerais); *habemos* (hemos); *liciones* (lecciones); *trujiste/ trujo* (trajiste/trajo). In the case of *efeto* vs. *efecto*, *aceto* vs. *acepto*, we modernize the form unless it affects the rhyme, in which case we note it.

Readers will notice other variations from modern usage that are standard poetic forms of the time:

- Cases of assimilation, in which the final 'r' of an infinitive can change to an 'l' when a pronoun is attached to the infinitive, usually for purposes of maintaining the rhyme. Examples are: *amarla* → *amalla*, *pretenderla* → *pretendella*, *sacarla* → *sacalla*, *subirla* →*subilla*.
- Occasional elimination of the personal 'a' before infinitives or direct objects. We insert [a] if it is not present in 1653.

- Varying position of pronouns, sometimes before, sometimes after the verb (e.g., *dejárasme, te ve*).
- Use of the imperfect subjunctive when the meaning would require the use of a conditional form (*cumplieras* instead of *cumplirías*).
- Metathesis, in which the last letter of the verb and the first letter of the attached pronoun are switched (e.g., *dejadle* → *dejalde*, *perdonadle* → *perdonalde*).
- Apocopation, or the omission of the final sound or sounds of a word, is not always used when modern usage would expect it (*grande valor* instead of *gran valor*); however, some words are apocopated to fit the syllable count (*casa* → *ca, quienes* → *quien*).

Other differences that are less frequent that might cause the reader to question the text are variations of verb forms, often in the service of rhyme or meter, a characteristic *leismo* (using the pronoun *le* instead of the modern usage of *lo*), eliminating a form of *haber* [*he, ha*] before a past participle beginning with 'a', use of *en* instead of *a* or *de* before an object (e.g., *Yo adoro en Estefanía* or *hablando a su padre en ti*).

Editions of *La discreta enamorada*
We consulted the following editions in preparing our own.

Manuscripts
1735, copista Isidro Rodríguez, Biblioteca Palatina, Parma (CC V 28932.19).
1851(?), Biblioteca Nacional de España (MSS/15232). Available online at <http://bdh.bne.es/bnesearch/detalle/bdh0000050968>.

Printed editions[70]
1653, in *Parte tercera de comedias de los meiores ingenios de España* (Madrid: Melchor Sánchez). Available online at http://bdh.bne.es/bnesearch/detalle/bdh0000073320.
1853, in *Comedias escogidas de Frey Lope Felix de Vega Carpio*, ordenadas

---

70 The following editions follow the 1653 edition closely or mainly: both manuscripts (1753 Parma and 1851? BNE), 1928 Tenreiro, 1955 Guarner, 1990 Pedraza, 1998 Gómez.

por Juan Eugenio Hartzenbusch. Biblioteca de Autores Españoles vol. 24 (Madrid: Rivadeneyra).

1876, 1899, in *Biblioteca Universal. Colección de los mejores autores antiguos y modernos nacionales y extranjeros*, vol. XXV. (Madrid: [Hernando]).

1910, in *Lope de Vega. Comedias* (Valencia: Prometeo).

1913, in *Obras de Lope de Vega publicadas por la Real Academia Española*, vol. XIV, Comedias novelescas, segunda sección (Madrid: Rivadeneyra). Prepared by Marcelino Menéndez Pelayo, who died before completing an introduction.

1928. ed. R. M. Tenreiro. (Madrid: Compañía Ibero-Americana de Publicaciones).

1928. Colección Universal. (Madrid: Espasa-Calpe).

1940. Edición anotada. (Buenos Aires: Sopena).

1948. (Buenos Aires: Espasa-Calpe).

1955. ed. Luis Guarner. Colección Obras Maestras. (Barcelona: Editorial Iberia).

1971, in *Obras de Lope de Vega*, tomo XXXI: Comedias novelescas. Biblioteca de Autores Españoles vol. 247. (Madrid: Atlas,). See 1913.

1990, in *Lope de Vega esencial*, ed. Felipe Pedraza. (Madrid: Taurus).

1998, in *Obras completas de Lope de Vega*, vol. 15. ed. Jesús Gómez et al. (Madrid: Turner).

2012. (Barcelona: Linkgua Teatro).

Other editions[71]

In addition, we consulted the following editions, one unpublished and the others posted online. (All are based on the 1653 edition):

1971. ed. José Angel Uriarte (Univ. de Deusto: *Memoria de licenciatura*).

1984. ed. Vern Williamsen (AHCT online)

2019. ed. Gemma Burgos (Colección EMOTHE. Biblioteca Digital ARTELOPE).

---

71   We did not include Francisco Romero's version (available on the Biblioteca Virtual Miguel de Cervantes website) since it is vastly reduced (by over 1000 lines), presumably for performance.

Translator's Note

My English version of Lope de Vega's sparkling comedy had its origin in a workshop on literary translation that I attended a few years ago at the annual meeting of the Association for Hispanic Classical Theater in El Paso. The leader of the workshop was the eminent translator David Johnston, whose work I have long admired. Although Johnston chose to conduct the session mainly as a practicum, with each participant responsible for translating a brief passage from a Golden Age play to be submitted to others for comments and suggestions, over the course of two hours he made observations that taken together amounted to a précis of his personal theory of theatrical translation.

Among the remarks that have remained with me is that every act of translation may usefully be thought of as double-faceted conversation; on the one hand, a conversation between two languages, each with its own particularities, limitations, strengths and weaknesses; and on the other a conversation between two worlds, each of which is located in a specific place and a particular moment in time, the here and now, and the there and then. Out of these encounters comes enlightenment, increased understanding of the values, beliefs, and cultural assumptions both of the inhabitants of the other world, and those of one's own.

Illumination, then, is a major part of the theatrical event, but it is not the only important element. Also significant are the experience of being moved, entertained, and engaged, and, for a few moments anyway, absorbed into the community of fellow playgoers. Undergoing such an experience requires that the translator understand the concerns and preoccupations of the audience for which he or she is writing, and be able to speak to it in its own language, with words and terms that it will grasp readily.

Stimulated by Johnston's observations, on the flight home from the AHCT conference I began to consider the possibility of undertaking to translate a lively play that would appeal to contemporary audiences. The play that I quickly hit upon was Lope's *La discreta enamorada*. The kind of translation that I wished to write was also clear in my mind. It was not to be an 'academic' or literal version, aiming for 'fidelity' to the original text, however that might be defined. It was to be, rather, 'stageable' or 'playable'. It does not pretend to be faithful to the original next, but rather to engage the audience on its own terms, to which end it does not shy from colloquialisms nor from modern-day slang and diction. It recognizes that just as the character of audiences changes over time, so must the nature of the translations employed to bring older works to life on modern stages. The history of translations is thus the history of adaptations, each one fitted to the expectations and experiences of its particular group of spectators.

Although the translation/adaptation that follows is meant to be an acting version of Lope's play and is for the most part not literal, I like to think that it is broadly true to the sense of Lope's text. My intention throughout was to write in a language recognizable as modern English, although the tone is often more formal than would be common these days. I haven't avoided that elevation because I think it gives a feeling of 'foreignness' suggestive of seventeenth-century Spanish culture.

My text is broadly metrical in the sense that I've rendered Lope's eight and eleven syllable lines into lines of more or less equal length. Except in the two sonnets and the song at the beginning of Act 2, I've made no effort to rhyme, although sometimes it has popped up more or less spontaneously.

It is my hope that I've captured something of the humor of the play, as well as the energy, speed, and elliptical feeling of the dialogue. I also hope that I've conveyed at least some of the quality of the different voices, ranging from the most colloquial (Hernando) to the most formal (the Captain). I've also tried to be attentive to the rapid changes of register among the voices and even within individual speeches. That, too, is found in Lope's play in abundance, and adds to the feeling of hurry and impatience that characterizes this delightful work.

THE CLEVEREST GIRL IN MADRID

LA DISCRETA ENAMORADA

Personas que hablan en ella

Belisa, viuda.
Fenisa, su hija.
El Capitán Bernardo.
Lucindo, su hijo.
Hernando.
Leonardo, su criado.
Gerarda, dama.
Doristeo, gentilhombre.
Finardo, su amigo.
Fulminato.
MÚSICOS.

The Characters of the Play

Belisa, a widow
Fenisa, her daughter
Captain Bernardo
Lucindo, his son
Hernando, a servant
Doristeo, a nobleman
Finardo, a nobleman
Gerarda, a courtesan
Leonardo, a servant (non-speaking)
Fulminato, a servant
Liseo, a musician
Fabio, a musician

JORNADA PRIMERA

Salen Belisa, viuda, Fenisa, dama, su hija.

BELISA	Baja los ojos al suelo,	*redondillas*
	porque sólo has de mirar	
	la tierra que has de pisar.	
FENISA	¿Que no he de mirar al cielo?	
BELISA	No repliques, bachillera.	5
FENISA	Pues ¿no quieres que me asombre?	
	Crïó Dios derecho al hombre	
	porque el cielo ver pudiera;	
	y de su poder sagrado	
	fue advertencia singular,	10
	para que viese el lugar	
	para donde fue crïado.	
	Los animales, que el cielo	
	para la tierra crïó,	
	miren el suelo; mas yo	15
	¿por qué he de mirar al suelo?	
BELISA	Mirar al cielo podrás	
	con sólo el entendimiento;	
	que un honesto pensamiento	
	mira la tierra no más.	20
	La vergüenza en la doncella	
	es un tesoro divino.	
	Con ella a mil bienes vino,	
	y a dos mil males sin ella.	
	Cuando quieras contemplar	25
	en el cielo, en tu aposento	
	con mucho recogimiento,	
	tendrás, Fenisa, lugar.	
	Desde allí contemplarás	
	de su grandeza el proceso.	30

ACT ONE

The action takes place in Madrid. The time is the early seventeenth century.
In the street.
Enter Belisa and Fenisa.

BELISA	Finea, I've told you, eyes down!	
	When in the street you are to look	
	Only at the ground you walk on.	
FENISA	You mean I can't look at the sky?	
BELISA	Don't argue with me, young lady!	5
FENISA	But why? Why may I not contemplate	
	The wonder of the sky? God made	
	Man upright so that he could see	
	The heavens, that glorious sign	
	Of His sacred power, and thus	10
	Behold the celestial home he hopes	
	To gain while toiling here below.	
	Animals, which God created	
	For the purpose of life on earth,	
	Let them cast their eyes on the ground.	15
	But why must I also look down?	
BELISA	You can gaze upon the heavens	
	With your understanding alone.	
	Honest and godly looks incline	
	Downward, never the other way.	20
	A young girl given a good name	
	Owns a jewel of great value;	
	With it come a thousand good things,	
	And without it a thousand ills.	
	If you should wish to meditate	25
	On the heavens, you may do so,	
	Daughter, secluded in your room	
	At home, safe, quiet, and alone.	
	There you may reflect all you want	
	On the majesty of God's work.	30

FENISA	No soy monja, ni profeso
	las liciones que me das,
	y si para atormentarme
	me trujiste al jubileo,
	más cumplieras tu deseo	35
	pudiendo en casa encerrarme.
	Dejárasme con diez llaves.
BELISA	Estremos haces agora.
FENISA	Pues ¿no he de sentir, señora,
	que por momentos me acabes?	40
	Con mis ojos vas riñendo.
	¿En qué te dan ocasión?
BELISA	Por ser santa la estación,
	voy tus ojos componiendo.
	Y no recibas enojo;	45
	que doncellas y hermosuras
	son como las criaturas,
	que suelen morirse de ojo.
	Hay mancebete en Madrid,
	que, si te mira al soslayo,	50
	hará el efecto del rayo.
FENISA	El efecto me decid.
BELISA	Abrasarte el corazón,
	dejando sano el vestido.
FENISA	Ya sabes tú que no he sido	55
	de tan tierna condición.
BELISA	Decía tu abuela honrada
	que una doncella altanera
	era en la calle una fiera
	de cazadores cercada.	60
	Piérdese cuando la alaban,
	ríndese cuando suspiran;
	que cuantos ojos la miran,
	con tantas flechas la clavan.
FENISA	Pues ¿cuándo se ha de casar	65
	una mujer nunca vista?
BELISA	Eso no ha de ser conquista;
	que es imposible acertar.

FENISA	I'm not a nun, Mother, and I
	Don't assent to all your teachings.
	And if you brought me here today
	Just to torture and torment me,
	You could have better achieved your 35
	Wishes by leaving me at home,
	Locked up in my room with ten keys.
BELISA	Now you're being ridiculous!
FENISA	But how can I not be upset
	When you go on picking at me? 40
	You're always reproaching my eyes;
	What offense have they given you?
BELISA	You need to watch where you're looking,
	Because these are high holy days.
	And please don't be angry with me; 45
	Young ladies and beautiful girls
	are like helpless creatures who
	Die when struck by the evil eye.
	There are young gallants in Madrid
	Who, merely by glancing at you, 50
	Produce an effect like lightning.
FENISA	Yes? What kind of effect is that?
BELISA	They burn your heart to a cinder,
	But leave the clothes you wear untouched.
FENISA	I'm not a mere child. I know all 55
	About the ways and tricks of men.
BELISA	Your sainted grandmother would say
	A proud, young girl seen on the street
	Will draw a pack of men just like
	A poor beast pursued by hunters. 60
	When praised she forgets who she is;
	When they sigh she gives in to them.
	All the sly glances she receives
	Are like arrows that pierce her heart.
FENISA	If she is never seen by men 65
	How is a woman to marry?
BELISA	It's not a matter of conquest;
	That's a game that cannot be won.

FENISA	Pues ¿qué ha de ser?
BELISA	Buena fama
	de virtud y de nobleza.

70

FENISA	Donde falta la riqueza
	mucho la hermosura [llama];
	que ya no quieren los hombres
	sola virtud.
BELISA	Pues ¿qué?
FENISA	Hacienda.

Salen Lucindo, Gerarda y Hernando, criado de Lucindo.

GERARDA	¿Que soy tu querida prenda?
LUCINDO	Así es razón que te nombres.
GERARDA	Galán de palabras vienes.
LUCINDO	Ando al uso.
FENISA	Éste es Lucindo.
GERARDA	Luego ¿préciaste de lindo?
LUCINDO	¿De lindo? Donaire tienes.
	Préciome de hombre.
FENISA	¡Ay de mí!
	Locamente imaginé
	poner en hombre la fe,
	que con el alma le di,
	no habiendo nacido dél
	la pretensión de mi amor.
GERARDA	Para un amante hablador
	soy en las tretas crüel;
	que conmigo no hay chacota,
	por vida del gusto mío.
LUCINDO	De tus locuras me río.
GERARDA	¡Qué gato de a[l]galia azota!
	Por su vida, que no saque
	con arrobas de rigor,
	un adarme de mi amor.
LUCINDO	Tu rigor mi amor aplaque;
	que alabarte una mujer
	que pasaba junto a ti,

75

80

85

90

95

FENISA	Then what is it a matter of?	
BELISA	A reputation for virtue	
	And nobility of the soul.	70
FENISA	When a girl is lacking in means	
	Beauty has many attractions;	
	Men these days are not looking just	
	For virtue.	
BELISA	What else?	
FENISA	A dowry.	

Enter Lucindo, Gerarda, and Hernando. They remain on one side of the street, distant from Belisa and Fenisa.

GERARDA	You say I'm your dearest treasure?	75
LUCINDO	So you should consider yourself.	
GERARDA	Aren't you the smooth talker today!	
LUCINDO	It's all the style.	
FENISA	*(Aside.)* (There's Lucindo.)	
GERARDA	You confess that you're a dandy?	
LUCINDO	A dandy? You must be joking.	80
	I confess I am a man!	
FENISA	*(Aside.)* (Dear God,	
	How mad can I possibly be,	
	To have placed my faith in someone,	
	To have given him all my soul,	
	Without a shred of evidence	85
	That he's even aware of me.)	
GERARDA	For a lover full of speeches	
	My cruelty has no limits;	
	A pretty song-and-dance has for	
	Me no appeal whatsoever.	90
LUCINDO	What drivel! Your words make me laugh.	
GERARDA	And you are beating a dead cat!	
	Insult me if you will, but be	
	Aware that a pound of harsh words	
	Will not get you one ounce of love.	95
LUCINDO	Let my love appease your anger.	
	If I happened to compliment,	
	Without giving it any thought,	

	no haciendo malicia en mí,	
	¿qué delito puede ser?	100
	Y ya te dije que tú	
	eras mi querida prenda.	
GERARDA	Vaya a poner esa tienda	
	a las Indias del Perú.	
	Todas esas niñerías	105
	[de] cuentas y de espejuelos	
	para bobas son anzuelos;	
	no conmigo argenterías.	
	Oro macizo de amor	
	me han de dar, [no] plomo, a mí.	110
FENISA	¿Que a quien no sabe de mí	
	amase con tal rigor?	
	¿Que no me conozca este hombre,	
	y que me muera por él?	

Salen Doristeo y Finardo.

FINARDO	Por aquí la vi con él.	115
DORISTEO	Y ¿es galán?	
FINARDO	Es gentilhombre.	
DORISTEO	¿Si son estos?	
FINARDO	Estos son.	
GERARDA	¿Ve aquel mancebo que viene?	
LUCINDO	Sí veo.	
GERARDA	Pues aquél tiene	
	de mis veras posesión.	120
	Cuanto [te] dije es fingido;	
	cuanto [te] quise es burlando.	
	Voyme; que me está aguardando.	

Pásase al otro.

LUCINDO	¿Qué haré?	
HERNANDO	Mosquetazo ha sido.	
LUCINDO	¿Quitarele la mujer?	125
	¿Acuchillarele, Hernando?	
HERNANDO	¿Quiéresla?	

	A young woman who passed us by,	
	Just what crime have I committed?	100
	Didn't I already tell you	
	That you are my precious treasure?	
GERARDA	Go peddle those wares somewhere else;	
	They'll fetch a good price in Peru.	
	All that ludicrous flattery	105
	Is nothing but cheap jewelry	
	Designed to catch half-wits and fools.	
	Don't come to me with silver rings	
	Eighteen carat gold is my thing;	
	That's what I want, and nothing less.	110
FENISA	*(Aside.)* (How can I possibly love a	
	Man who's oblivious of me?	
	He doesn't know me from Adam,	
	Yet here I am, dying for him.)	

Enter Doristeo and Finardo, forming a third group. Belisa and Fenisa remain on one side. Lucindo, Gerarda, and Hernando on the other.

FINARDO	I saw her with him around here.	115
DORISTEO	Is he gallant?	
FINARDO	A gentleman.	
DORISTEO	Are those the two over there?	
FINARDO	Yes.	
GERARDA	Do you see the man who's coming?	
LUCINDO	That one? Of course.	
GERARDA	Well, he's the one	
	To whom I now give my true self.	120
	Everything I told you is false;	
	My love for you was just pretense.	
	But I must go. He's waiting there.	

Gerarda moves over to Doristeo.

LUCINDO	*(To Hernando.)* What should I do?	
HERNANDO	She shot you down!	
LUCINDO	Should I snatch her away from him?	125
	Should I draw my dagger and fight?	
HERNANDO	Do you love her?	

LUCINDO	Estoyme abrasando.
HERNANDO	Agua será menester.
	¡Que nadie merezca [amor]
	sino es las libres mujeres! 130
GERARDA	Digo que mis ojos eres.
DORISTEO	Templando vas mi rigor.
	Como acompañarte vi
	este galán majadero,
	preciado de caballero, 135
	notable enojo sentí;
	mas en ver que le has dejado,
	brazos y gracias te doy.
GERARDA	Ven[te] conmigo. [Que voy.]
DORISTEO	¿Adónde?
GERARDA	[Hacia e]l Prado. 140

Vanse los dos.

LUCINDO	¿Fuéronse?
HERNANDO	Con mucha prisa.
	No te aflijas, que es martelo.
LUCINDO	¿Quién es aquélla?
HERNANDO	Recelo
	que [es la] vecina Fenisa;
	pero tiene una giganta 145
	por madre; que es emprender
	a Irlanda.
FENISA	Nunca mujer
	se puso a locura tanta.
	¡A un hombre que no me ha visto,
	ni se acuerda si nací, 150
	quiero bien!
LUCINDO	Nunca la vi.
FENISA	¡Qué mal mi inquietud resisto!
	¿Cómo le daré ocasión
	para que el rostro me vea?
	Amor mil cosas rodea. 155
	Todas sin remedio son.

LUCINDO	I'm on fire!
HERNANDO	In that case, I'd call for water.
	Look, the only girls you should love
	Are the ones who are free as birds. 130
GERARDA	*(To Doristeo.)* I've said you're the light of my eyes.
DORISTEO	All right; I'm starting to calm down.
	When I saw you with that young man,
	That pompous and callow fellow
	Who presumes to be a gentleman, 135
	I admit I got a bit steamed;
	But now that I see you've left him,
	I give you my arms and my thanks.
GERARDA	I have to leave. Do come with me.
DORISTEO	Yes, of course. Where?
GERARDA	I'm going home. 140

Exit Gerarda, Doristeo, and Finardo. Remaining on one side are Belisa and Fenisa. On the other, Lucindo and Hernando also remain.

LUCINDO	Did they leave?
HERNANDO	As fast as they could.
	She's trying to make you jealous.
LUCINDO	Who's that young woman?
HERNANDO	I suspect
	That it's your neighbor, Fenisa.
	Her mother stands guard at their door; 145
	You'd sooner sneak by Cerberus
	Than get by her.
FENISA	*(Aside.)* Was there ever
	A woman as senseless as I?
	I love a man who not only
	Has never seen me, he doesn't 150
	Know I exist.)
LUCINDO	I've never seen her.
FENISA	*(Aside.)* (I just can't resist what I feel.
	I need to think of something so
	He'll be able to see my face.
	Love hatches many stratagems 155
	But most will likely come to naught.)

HERNANDO	Si vieses esta doncella,
	te doy palabra, señor,
	que olvides tu loco amor,
	porque es sabia, honesta y bella; 160
	aunque no sé qué he pensado
	de tu padre.
LUCINDO	¿De mi padre?
HERNANDO	Pero quizá con su madre
	casarse tiene pensado,
	y aun es más puesto en razón. 165
LUCINDO	¿Casarse mi padre agora?
HERNANDO	Habla y mira a esta señora,
	que es de rara perfección.
LUCINDO	Llevome el alma Gerarda;
	celos me tienen sin mí. 170
	¿Qué quieres que mire aquí?
HERNANDO	Esta hermosura gallarda.
LUCINDO	No hay vista en hombre celoso;
	todo le parece mal.
FENISA	Ya he pensado traza igual 175
	a mi designio amoroso.
	Pasaré junto a Lucindo,
	dejaré el lienzo caer,
	y al dármele, podrá ser
	mire el alma que le rindo; 180
	que si a los ojos me mira,
	verá toda el alma en ellos.
HERNANDO	Mira aquellos ojos bellos,
	donde amor, de amor suspira.
BELISA	Vámonos, hija; que es hora 185
	de recogernos a casa.
HERNANDO	Ya junto a nosotros pasa;
	mira su belleza agora.

Pasa, y deja caer el lienzo.

LUCINDO	Un ángel me ha parecido.
HERNANDO	El lienzo se le cayó. 190
LUCINDO	Quedo; darésele yo.
	Que volváis el rostro os pido.

HERNANDO	If you got a good look at that	
	Young lady, I assure you, sir,	
	That you'd forget your foolish love.	
	She's clever, chaste, and beautiful –	160
	Although now that I think of it,	
	Your father...	
LUCINDO	Yes, what about him?	
HERNANDO	But it could be it's her mother	
	That he's proposing to marry,	
	Which would be more reasonable.	165
LUCINDO	My father, marry at his age?	
HERNANDO	Just go speak to that young lady;	
	You'll see she's perfection itself.	
LUCINDO	Gerarda has captured my soul.	
	I'm so jealous I'm not myself.	170
	What do you want me to look at?	
HERNANDO	Her beauty that's beyond compare!	
LUCINDO	A jealous man is blind to all;	
	Everything seems worthless to him.	
FENISA	*(Aside.)* (I think I have the perfect plan	175
	To achieve the goal I'm after.	
	I'll walk by Lucindo and then	
	Drop my handkerchief to the ground;	
	When he returns it, it may be	
	He'll realize that I love him.	180
	For if he looks me in the eyes	
	He can't miss my soul burning there.)	
HERNANDO	Just look at those beautiful eyes;	
	Don't you see how they sigh with love?	
BELISA	Come now, daughter; the hour is late.	185
	It's time that we're at home again.	
HERNANDO	She's walking in this direction;	
	What a sight for sore eyes she is!	

Belisa and Fenisa pass by, and Fenisa drops her handkerchief.

LUCINDO	She's like a beautiful angel!	
BELISA	Look! She just dropped her handkerchief.	190
LUCINDO	Yes, I can see. I'll give it back.	
	I beg you, let me see your face.	

Alza el lienzo.

FENISA	¿Qué es, señor, lo que mandáis?
LUCINDO	Este lienzo se os cayó.
FENISA	¿A mí? Sospecho que no.
	Pero esperad.

195

Desenfá[l]dase toda, y descúbrese.

LUCINDO	¿Qué buscáis?
FENISA	Si tengo en la manga el mío.
BELISA	¿Qué es eso?
FENISA	En ésta no está.
BELISA	¿Qué es eso?
FENISA	El lienzo me [da].
BELISA	Pues ¿es tuyo?
LUCINDO	¡Gentil brío!
FENISA	Eso es lo que ando mirando.
	En ésta no está tampoco.
HERNANDO	Volver puede un hombre loco
	aquel mirar suave y blando.
FENISA	Miraré las faldriqueras.
BELISA	Acaba.
FENISA	Ya me doy prisa.
	No está aquí.
BELISA	Vamos, Fenisa.
FENISA	Ni en estotra está.
BELISA	¿Qué esperas?
FENISA	¿Tiene unas randas?
LUCINDO	Sí tiene.
FENISA	¿Y encaje?
LUCINDO	¿No lo miráis?
BELISA	Despacio en la calle estáis,
	donde todo el mundo viene.
FENISA	Pues ¿quiere v[uestra] m[erced]
	que lleve lo que no es mío?
LUCINDO	Señora, de vos le fío.
FENISA	Haceisme mucha merced.
	¿Tiene un poco descosido
	de una randa?

200

205

210

215

He picks up the handkerchief and addresses Finea.

FENISA	What is it that you're asking, sir?
LUCINDO	It seems you've dropped your handkerchief.
FENISA	You say *I* did? I don't think so. 195
	But wait...

She shakes out her skirts, revealing a bit of ankle, allows her veil to drop, and hikes up her sleeves.

LUCINDO	What are you looking for?
FENISA	To see if mine is in my sleeve.
BELISA	What's all this?
FENISA	It's not in this one.
BELISA	What's going on?
FENISA	He gave me this.
BELISA	Is it yours?
LUCINDO	*(Aside.)* (What spirit she has!) 200
FENISA	That's what I'm trying to find out.
	Well, it's not in this sleeve either.
HERNANDO	The kind, gentle look of her eye
	Could drive a man out of his mind.
FENISA	I'll check the pockets of my skirt. 205
BELISA	Stop that at once!
FENISA	I'm hurrying.
	It's not here.
BELISA	Fenisa, let's go.
FENISA	Not here either.
BELISA	What's holding you?
FENISA	Is there edging?
LUCINDO	Yes, there is.
FENISA	Made out of lace?
LUCINDO	Don't you see it? 210
BELISA	You're making a scene in the street,
	Where you'll be seen by all the world.
FENISA	But, sir, is it really your wish
	That I should take what isn't mine?
LUCINDO	My lady, you have all my trust. 215
FENISA	You do me a great courtesy.
	Are the stitches of the edging
	Somewhat undone?

LUCINDO	Sí, sospecho.
FENISA	¿A qué lado?
BELISA	Es sin provecho.
LUCINDO	Sospecho que de vos ha sido.

220

BELISA	Señor, deja[d]nos pasar.

Poned el lienzo en la pila
del agua bendita.

FENISA	Afila

Amor, tu flecha al tirar.

BELISA	Vamos.
FENISA	Yo voy.
HERNANDO	¿No es hermosa?

225

LUCINDO	Celos, ¿por qué me cegáis?

Vuelve Fenisa.

FENISA	¡Ah, señor!
LUCINDO	¿Qué me mandáis?
FENISA	Advertiros de una cosa:

   si de aqueste lienzo acaso
parece más cierto dueño,

230

que mi palabra os empeño...
Iba a decir que me abraso. *Aparte.*
   ...que no sé cierto si es mío;
diréis que vivo en la calle
de los Jardines...

HERNANDO	¡Qué talle!

235

¡Qué gracia! ¡Qué rico brío!

FENISA	...enfrente del Capitán

Bernardo Lucindo.

LUCINDO	El mismo

es mi padre.

FENISA	¡Ay dulce abismo

donde abrasándome están!

240

BELISA	¿Estás loca?
FENISA	Ya me voy;

que aqueste hidalgo decía
que es mi vecino.

LUCINDO	It looks that way.	
FENISA	On which side?	
BELISA	We're getting nowhere.	
LUCINDO	Dear lady, I'm certain it's yours.	220
BELISA	Sir, we must go. Please let us by.	
	Just leave the handkerchief by the	
	Font in the parish church.	
FENISA	*(Aside.)* (Cupid,	
	Now's the time to launch your arrows.)	
BELISA	Come!	
FENISA	I'm coming.	
HERNANDO	What a woman!	225
LUCINDO	Jealousy, why do you blind me?	

Fenisa starts to leave, turns and returns.

FENISA	Sir?	
LUCINDO	What is your wish, my lady?	
FENISA	I only wanted to say this:	
	If someone with a better claim	
	To this handkerchief should appear,	230
	And once more I give you my word…	
	(Aside.) (I almost said give you my love.)	
	…That I'm not certain that it's mine,	
	Tell her that the house where I live	
	Is on Garden Street…	
HERNANDO	What boldness,	235
	What cleverness, what a figure!	
FENISA	…Across from the house of Captain	
	Bernardo Lucindo.	
LUCINDO	Really?	
	He's my father!	
FENISA	*(Aside.)* (Oh, sweet abyss!	
	I'm already burning with love!)	240
BELISA	Are you quite mad?	
FENISA	I'm coming now;	
	This gentleman was just saying	
	That he's our neighbor.	

BELISA   ¡Porfía!
                    Vamos.
FENISA   ¡Qué perdida estoy!

Vanse las dos.

HERNANDO   ¿Qué te parece?
LUCINDO   Que es bella,   245
                    cortés, discreta y gallarda;
                    mas quiero bien a Gerarda,
                    y vase el alma tras ella.
                        Celos es suelo traidor,
                    resbaladizo de [suerte]   250
                    que hará caer al más fuerte
                    en los lodos del amor.
                        Terrible cosa es mirar
                    una mujer desdeñosa
                    hablar otro hombre celosa,   255
                    cuando se quiere vengar.
                        Aunque mi amor fuera poco,
                    que poco debe de ser,
                    ver tan libre una mujer
                    bastaba [a] volverme loco.   260
HERNANDO   Mujeres libres, señor,
                    son siempre las más queridas,
                    y aún iba a decir perdidas,
                    pues han perdido el honor.
                        Llora la mujer honrada   265
                    el siempre injusto desdén
                    del hombre que quiere bien;
                    y a él no se le da nada,
                        porque sabe que ha de estar
                    pudriéndose en su aposento;   270
                    pero cuando el pensamiento
                    se pone aquí no hay burlar;
                        que apenas con los enojos
                    sacarás de casa el pie,
                    cuando consolada esté   275
                    con mil hombres a tus ojos.

BELISA   Will you stop!
            Let's go!
FENISA   *(Aside.)* (There's no hope for me now.)

Exit Fenisa and Belisa.

HERNANDO What do you think?
LUCINDO   She's enchanting,   245
            Beautiful, discreet, and clever,
            But I'm in love with Gerarda,
            And I've given my soul to her.
            Jealousy's a treacherous slope,
            So shifting and so slippery   250
            That it will trip up the strongest
            And cast them into love's deep mire.
            It's a terrible thing to watch
            An arrogant, jealous woman
            Speak to another man because   255
            She wants vengeance on her lover.
            Although my love may have been spare,
            And spare is what I'd say it was,
            It was enough to drive me mad
            When I saw her frivolous ways.   260
HERNANDO Women of easy virtue, sir,
            Are always those whom men desire;
            But they deserve to be called lost,
            Because what they've lost is honor.
            A woman of unstained virtue   265
            Weeps over the unjust disdain
            Of the man she loves and desires,
            And she gives up nothing to him,
            Because she knows she must remain
            Alone and wretched in her room.   270
            But woe to those who think too much
            And contemplate what freedom brings.
            Focused on their unjust prison,
            They'll find a way to slip their ties
            And seek new life out on the street,   275
            Where men will bow down at their feet.

LUCINDO	Por eso el amor no dura	
	en libres, sino en honradas.	
HERNANDO	Cuelgan de celos y espadas	
	hombres de poca cordura,	280
	quiero decir poca edad.	
	Ya espero verte algún día	
	lejos de aquesta porfía	
	y cerca desta verdad.	
LUCINDO	Har[t]as causas me retiran.	285
HERNANDO	Una mujer libre y loca	
	es como mona, que coca	
	a los niños que la miran;	
	pero cuando llega el hombre	
	que tiene gobierno y palo	290
	espúlgale con regalo,	
	y no hay voz que no le asombre.	
	A los mozos sin consejo	
	las mujeres hacen cocos,	
	porque son niños y locos;	295
	no al hombre maduro y viejo.	
	Ya te ha visto en los anzuelos;	
	y aunque no puede sacarte,	
	alarga cuerda, con darte	
	celos, celos y más celos.	300
LUCINDO	¿Qué he de hacer?	
HERNANDO	Buscar, señor,	
	una bella [contra]cifra.	
LUCINDO	¿Luego el amor se descifra?	
HERNANDO	Sí.	
LUCINDO	¿Con qué?	
HERNANDO	Con otro amor.	
LUCINDO	No tratemos de eso agora;	305
	vamos a ver en qué para.	
HERNANDO	¿Ves cómo es cosa muy clara	
	que con celos te enamora?	
	¡Qué bien, Lucindo, un discreto	
	cañas de pescar [los] llama!	310
	Pescan honra, hacienda y fama,	

LUCINDO	That's why love is never lasting
	For loose women, only the pure.
HERNANDO	Jealousy and swords are always
	A big deal for men who lack sense –
	Or should I say experience.
	I still hope to see you someday
	Sprung from this trap in which you're stuck,
	Set free by my words of wisdom.
LUCINDO	Many things are holding me back.
HERNANDO	A woman who's loose and foolish
	Is like a monkey who gestures
	"Come here", when kids are watching her.
	But if a man should come along,
	Who's firm and carries a big stick,
	She'll brush and groom him with respect
	And listen well to all he says.
	With young men not yet fully formed
	Women tell jokes and fool around,
	Because they're boys, wild and crazy;
	Not with the man who's more mature.
	Gerarda's tossing you the bait,
	And although she's not caught you yet,
	She's giving you line, making you
	Jealous, jealous, and more jealous.
LUCINDO	What should I do?
HERNANDO	Love's a puzzle,
	Sir; look for the key to solve it.
LUCINDO	All my troubles can be resolved?
HERNANDO	Yes.
LUCINDO	How so?
HERNANDO	With another love.
LUCINDO	I don't want to hear of that now.
	Let's wait and see how this one ends.
HERNANDO	Don't you see that it's only out
	Of jealousy that you love her?
	A wise man spoke well, Lucindo,
	When he called it a fishing cane.
	What a woman's angling for is

Line numbers: 280, 285, 290, 295, 300, 305, 310

aunque cañas en efeto.
   ¿No te afrentas que una cosa
que a todo viento blandea,
para estribarte sea   315
enemiga poderosa?
   A tu hacienda pone cebo,
de celos hace seda[l];
pues ¿cómo que en hilo igual
cuelgue un discreto mancebo?   320
   Lo que aquel sabio decía
por las leyes, muy mejor
por la mujer de amor
agora decir podía.
   Son como telas de araña,   325
pescan moscas, débil gente;
mas no el animal valiente,
que las rompe y desmaraña.
   Afréntate de que yo
te enseño el vivir.

LUCINDO	No seas 330

pesado: mientras me veas
donde el amor me enlazó,
   de aquella tela de araña
soy mosca.

HERNANDO   ¡Y qué moscatel!
LUCINDO Ya soy pez simple y fïel   335
del cebo de aquella caña.
   Vamos; volverela a ver;
que me ha picado en el dedo
del corazón.

HERNANDO   Tengo miedo
que algo te ha de suceder.   340
LUCINDO   A ver vuelvo mis enojos.
HERNANDO ¡Jesús, qué necios desvelos!
LUCINDO Diome pimienta de celos;
voy a beber por los ojos.

Vanse, y sale Belisa, y Fenisa.

Honor, wealth, and reputation.
Aren't you insulted that a cane
That bends in the wind is yet so
Strong that it can throw you over, 315
Like a powerful enemy?
I tell you she's after your wealth;
Jealousy's the line on her pole.
How can someone as smart as you
Get hooked on such a tiny thread? 320
What another wise man proclaimed
About the law could be applied
As well if not even better
To women whose business is love.
They're exactly like spider webs, 325
Used to catch flies, those who are weak,
But not the animal that's strong.
He'll break through and destroy the web.
You should be ashamed that it's me
Teaching you how to live.

LUCINDO   Don't be 330
An ass. As long as you see me
In love's embrace, know that I'm just
a poor fly, eternally trapped
In the spider's web.

HERNANDO   Fly, indeed!
LUCINDO You're right; I'm just a simple fish, 335
Caught there on the bait of her pole.
Let's go; I must see her again.
She's pierced me right in the middle
Of my heart.

HERNANDO   I'm really afraid
That something bad will happen here. 340
LUCINDO Now I'm feeling angry again.
HERNANDO Lord, what a foolish obsession.
LUCINDO Jealousy burns me with a fire
That only seeing her can put out.

Exit Lucindo and Hernando.
A room in the house of Belisa.
Enter Belisa and Fenisa.

BELISA	¿Haste quitado tu manto?	345
FENISA	Quitado, señora, está.	
BELISA	Pues toma ese manto allá.	
FENISA	De tu cólera me espanto.	

    ¡Válgame Dios! ¿Qué te hago?
Con cualquier cosa te ofendo.   350

BELISA ¿Tú piensas que no te entiendo?
Yo tengo mi justo pago.
    Si yo te cerrase en casa,
pocas veces me [darías]
estos disgustos.

FENISA   Los días   355
que esto por milagro pasa,
    que al fin son de un jubileo,
tan caros me han de costar,
que te tengo de rogar
que me encierres.

BELISA   No lo creo.   360

FENISA ¿De qué te quejas de mí,
que siempre me andas riñendo?

BELISA De tu libertad me ofendo.

FENISA ¿Libertad?

BELISA   ¿Yo no lo vi?

FENISA ¿Qué mancebo me pasea   365
destos que van dando el talle?
¿Qué [guijas] desde la calle
me arroja, porque le vea?
    ¿Qué seña me has visto hacer
en la iglesia? ¿Quién me sigue   370
que a estar celosa te obligue?
¿Qué vieja me vino a ver?
    ¿Qué billetes me has hallado
con palabras deshonestas?
¿Qué pluma para respuestas,   375
qué tintero me has quebrado?
    ¿Qué cinta, que no sea tuya
o comprada por tu mano?
¿Qué chapín, qué toca?

BELISA	Where's your cloak? Did you remove it?	345
FENISA	Yes, Mother, I removed my cloak.	
BELISA	Take mine, then, and put it away.	
FENISA	Your constant anger frightens me.	
	Dear God, what have I done to you?	
	You take offense at everything.	350
BELISA	You think I don't understand you?	
	I'm getting just what I deserve.	
	If I confined you to the house	
	You'd not be able to cause me	
	All these upsets.	
FENISA	The days when, by	355
	Some miracle, I leave the house –	
	Such as these, the high holy days –	
	Cost me so dearly every time	
	That I must beg of you to please	
	Lock me up.	
BELISA	That's not what you want.	360
FENISA	What, exactly, is your complaint	
	That you keep on scolding me?	
BELISA	It's your free ways that offend me.	
FENISA	My free ways?	
BELISA	Did I not see it?	
FENISA	Oh? What handsome, gallant young man	365
	Has strolled by to show me his charms?	
	Who's tossed pebbles at my window	
	To get me to look out at him?	
	What secret signs have I given	
	In church? Who's always stalking me	370
	That you must be so vigilant?	
	What procuress came to visit?	
	What billets-doux with impure and	
	Lying words did you discover?	
	What pen to write a bold reply,	375
	What inkwell did you smash to bits?	
	What ribbon, except one of yours,	
	Or one that you yourself had bought?	
	What clogs? What headscarf?	

BELISA	En vano
	quieres que mi honor te arguya.
	No me quejo de que sea
	verdadera la ocasión.
FENISA	Pues ¿qué es esto? ¿Prevención?
BELISA	Mi honor [el] tuyo desea.
	Querría que te guardases
	deso mismo que me adviertes,
	y que a estas puertas más fuertes
	nuevos candados echases.
FENISA	Tanto me podrás guardar...
BELISA	¿Qué dices?
FENISA	Que haré tu gusto;
	pero cáusame disgusto
	tanto gruñi[r] y encerrar.
	¿Fuiste santa, por tu vida,
	en tu tierna edad?
BELISA	Fui ejemplo
	en casa, en calle y en templo,
	de una mujer recogida.
	Los ojos tuve con llave.
FENISA	¿Cómo te casaste?
BELISA	El cielo
	vio mi virtud y mi celo;
	que el cielo todo lo sabe.
FENISA	Mi tía me dijo a mí
	que hacías mil oraciones
	y andabas por estaciones.
BELISA	¿Yo, para casarme?
FENISA	Sí;
	y mil viernes ayunabas,
	a un padre del yermo igual;
	y haciendo esto, es señal
	que casarte deseabas.
BELISA	Nunca tal imaginé.
	Miente, por tu vida y mía;
	que antes monja ser quería,
	y sin gusto me casé.

380

385

390

395

400

405

410

BELISA	When honor's
	At stake, never doubt my concern. 380
	Besides, I've never said those things
	Have ever really taken place.
FENISA	What's it about then? Prevention?
BELISA	My honor and yours are bonded.
	My wish is that you be on guard 385
	Against those things you have mentioned,
	And that on all your strongest doors,
	You put even sturdier locks.
FENISA	*(Aside.)* (And that's how you would keep me safe?)
BELISA	What's that?
FENISA	I'll do as you want; 390
	But I simply cannot abide
	Your harping and being closed up.
	Tell the truth; in your maiden years
	Were you a saint?
BELISA	At home, in church,
	On the street, I was the model 395
	Of a cloistered and godly life.
	My eyes were shut tight with a key.
FENISA	Then how did you marry?
BELISA	Heaven
	Saw my virtue and my fervor;
	Heaven, we know, knows everything. 400
FENISA	My aunt, your sister, told me once
	That you said prayers a thousand times
	And did the stations of the cross.
BELISA	I did? To get a husband?
FENISA	Yes.
	And that on Fridays you fasted 405
	Like one of those desert hermits,
	And so made it quite clear to all
	That you wanted to get married.
BELISA	Never once did that cross my mind.
	I swear on my life, and yours too, 410
	She lies; I hoped to be a nun,
	And married against my wishes.

FENISA	Pues ¿cómo fuiste celosa
	de mi padre, que Dios haya?
BELISA	Porque no había joya o saya,
	plata en casa, ni otra cosa,
	que no diese a cierta dama.
	Hacía aquel sentimiento
	por vosotras.
FENISA	Golpes siento.
BELISA	Mira, Fenisa, quién llama.
FENISA	Por entre la reja vi
	el Capitán tu vecino.
BELISA	Ya lo que quiere adivino.
FENISA	¿Ya lo sabes? ¿Cómo ansí?
BELISA	[Ha] días que da en mirarme.
	Creo que me quiere bien;
	yo le he mostrado desdén,
	y querrá en bodas hablarme.
	Y por tu vida, Fenisa,
	que no me estuviese mal;
	que es un hombre principal.
FENISA	Perdona, madre, esta risa.
BELISA	¿De qué te ríes?
FENISA	De ver
	la santidad que tendrías
	cuando más moza serías;
	que ejemplo debió de ser
	en casa, en calle y en templo.
	De llamar el Capitán,
	¿esos bostezos te dan?
	Tomar quiero el buen ejemplo.
BELISA	Loca, es un hombre muy rico,
	y esta casa está sin hombre;
	serate padre en el nombre.
FENISA	Que me escuches te suplico.
	¿Es para guardarme a mí?
BELISA	No es otra mi prevención

Los números de verso que aparecen al margen derecho: 415, 420, 425, 430, 435, 440, 445.

FENISA	Well then what made you so jealous
	Of father, may God preserve him?
BELISA	Because there was barely a jewel, 415
	Or gown, or piece of silver that
	Didn't end up with his mistress!
	My jealousy came from concern
	For your welfare.
FENISA	I hear a knock.
BELISA	Go see who it is, Fenisa. 420

Fenisa goes to the window and returns.

FENISA	Through the window grille I could see
	Your neighbor, Captain Bernardo.
BELISA	Really? I can guess what he wants.
FENISA	How can you possibly know that?
BELISA	Because he's been looking at me 425
	For days. I believe he loves me.
	I treated him with disdain so
	He must have come here to propose.
	And, upon your soul, Fenisa,
	That would not do me ill. He's an 430
	Exceedingly distinguished man.
FENISA	Pardon me for laughing, Mother.
BELISA	What are you laughing at?
FENISA	Hearing
	How saintly was your life when you
	Were more or less my present age. 435
	The fine model you must have been
	At home, in church, and on the street…
	And then the Captain comes calling,
	And you have all these ideas?
	I must follow your example. 440
BELISA	Don't be foolish! He's a rich man,
	And there's no other in the house.
	He would be a father to you.
FENISA	Mother, listen, I beg of you.
	Is this to keep an eye on me? 445
BELISA	My only intention is that

	que ver en casa un varón	
	que te guarde y honre a ti.	
FENISA	Pues, cásame a mí primero,	
	y guárdeme mi marido.	450
BELISA	Cuando se hubiera ofrecido,	
	lo hiciera, y hacerlo espero.	
FENISA	Yo en los términos te arguyo.	
BELISA	Éste guardará tu honor.	
FENISA	¿No me guardara mejor	455
	mi marido que no el tuyo?	
BELISA	Hijo tiene, y ser podría	
	concertar esto también.	
FENISA	¡Ay, mi Lucindo y mi bien!	
	¡Quién viese tan dulce día!	460

Sale Bernardo, viejo, muy galán, con su gorra de plumas, espada y daga; en fin, como Capitán a lo antiguo; [criados]

CAPITÁN	Como en salirse tardaban,	
	la licencia no aguardé;	
	porque en eso imaginé,	
	señoras, que me la daban.	
	Fuera de que el ser vecino	465
	desde que vine de Flandes,	
	me alienta a cosas más grandes.	
BELISA	Lo que me quiere imagino.	
	Agravio se nos hiciera,	
	si v[uestra] m[erced] no entrara,	470
	y en esta casa mandara	
	como si en la suya fuera.	
	Llega esas sillas, Fenisa.	

Siéntase el Capitán

CAPITÁN	Vosotros, salíos allá.

[Vanse los criados.]

BELISA	Pena, Fenisa, me da	475
	que me cogiese de prisa.	
	¿Está bien puesta esta toca?	

	There should be a man living here	
	To guard you and defend your honor.	
FENISA	In that case, let me get married,	
	And let my husband protect me.	450
BELISA	If someone had made an offer,	
	I'd do so, and I still hope to.	
FENISA	I'm not sure I can believe that.	
BELISA	The Captain would guard your honor.	
FENISA	Wouldn't a husband of my own	455
	Watch over me better than yours?	
BELISA	The Captain has a son; perhaps	
	Something could be arranged with him.	
FENISA	*(Aside.)* (Oh, my Lucindo, my true love!	
	Who ever saw so sweet a day!)	460

Captain Bernardo enters. He is elderly, and very gallant, with a plumed hat, sword, and dagger, like a captain of the old style. Fulminato and another servant enter with him.

CAPTAIN	Since nobody came to the door,	
	I entered without permission.	
	Please do forgive me, dear ladies;	
	I was sure you'd want to give it.	
	As you know I've been your neighbor,	465
	Since my return from Flanders, but	
	Now greater matters bring me here.	
BELISA	*(Aside.)* (I can see how much he loves me.)	
	We would have been most offended,	
	Kind sir, if you had not come in	470
	And treated this humble abode	
	Just as if it were your own home.	
	Fenisa, bring some chairs over.	

The Captain sits down.

| **CAPTAIN** | *(To the servants.)* You may leave us now, both of you. | |

Exit the servants. Belisa and Fenisa move away to speak in private.

BELISA	I'm so embarrassed, Fenisa,	475
	That he caught me quite unprepared.	
	Is my headdress on properly?	

FENISA	Nunca mejor te la vi.
BELISA	¿Tengo alegre el rostro?
FENISA	Sí.
BELISA	¿Parécete que provoca?

480

FENISA	Sí, madre.
BELISA	¿A qué?
FENISA	A devoción.
BELISA	¡Maldita seas, amén!
	Nunca me has querido bien.
FENISA	¡Oh, santas de privación!

Cuando no pueden comer   485
les pesa de ver con dientes
a las otras. ¿Qué esto intentes?
No me espanto; eres mujer.

BELISA	Hoy me descuidé en prenderme

un poquito de salud.   490

FENISA	No tengas tanta inquietud.
BELISA	¿Cómo?
FENISA	Tu galán se duerme.
BELISA	Ahora bien, voy a sentarme.
FENISA	La vergüenza de su amor

te dará, madre, color.   495

Siéntase Belisa.

BELISA	Ya, señor, podéis hablarme.	
CAPITÁN	Belisa, el ser vecino, que en efeto,	*tercetos*

me obliga a reparar en vuestra casa,
de su virtud me ha dado buen [conceto].
Veo tarde y mañana cuanto pasa;   500
tras esto, sé de coro su nobleza,
como suele informarse quien se casa;
    y como la virtud y la belleza
sean despertadores del sentido,
aunque duerme la edad con más pereza,   505
    yo me [he] animado a daros un marido
tal como yo, que tengo menos años
de los que habéis, de verme, conocido;
    sino que esto de andar reinos extraños

FENISA	I've never seen it look better.
BELISA	My expression, is it ... happy?
FENISA	Yes
BELISA	And does it ... incite? 480
FENISA	Yes, mother.
BELISA	To what?
FENISA	To profound devotion.
BELISA	A curse upon you, Fenisa!
	I know that you've never loved me.
FENISA	*(Aside.)* (Oh, these saints of self-privation!
	When they can no longer eat 485
	It grieves them to see that others
	Still have teeth. Is that your problem?
	You are a woman after all.)
BELISA	I'm afraid that I neglected
	To put on any rouge today. 490
FENISA	I wouldn't worry about that.
BELISA	Why not?
FENISA	Your suitor is asleep.
BELISA	All right; I'm ready to sit down.
FENISA	*(Aside.)* (The shame of this rash love, Mother,
	Is certain to color your cheeks.) 495

Belisa sits down.

BELISA	Now, sir, let us resume our talk.
CAPTAIN	My dear Belisa, being your close neighbor –
	And thus cognizant of doings in your house –
	I have come to think highly of your virtue.
	Morning and night I can see what's happening. 500
	What's more, I'm aware of your noble ancestry,
	Since, like future spouses, I've informed myself;
	And because heritage, virtue, and beauty
	Are what awaken interest and the senses,
	Even in those aged souls, quick to nod off, 505
	I have dared to present you here a husband –
	Myself – , who am considerably younger
	Than you have no doubt supposed from seeing me.
	It's because the years I spent as a soldier

con las armas, dormir en la campaña,   510
caminos, velas, militares daños,
   correr la posta a Flandes desde España,
consumen la robusta gallardía
que los floridos años acompaña.
   Dios haya a Carlos Quinto, que decía   515
que la posta y la mar le envejecieron,
cuando apenas cuarenta y seis cumplía.
   Yo nací el año de sesenta, y fueron
el Duque y la Duquesa mis padrinos,
cuyas Albas tal luz a España dieron.   520
   Heme hallado en jornadas y caminos,
que si fueran de bronce me acabaran.
En fin, señoras, somos hoy vecinos.
   Mucho los viejos una casa amparan;
los mozos son polilla de la hacienda,   525
que unos [a] andar comienzan y otros paran.
   Mi edad no es bien vuestra virtud ofenda;
que estoy muy ágil, fuerte, como y duermo,
y sé a un caballo gobernar la rienda.
   Yo pienso que en mi vida he estado enfermo; 530
sólo mano enemiga me ha sangrado,
y un desafío público en Palermo.
   Ese hijuelo que tengo es bien crïado,
mañana le darán una bandera,
y un hábito le tengo negociado.   535
   No dará pesadumbre.

FENISA
              ¡A Dios pluguiera
que ya estuviera en casa!

CAPITÁN
                  Finalmente,
se irá Lucindo por momentos fuera.
   Suplícoos, pues, Belisa, humildemente,
que me deis a Fenisa, vuestra hija,   540
que yo pienso dotarla honestamente,
   para que ella gobierne, mande y rija
no poca hacienda que ganó mi espada,
si no es que mi cansada edad la aflija;
que muy presto verá que no es cansada.   545

In foreign lands, bearing arms, sleeping in fields,   510
On the road, on board ship, wounded in battle,
Carrying dispatches to Flanders from Spain,
Have taken a toll on the constitution
That I had in the long-gone days of my youth.
May God preserve the emperor Charles, who said   515
It was life on the road and on the sea that
Made him old when he was only forty-six.
I was born in 1560, and I claim
As godparents the Duke and Duchess of Alba,
Whose light is a shining glory of our Spain.   520
So here I am, forged by those days and travels
That, were they made of bronze, would have finished me.
In short, dear ladies, we are now close neighbors.
Older men are the protectors of a home;
Younger men eat through its contents just like moths, 525
Arriving, leaving, and never in one place.
Don't let my age offend your sense of what's right.
I'm strong and as yet fit; I eat and sleep well,
And I'm still one of the best horsemen around.
I've hardly been unwell a day in my life   530
And I've never lost blood except in battle,
Not including a duel in Palermo.
That young son of mine has been ably brought up.
Tomorrow he'll be made second lieutenant,
And soon thereafter he is to be knighted.   535
He'll never cause you sorrow.

FENISA   *(Aside.)*   (I wish to God
That he were here now.)

CAPTAIN   However, Lucindo
Will soon be leaving to take up his duties.
Thus, I do humbly beg of you, Belisa,
That you here give me the hand of your daughter.   540
I propose to endow her most handsomely,
So that she may govern and administer
The not insubstantial wealth my sword has won,
Unless she be troubled by my well-worn years,
Which as she'll soon learn are hardly worn at all.   545

BELISA	¡A mi hija, Capitán,	*redondillas*
	me pide vuestra merced!	
CAPITÁN	Y tendré a mucha merced,	
	si esas manos me la dan.	
FENISA	Triste de mí! ¿Qué es aquesto?	550

Pensé que a mi madre amaba,
y que ya Lucindo estaba
a mi remedio dispuesto.
    Sueño fue mi fantasía
en una ocasión tan alta,   555
pues la gloria que me falta,
soñaba yo que tenía.

BELISA   Pensé que vuestro deseo
a quererme se inclinaba.

CAPITÁN No, Belisa.

BELISA   Alegre estaba,   560
y lo estoy de lo que veo.
    Hija, ya ves su intención.

FENISA La fe que tuve en mi bien
me hizo tener también
alegre mi corazón.   565
    Mas como era fe engañada
del sueño que imaginé,
fe falsa y fingida fue,
fe traidora y fe burlada,
    fe de un sueño que [dormía];   570
y si soñada ha de ser,
yo juro de no creer
más a la fe. Madre mía.
    pensé que fuérades vos
la novia del Capitán.   575

BELISA Lejos sus intentos van,
y estoy corrida, por Dios.

FENISA   ¡Ay, sueño de mi afición!
¡Qué bien, pues que me engañé
por vuestras burlas, diré   580
que los sueños sueños son!

BELISA	Then it's my daughter's hand, Captain,
	That you're requesting in marriage?
CAPTAIN	And I would be deeply honored
	If you saw fit to give it to me.
FENISA	*(Aside.) (*Dear God, help me! What's happening? 550
	I thought it was Mother he loved,
	And that Lucindo was the one
	Who would bring an end to my plight.
	But everything I dreamed was just
	A product of my fantasy, 555
	And the glorious end of it
	Has vanished like the dream itself.)
BELISA	I somehow thought that your desire
	Was placed on me, not Fenisa.
CAPTAIN	No, Belisa.
BELISA	I was so pleased... 560
	And still am, I hasten to say.
	Daughter, you've heard his proposal.

The Captain withdraws, allowing Belisa and Fenisa to speak in private.

FENISA	*(Aside.)* (The faith I had in my future
	Was what moved my soul to take flight
	And my heart to fill with gladness. 565
	But that faith was an illusion,
	Conjured up by my fantasy,
	It was false and fictitious faith,
	Fraudulent, phony and fake faith,
	Faith of the dream I was dreaming; 570
	And if it was only a dream,
	Then I swear never to have faith
	In faith again.) Mother, dearest,
	I was sure that you were the one
	Whom the Captain wished to marry. 575
BELISA	His intentions are otherwise,
	And, God knows, I'm quite embarrassed.
FENISA	*(Aside).* (Oh Love, that I dreamt in my dreams!
	How fitting, since I was deceived
	By your tricks, I now say, as one 580
	Often hears, "even dreams are dreams."

BELISA	Fenisa, aunque estoy corrida
	de haber pensado casarme,
	no lo estoy de imaginarme
	de tu verde edad vencida. 585
	Discreta eres; procura
	persuadirte a lo que ves.
FENISA	Si a tu edad vence interés,
	a mi edad vence hermosura.
	Los viejos, que habéis gozado 590
	vuestros años, atendéis
	a lo que gozar podéis
	con avariento cuidado.
	Queréis regalo, dinero,
	descanso y ociosidad, 595
	y envidiando nuestra edad,
	esto pretendéis primero.
	Desobedecerte fuera
	cosa indigna a mi virtud;
	pero fáltame salud. 600
	El término considera,
	y pídele por un mes,
	mientras se concierta todo.
BELISA	Yo lo sabré hacer de modo,
	que muchas gracias me des. 605

Llegale [a] hablar.

FENISA	Discreta he sido en decir
	que este casamiento [aceto],
	pues de mi amor el [efeto]
	[puedo] por él conseguir;
	que si luego le negara 610
	y con disgusto se fuera,
	tarde a mi Lucindo viera,
	tarde a mi Lucindo hablara.
	Con entrar su padre aquí,
	habrá comunicación. 615

Hablan los dos a solas.

BELISA	Fenisa, although I'm ashamed	
	To have had thoughts of marrying,	
	I'm not ashamed for believing	
	It was your youth that bested me.	585
	You're prudent; do persuade yourself	
	To accept what you've been offered.	
FENISA	If at your age it's safe refuge	
	That counts, at my age it's beauty.	
	You old people, who have been blessed	590
	With many years, give much thought to	
	The best way to enjoy the things	
	That you've always held in regard.	
	What you want are wealth and leisure,	
	Robust health and a good night's sleep.	595
	And being jealous of our youth,	
	No doubt you'd like to have that too.	
	To disobey you in this would	
	Be unworthy of my virtue;	
	But right now I'm not at my best,	600
	And it's better not to rush things,	
	So ask him for a month's delay	
	While proper arrangements are made.	
BELISA	I'll do it in such a manner	
	That later you'll surely thank me.	605

Belisa goes to speak to the Captain.

FENISA	*(Aside.)* (It was really clever to say	
	That I accept his proposal,	
	Because now I'll be able	
	To get what I've set my sights on.	
	If I had turned the Captain down,	610
	And he left the house in a huff,	
	There's no way I could see my love,	
	And no way I could speak to him.	
	Now when his father comes calling	
	We'll use him as our middleman.)	615

CAPITÁN	Todas esas cosas son
	de gran gusto para mí.
	El término acepto, y digo
	que un mes la quiero esperar.
	Pero déjamele hablar. 620
FENISA	¡Qué notable intento sigo!
CAPITÁN	Nunca desa discreción
	en Madrid tan celebrada,
	salió, mi Fenisa amada,
	más cuerda resolución. 625
	Tu virtud he confirmado;
	que no apetecer tu edad
	muestra bien la calidad
	de ese pensamiento honrado.
	Haré de hoy más, pues me honra 630
	tanto el saber que te igualo,
	un padre de tu regalo
	y un alcaide de tu honra.
	Y dándome Dios salud,
	esta misma barba anciana 635
	servirá de barbacana
	al fuerte de tu virtud.
	Y si esta nieve no trata
	bien el juvenil decoro,
	[juntando a tus hebras de oro] 640
	estos cabellos de plata,
	supliré en regalo y galas
	los defectos de la edad.
[FENISA]	Con tu honor y calidad,
	señor, mis años igualas. 645
	Deja la humildad aquí,
	pues ya soy tuya.
CAPITÁN	¿«Soy tuya»
	dijiste?
FENISA	Sí, ya no es suya
	quien se ha de llamar de ti.

CAPTAIN   All of those things that you mentioned
              Are proper and to my liking.
              I accept the delay, and vow
              That we will marry in one month.
              But now do let me speak to her.   620
FENISA   *(Aside.)* (What a brilliant plan I've devised!)

The Captain and Fenisa now speak together.

CAPTAIN   Never, dear Fenisa, has your
              Prudence, so much celebrated
              In Madrid, hit upon a more
              Level-headed plan of action.   625
              Your discretion is now quite clear.
              Even though you're still young in years
              You're not mad for money, which shows
              The correctness of your thinking.
              I'm honored that you have found me   630
              Worthy, and I will always be
              For you the guardian of your wealth
              And the protector of your honor.
              And should God grant me ample health,
              This beard that has seen many years   635
              Will be the unyielding bulwark
              Of the fortress of your virtue.
              And if the snow that crowns my head
              Accords ill with your youthful bloom,
              My silver hairs in poor contrast   640
              With your locks of glistening gold,
              I will redress the flaws of age
              With treasure and generous gifts.
FENISA   Sir, your honor and manifest worth
              Are more than a match for my youth.   645
              Please, enough of this humble talk,
              For I'm already yours.
CAPTAIN   Did you
              Say "I'm yours"?
FENISA   Yes, and from now on
              I'd like you to be less formal.

CAPITÁN	¿Otro favor? ¡Pesia tal!	650
	¡No fuera en Flandes aquesto	
	para que se echara el resto	
	con un festín general!	
	Torneo había de haber,	
	por vida del Capitán;	655
	y si licencia me dan,	
	en Madrid le pienso hacer.	
FENISA	Suplícoos, por vida mía,	
	la corte no alborotéis.	
CAPITÁN	Haré lo que me [mandéis],	660
	dulce esposa y prenda mía;	
	mas si no fuera por vos...	
FENISA	Un poco tengo que hablaros.	
CAPITÁN	Yo mucho que regalaros.	
FENISA	Mil años os guarde Dios.	665

Yo no sabía que era vuestro hijo *Aparte. Versos sueltos*
Lucindo, un caballero que solía
entrar en vuestra casa algunas veces.
Mi madre me lo dijo cuando entrábades;
y pues es vuestro hijo y vos mi esposo,   670
que lo seréis si Dios fuere servido
y me diere salud para gozaros.

CAPITÁN	¡Qué palabras tan dulces! Por Dios vivo,	
	que el sol de aquella boca de claveles	
	la nieve de las canas me derrit[e].	675
FENISA	Digo, señor, que importará atajar[l]e	
	la loca pretensión con que me sirve.	
CAPITÁN	¿Mi hijo os sirve?	
FENISA	Si el servirme fuera	
	con la cordura y cortesía lícita	
	a una mujer de mis iguales prendas,	680
	no me quejara con melindres vanos;	
	que nunca me precié de gusto hipócrita.	
CAPITÁN	Pues ¿cómo os sirve?	
FENISA	Con papeles locos,	
	por manos de terceras, que a mi casa	
	viene[n] con mil achaques [e] invenciones,	685

CAPTAIN	You'd allow that? Well, I'll be damned!	650
	During my service in Flanders	
	Occasions such as this never	
	Passed without great celebration.	
	I swear, on my Captain's honor,	
	There's going to be a tournament,	655
	And if I'm granted permission,	
	We'll have it right here in Madrid.	
FENISA	I beg you, for the love of God,	
	Please don't stir up the whole city.	
CAPTAIN	I'll do whatever you should ask,	660
	My sweet wife and dearest treasure,	
	But, if it were not you asking...	
FENISA	Sir, there's something we must discuss.	
CAPTAIN	Whatever you wish, dearest one.	
FENISA	Thank you, and may God preserve you.	665
	I was quite unaware, sir, that Lucindo,	
	A young gallant whom we've seen going into	
	And coming out of your house, was your son. My	
	Mother informed me of that a while ago.	
	Since, then, he is your son, and you my husband –	670
	Which you will indeed be if it so please God	
	And He afford me the necessary health...	
CAPTAIN	What sweet words you speak! By the good Lord above	
	I swear the sun of your two flaming-red lips	
	Is melting the snow you can see in my hair.	675
FENISA	My point is that you must put an end at once	
	To his crazy, outrageous pursuit of me.	
CAPTAIN	What? My son is pursuing you?	
FENISA	If it were	
	With good sense and the fond courtesy proper	
	To a woman of my station and virtues,	680
	I would not complain, for that would be petty;	
	I've never been one to play the hypocrite.	
CAPTAIN	But how does he pursue you?	
FENISA	With mad letters	
	Brought here by others, who show up at the house	
	With a thousand excuses and inventions.	685

echando mil amigas por terceras;
y en todo aquesto, ni por pensamiento
se le acuerda a tratar de casamiento.

CAPITÁN   Es loco el mozo; perdonalde, os ruego;
que yo saldré fiador que no os enoje   690
de aquí adelante.

FENISA   Pues que ya es mi hijo,
os suplico, señor, que cuerdamente
le digáis que me quejo deste agravio,
y fíolo de vos, pues sois tan sabio.

CAPITÁN   Deja[d]me ese cuidado. El cielo os guarde.   695
Belisa, yo le he dicho a mi Fenisa
que pienso regalarla, y que no quiero
vida por otra cosa. A Dios te queda,
que yo volveré a verte; pero advierte
que me has de dar licencia para verte.   700

BELISA   Guárdate el cielo.
                             Gran ventura ha sido,
Fenisa, la que el cielo nos ha dado.

FENISA   ¿Estás contenta?

BELISA   ¿No lo ves?

FENISA   Sospecho
que disimulas el pesar que tienes.

BELISA   ¿Cómo?

FENISA   Porque quisieras tú casarte.   705

BELISA   Malicia tuya. Ven.

FENISA   ¡Ay, mi Lucindo!
Si no me entiendes con aqueste enredo,
no eres discreto ni en Madrid nacido;
mas si me entiendes, y a buscarme vienes,
tú naciste en Madrid, discreción tienes.   710

Vanse, y salen Lucindo y Hernando.

	He turns my dearest friends into go-betweens!	
	And despite all this traffic it has never	
	Occurred to him to speak of matrimony.	
CAPTAIN	The boy is out of his mind; please forgive him.	
	I give you my pledge that he will no longer	690
	Cause you vexation.	

FENISA   Since he's now my son, too,
I must request that you inform him at once
That I am offended by his behavior.
I entrust him, sir, to your wise governance.

CAPTAIN   I accept my duty. May God be with you.   695
             (To Belisa.) Dear Belisa, I have said to your daughter
             That as her husband I will forever be
             Most generous, for that is what life is for.
             Good-by for now; I will call here again soon,
             If I have your kind permission to do so.   700

BELISA   Heaven preserve you.

Exit the Captain.

                                      The good Lord, Fenisa,
             Has blessed us with marvelous fortune today.

FENISA   Are you happy?

BELISA   Can you not see?

FENISA   I suspect
             That you're concealing the sadness that you feel.

BELISA   How so?

FENISA   Because you were hoping to marry.   705

BELISA   Don't be malicious! Come.

FENISA   *(Aside.)*   (Oh, my Lucindo!
             If you can't follow this little scheme I've hatched
             You're neither clever nor a son of Madrid;
             But if you do understand, and come looking,
             Born in Madrid you were, and blessed
                 with sharp wits!)   710

Exit Fenisa and Belisa.

LUCINDO	Aún no sale aquel galán.	*quintillas*
HERNANDO	¿Qué es salir? Está despacio.	
LUCINDO	Mis celos no me le dan.	
HERNANDO	Es esta casa un palacio;	
	mostrándosele estarán.	715
	En sólo ver niñerías	
	hay dos semanas enteras.	
	Andarán las galerías.	
	Mejor esté yo en galeras,	
	que la sirviera dos días.	720
LUCINDO	Si en galeras de Gerarda	
	anda al remo este dichoso,	
	que agora en salir se tarda,	
	no sé yo cuál envidioso	
	a la ribera le aguarda.	725
	Ay de mí, Hernando, que quiero	
	una mujer diestra, astuta,	
	de amor vano y lisonjero,	
	despejada y resoluta,	
	y con [un] alma de acero.	730
HERNANDO	Que el amor cause afición	
	está muy puesto en razón;	
	pero que el ser muy querido	
	descuido engendre y olvido,	
	efectos bastardos son.	735
LUCINDO	Él sale, y ella se ha puesto	
	a la ventana.	
HERNANDO	Querrá	
	verle galán y dispuesto.	

Gerarda en el alto, y Doristeo sale con Finardo

GERARDA	Lucindo en la calle está.	
LUCINDO	¡Tantas desdichas! ¿Qué es esto?	740
DORISTEO	¿No es gallarda?	
FINARDO	Es extremada.	
	¡Qué discreta y qué cortés!	

The street in front of Gerarda's house.
Enter Lucindo and Hernando.

LUCINDO	That fellow still hasn't come out.
HERNANDO	Calm down. You need to be patient.
LUCINDO	My jealousy doesn't let me.
HERNANDO	What a house! More like a palace!

They must be showing him around.   715
Just to see the lady's baubles
Would take three weeks, or maybe more.
And think of all the galleries …
Speaking of which, I'd rather be
A galley slave than serve Madame!   720

LUCINDO   If it's in Gerarda's galley
That that most fortunate fellow
Is presently working his oar,
Imagine all the envy felt
By his friends waiting on the shore.   725
God help me, Hernando, I love
A woman who's smart and astute,
In love both vain and flattering,
Free in her ways, yet resolute,
And possessed of a soul of steel!   730

HERNANDO   That love arouses affection
Is a normal state of affairs;
But that being desired should be
The cause of coldness and disdain,
That's not so easy to explain.   735

LUCINDO   He's leaving now, and she's appeared
At the window.

HERNANDO   I guess she wants
One last glimpse of her young gallant.

Enter Doristeo and Finardo from the house of Gerarda, who appears at her window.

GERARDA	*(Aside.)* (Lucindo is there in the street.)	
LUCINDO	*(Aside.)* (More damnable luck! What is this?)	740
DORISTEO	Isn't she beautiful?	
FINARDO	Indeed!	

Also discreet and most charming.

DORISTEO	Todo en su talle me agrada.
FINARDO	¿Si es éste Lucindo?
DORISTEO	Él es.
FINARDO	¿Si viene a sacar la espada?

745

DORISTEO	Venga a lo que más quisiere;
	yo sé que es aborrecido.
GERARDA	Celoso está; desespere;
	que por desdenes y olvido
	yo sé lo que un hombre quiere.

750

Mas para picarle más,
quiero hablar con Doristeo,
a quien no quise jamás;
que por abreviar rodeo,
y por saltar vuelvo atrás.

755

	¡Ah, caballero!
LUCINDO	¿Es a mí?
GERARDA	No os llamo, señor, a vos.
DORISTEO	¿Y a mí, señora?
GERARDA	A vos, sí.
LUCINDO	¿No ves aquello?
HERNANDO	Por Dios,
	que es infamia estar aquí.

760

LUCINDO	Buscaremos invención
	para que entienda que vengo
	aquí con otra ocasión.
GERARDA	Salir esta noche tengo;
	acompañarme es razón.

765

DORISTEO	¿Dónde iréis?
GERARDA	Pienso que al Prado.
	Venid por mí.
DORISTEO	Yo vendré.
LUCINDO	Ir al Prado han concertado.
HERNANDO	Tú fueras mejor, a fe.
	Tus mismos celos te han dado.

770

DORISTEO	¿Qué me mandáis más?
GERARDA	Serviros.
DORISTEO	Adiós.
FINARDO	¿No nos quiere nada?

DORISTEO	I like everything about her.
FINARDO	Could that be Lucindo?
DORISTEO	It is.
FINARDO	Do you think he's come to challenge you? 745
DORISTEO	That's his choice. I couldn't care less.
	I know Gerarda detests him.
GERARDA	*(Aside.)* (He's jealous; he's really frantic.
	It's clear that contempt and neglect
	Will always do the trick with men. 750
	But just to spur him on a bit,
	I'll call now to Doristeo,
	Who doesn't mean a thing to me;
	To be brief I'll jabber away,
	And to move along I'll turn back.) 755
	Oh, sir!
LUCINDO	Are you speaking to me?
GERARDA	No, I wasn't speaking to you.
DORISTEO	Was it me, my lady?
GERARDA	Yes, you.
LUCINDO	Do you see that?
HERNANDO	It's very clear
	She wants to humiliate you. 760
LUCINDO	We'll have to concoct a story
	To convince her that my purpose
	Here is not what she supposes.
GERARDA	*(To Doristeo.)* I'll be going out this evening;
	I expect you to escort me. 765
DORISTEO	Yes, where?
GERARDA	The park of the Prado.
	Come by for me.
DORISTEO	With great pleasure.
LUCINDO	It seems they're off to the Prado.
HERNANDO	Better it should have been you.
	Your jealousy has earned the favor. 770
DORISTEO	What more do you ask?
GERARDA	Just your service.
DORISTEO	Good-by, then.
FINARDO	Is that all she wants?

DORISTEO ¿Puedo irme?
FINARDO   Podéis iros.

Vanse los dos.

LUCINDO ¡Que no he sacado la espada,
haciéndome tantos tiros!   775
          Pues ¡vive Dios, que he de darte
celos, por ver si con celos
puedo a quererme obligarte,
ya que no quieren los cielos
que pueda amando obligarte!   780
HERNANDO ¿Cómo se los piensas dar?
LUCINDO Quiero esta noche llevar
al Prado alguna mujer,
adonde me pueda ver
hablar, requebrar y amar.   785
HERNANDO Y ¿quién ha de ser?
LUCINDO   No sé.
HERNANDO Hallarla será imposible.
LUCINDO No importa. Yo te pondré
un manto.
HERNANDO   Doña Terrible
me podrás llamar.
LUCINDO   Sí, haré.   790
HERNANDO ¡Estás loco!
LUCINDO   Pues, ¿qué importa?
HERNANDO ¿No importa, si topo acaso
gente de palabras corta?
LUCINDO Saldré yo muy presto al paso.
Hernando, la voz reporta.   795
          Llega, y habla esa mujer.
Pregunta si vio unas damas.
HERNANDO Bien dices, déjame hacer.
Pues no agradas, porque amas,
celos serán menester.   800
          ¡Ah, mi señora Gerarda!
GERARDA ¿Eres tú, Hernando?

DORISTEO	May I go now?
FINARDO	Yes, you may go.

Exit Doristeo and Finardo.
Lucindo and Hernando speak alone.

LUCINDO	What kept me from drawing my sword
	After the shots they took at me?

775

But, I swear, by God, I'll make you
Jealous. Then we'll find out whether
Jealousy moves you to love me,
Since it's clear that heaven has not
seen fit for my love to do so   780

HERNANDO So how will you make her jealous?
LUCINDO How, you ask? I'll go this evening
With some woman to the Prado,
And there Gerarda will see me
Talking, sighing, and making love.   785

HERNANDO And who's the woman?
LUCINDO   I don't know.
HERNANDO I doubt you'll find anyone willing.
LUCINDO It's not a problem. I'll just put
A cloak on you.

HERNANDO   And then call me
The Bearded Lady!

LUCINDO   Exactly!   790
HERNANDO You're crazy!
LUCINDO   What does it matter?
HERNANDO It matters if I stumble on
A pack of men up to no good.

LUCINDO Don't worry; I'll come to your aid.
And for God's sake, keep your voice down.   795
Now go speak with Gerarda. Ask
If she knows a certain lady.

HERNANDO I get it! I'll make up a name.
Since your love has failed to win her,
It's smart to try jealousy now.   800
(To Gerarda.) You there, my lady Gerarda!

GERARDA Is that you, Hernando?

HERNANDO	Yo soy.
GERARDA	Tengo qué hacer.
HERNANDO	Oye, aguarda.
GERARDA	¡Por ti en la ventana estoy!
HERNANDO	Eres discreta y gallarda.

     805

GERARDA   ¿Qué quieres?

HERNANDO   Saber querría
en qué casas destas vive
cierta doña Estefanía,
porque un loco no me prive
de la ración deste día;   810
    que me la mandó seguir,
y la perdí por mirarte.

GERARDA   ¡Oh, qué gracioso fingir!
Dígale a su Durandarte
que me suelo yo reír   815
    de tretillas tan groseras.
¡Ah, mi señor Beltenebros!
¿Para qué son las quimeras?
Trueque celos en requiebros;
lléguese, hablemos de veras.   820
    ¿De qué se finge valiente,
si está, de verme, temblando?
Muestre el pulso; a ver la frente.
¡Jesús, que se está abrasando!
¡Qué temerario accidente!   825
    ¡Hola!, lleva [a] aquel celoso
dos tragos de agua de azar.

HERNANDO   ¡Macacao!

GERARDA   ¡Cuento donoso!
¿Él me viene a [a]martelar?

LUCINDO   Corrido estoy.

HERNANDO   Yo furioso.   830
    ¿Conoces algún poeta?

LUCINDO   ¿Para qué?

HERNANDO   Para enviar

HERNANDO	Yes, ma'am.
GERARDA	I'm occupied now.
HERNANDO	Wait! Listen!
GERARDA	You can see I'm still here, can't you?
HERNANDO	How gracious and lovely you are!

805

GERARDA	What do you want?
HERNANDO	I'd like to know

In which of these buildings a lady
Named Estefanía resides,
So that crazy master of mine
Won't make me go hungry today.   810
He ordered me to follow her,
But I lost her, rapt in your charms.

GERARDA   What a witty liar you are!
Go tell that Romeo of yours
That his pathetic little stunts   815
Only make me laugh out loud.
(To Lucindo.) You over there, Sir Lancelot!
Why these absurd shenanigans?
Jealousy won't work; try flattery.
Come over here, and drop the games.   820
What's the point of feigning courage
If you tremble at sight of me?
Give me your pulse; your forehead, too.
God almighty! He's burning up!
What a dreadful development!   825
Someone bring that jealous fellow
Two swallows of orange water!

HERNANDO	Holy Moses!
GERARDA	*(To Hernando.)* Your tale's no good.

It's clear he's still pursuing me.

Lucindo and Hernando speak alone.

LUCINDO	Now I'm embarrassed.
HERNANDO	Me, I'm mad!

830

Do you know any good poets?

LUCINDO	Why do you ask?
HERNANDO	To send that witch

	una sátira en receta
	a esta bruja, o hazle dar
	una hermosa [cantaleta];	835
	haya pandorga esta noche;
	yo compraré los cencerros,
	aunque hasta el alba trasnoche;
	haya sábanas y entierros,
	campanillas, hacha y coche.	840
	¡Vive Dios!
LUCINDO	Calla, ignorante.
	¡Ah, mi bien, ah, mi Gerarda!
GERARDA	¿Llamas?

Vase.

LUCINDO	Quítate delante.
	¿Adónde te vas? Aguarda,
	oye la voz de tu amante.	845
	¿Para qué es matarme ansí?
HERNANDO	¿Vive Estefanía aquí?
LUCINDO	¿Quieres callar, bestia?
HERNANDO	No.
	Por aquí pienso que entró.
LUCINDO	¡Mi bien, duélete de mí!	850
HERNANDO	¡Tu padre!
LUCINDO	¡Válgame el cielo!

Sale el Capitán.

CAPITÁN	Todo hoy ando en busca tuya.
LUCINDO	Lo que me quieres recelo;
	que no es mucho que te arguya
	de mi inquietud y desvelo.	855
	Pero advierte, padre mío,
	que querer una mujer
	no es en mi edad desvarío,
	antes señal de tener
	generoso talle y brío.	860
	Si es porque no es muy honrada...
CAPITÁN	¿Cómo que honrada no es?

	Some nasty verses to get her goat,	
	Or give her a serenade that	
	She'll not forget in all her days.	835
	Listen; tonight we'll raise a row	
	That won't be over until dawn.	
	I'll get the cowbells; we'll also	
	Need handbells, torches, sheets for a	
	Fake burial and a carriage	840
	I can't wait!	
LUCINDO	Shut up, imbecile!	
	(To Gerarda.) Gerarda, Gerarda my love!	
GERARDA	Did someone call?	

Exit Gerarda.

LUCINDO	*(To Hernando.)* Out of my way.	
	(To Gerarda.) Where are you going? Wait, please wait,	
	And hear the voice of your lover.	845
	Why do you want to destroy me?	
HERNANDO	Does Estefanía live here?	
LUCINDO	Will you shut up, you nitwit?	
HERNANDO	No.	
	I'm sure this is where she went in.	
LUCINDO	My love, please take pity on me!	850
HERNANDO	It's your father!	
LUCINDO	Oh, Christ, not him!	

Enter Captain Bernardo.

CAPTAIN	I've been looking for you all day.	
LUCINDO	I can guess what you want of me;	
	I suppose the look on my face	
	And my nervousness give it away.	855
	But please keep in mind, Father, that	
	To love a woman at my age	
	Is not a mental disturbance	
	But a sign of normality	
	And a spirited character.	860
	I know her honor's less than pure…	
CAPTAIN	What? What do you mean, less than pure?	

	Lengua en escorpión bañada,	
	¿mereces besar sus pies,	
	ni aun tierra dellos pisada?	865
LUCINDO	Estoy con enojo agora	
	de mil celos que me ha dado,	
	con un hombre o dos que adora.	
CAPITÁN	¿Qué dices de hombre adorado,	
	y tan principal señora?	870
	Pero diraslo por mí,	
	a quien debe de adorar.	
LUCINDO	¿Que también te quiere a ti?	
CAPITÁN	¿No la merezco agradar?	
LUCINDO	Sí, señor.	
CAPITÁN	¿Mascas el sí?	875
LUCINDO	Pésame que hables con ella;	
	que es mujer que a veinte trata.	
CAPITÁN	¡Tu lengua pones en ella,	
	porque de celos te mata,	
	siendo tan noble doncella!	880
	¡Vive Dios, que si no fuera	
	por no dejar de casarme,	
	que una estocada te diera!	
LUCINDO	¿Casarte? Eso sí es matarme.	
	Padre, señor, considera...	885
CAPITÁN	¿Qué debo considerar?	
LUCINDO	Que es una mujer de amores.	
CAPITÁN	Dado me ha que sospechar,	
	pero póneme temores	
	por estorbarme el casar.	890
	Como el que con los espejos	
	puestos al sol da en los ojos	
	al que viene desde lejos,	
	quiere el necio darme enojos	
	con estos vanos consejos.	895
	Mas quiero volverle [a] hablar,	
	y decirle esta respuesta;	
	que me ha dado que pensar.	

Vase.

	You with the tongue of a scorpion,	
	Do you deserve to kiss her feet	
	Or even the ground she walks on?	865
LUCINDO	It's just that I'm really upset.	
	She's made me jealous of the man,	
	Or two, she now seems to adore.	
CAPTAIN	She's in love with another man,	
	That lady of spotless repute?	870
	But you must be speaking of me,	
	Whom, of course, she does love dearly.	
LUCINDO	You're saying she loves you as well?	
CAPTAIN	Don't I deserve to be favored?	
LUCINDO	*(Mumbling.)* Yes, sir.	
CAPTAIN	Is that so hard to say?	875
LUCINDO	I'm just sorry you talk to her;	
	You're one of many on her string.	
CAPTAIN	You only speak of her that way	
	Since you're dying of jealousy;	
	She, sir, is a noble lady!	880
	By God, if it were not that the	
	Wedding would have to be postponed	
	I'd run you through right here and now!	
LUCINDO	Wedding? That ends it all for me!	
	Father, sir, you must consider…	885
CAPTAIN	What is it I must consider?	
LUCINDO	That she's had many men before.	
CAPTAIN	*(Aside.)* (Now I'm beginning to wonder…	
	But I'm sure he's raising these doubts	
	Just so I'll renounce the marriage.	890
	Like the fellow with a mirror	
	Who uses it to reflect sun	
	In the eyes of someone coming,	
	The fool hopes to aggravate me	
	With his unproved, baseless warnings.	895
	But I should speak to her again	
	And tell her what Lucindo said;	
	He's definitely made me think.)	

Exit the Captain.

HERNANDO	¿Qué te parece?
LUCINDO	[Por ésta]
	hoy me tengo de matar. 900
	Rompe [esas] puertas.
HERNANDO	Aguarda.
LUCINDO	Sale aquí, infame Gerarda.
HERNANDO	Con más tiento; espera un poco.

Sale Gerarda.

GERARDA	¡Golpes en mi casa, loco!
LUCINDO	¿Qué respeto me acobarda, 905
	que no te quito la vida?
GERARDA	¡Daguita! ¡Oh, qué lindo cuento!
LUCINDO	¿Tú con mi padre, fingida,
	has tratado casamiento?
GERARDA	Tracilla es escogida. 910
	Si para volver acá
	buscas embustes, Lucindo,
	esto ¿en qué razón está?
LUCINDO	¿Por qué en mirarte me rindo?
	¿Por qué no te mato [ya]? 915
	¿No viste a mi padre aquí?
	Pues él me ha dicho, [crüel],
	que para matarme a mí,
	quieres casarte con él.
GERARDA	¿Yo, que en mi vida le vi? 920
	¿Diote la industria este necio
	para tener ocasión
	de hablarme?
HERNANDO	Menos desprecio;
	que no es aquesto invención,
	sino verdad.
GERARDA	No hablar recio. 925
HERNANDO	¿Por qué no? Con la verdad

HERNANDO   What do you think?
LUCINDO   That that woman
                 Is going to be the death of me.   900
                 Break the door down!

He pounds on the door.

HERNANDO   Hey, don't do that!
LUCINDO   Damn you, Gerarda, come out here!
HERNANDO   Take a deep breath and just calm down!

Gerarda comes out.

GERARDA   Mad man! Stop banging on my door!
LUCINDO   What small shred of respect keeps me   905
                 From killing you right here and now?

He pulls out a dagger.

GERARDA   A dagger? I can't believe this!
LUCINDO   Faithless woman! It's my father
                 That you're now planning to marry?
GERARDA   What a ludicrous invention!   910
                 If you were looking for pretexts
                 To come back here, Lucindo dear,
                 You could have done better than that!
LUCINDO   Why do I get weak just looking
                 At you? Why don't I kill you now?   915
                 Did you not see my father here?
                 He told me, to destroy my life
                 Forever, cruel man that he is,
                 That you're going to marry him.
GERARDA   I've never seen him in my life.   920
                 Is it that moron at your side
                 Who made all that up to get you
                 To come see me?
HERNANDO   Just a minute!
                 None of what he said was made up.
                 It's God's own truth.
GERARDA   Don't shout so much!   925
HERNANDO   Why not? When it's truth against lies,

	hable bajo la mentira,	
	la verdad con libertad.	
GERARDA	Tu desvergüenza me admira.	
LUCINDO	Y a mí tu temeridad.	930
	¿Cuándo viste al padre mío?	
	¿Dónde te habló?	
GERARDA	¿Qué es aquesto?	
	¿Hay más loco desvarío?	
LUCINDO	¿Posible es que has descompuesto	
	sus canas con ese brío?	935
	Demonios sois las mujeres.	
GERARDA	¡Muy ángeles son los hombres!	
	Lucindo, ¿para qué quieres	
	disfrazar con estos nombres,	
	que por mis desdenes mueres?	940
	¿Qué padre es éste? ¿No adviertes	
	que entiendo tus invenciones?	
LUCINDO	¡Plegue a Dios tal mal aciertes	
	en casarte, ya que pones	
	mi vida entre tantas muertes,	945
	que te viva dos mil años	
	el viejo por quien me dejas	
	en tanta[s] penas y daños,	
	y a quien por ojos y orejas	
	le has dado hechizos y engaños!	950
	¡Plegue a Dios! Mas ¿qué inhumanas	
	maldiciones puedo hacer	
	más que verte las mañanas,	
	como sierra, amanecer	
	con la nieve de sus canas?	955
	¿Qué más que ver un anciano	
	a tu lado hermoso y tierno,	
	de tu belleza tirano?	
	¡Qué gentil hielo en invierno,	
	y qué espantajo en verano!	960
	Adiós, madrast[r]a crüel;	
	que presto, estando con él,	
	te pesará el ver en vano	

It's lies that need to speak softly,
But the truth can always cry out.

GERARDA   Your impudence amazes me.

LUCINDO   As does me your audacity.   930
When did you see my father?
Where did you speak?

GERARDA   What's going on?
This is all completely crazy.

LUCINDO   I'm getting the idea that
You've turned his head with your boldness.   935
You women are truly devils!

GERARDA   And men are nothing but angels!
Lucindo, it's silly to use
All these names to hide the fact that
My disregard is killing you.   940
There's no father. Don't you see that
I'm on to your fabrications?

LUCINDO   I hope to God, since your marriage
Is so wrong and places my life
In great harm and mortal danger,   945
That your husband lives two thousand years.
Yes, the old man for whom you leave me
In such sorrow and misery,
And on whom you have cast a spell
That creeps in through both eyes and ears.   950
And I hope to God ... but what vile
Curses could equal the pleasure
Of knowing you'll wake up each day
Next to someone whose ancient head,
Like the mountains, is crowned with snow?   955
What could be better than seeing
At your youthful and lovely side
That old man, claiming your beauty.
He'll be like ice in the winter
And in summer a real scarecrow!   960
Good-by, then, cruel stepmother;
Very soon, after you've married
My father, what you'll be seeing

que te bese yo la mano,
y que tú la boca a él.   965
    ¡Jesús, qué mala elección!

GERARDA   Hernando, ¿es esto de veras,
o vuestras quimeras son?

HERNANDO   ¡Ojalá fueran quimeras!

GERARDA   Ya entiendo vuestra intención.   970
    Oísteisme concertar
ir al Prado aquesta noche,
y queréismelo estorbar.
Pues ¡por Dios, que ha de haber coche
y quien nos venga a cantar!   975
    Piquen, por hacerme gusto,
en casa de Estefanía.

LUCINDO   Matarete.

GERARDA   ¡Ay Dios, qué susto!

Vase.

HERNANDO   Entrose.

LUCINDO   ¿Cerraste, arpía?
¡Mal haya amor tan injusto!   980
    Abre esta puerta, mi bien.
Acecha por esta llave
si sus crïadas se ven.

HERNANDO   ¡Qué bien engañarte sabe!

LUCINDO   ¡Matarme sabe también!   985

HERNANDO   Al viejo ha desvanecido
para darte más enojos.

LUCINDO   Liviano en extremo ha sido;
mas ¿qué no podrán tus ojos,
dulce Argel de [mi sentido]?   990

Sale el Capitán.

CAPITÁN   ¿Estaste aquí todavía?   *romance a-a*

LUCINDO   Pues ¿eso, señor, te espanta?
Si con la mujer que adoro
en esos años te casas,
¿es mucho que me despida   995

	Is that I'll be kissing your hand,	
	And you'll be kissing his dried-up lips.	965
	Good God, what a bad choice you've made!	

GERARDA   Hernando, is all this for real,
Or are these just more of your tricks?

HERNANDO   You'd better believe it's for real.

GERARDA   I can see now what you're up to.   970
You overheard me arranging
To go to the Prado tonight,
And you're trying to prevent it.
Well, too bad! We'll go in a coach
And there'll be music and singing!   975
Now, just to give me pleasure go
Knock on Esfetanía's door.

LUCINDO   I'll kill you!

GERARDA   My lord, what a fright!

Exit Gerarda.

HERNANDO   She's gone.

LUCINDO   And locked the door, the tramp!
Damn this love that's ruining my life!   980
My darling, please open the door.
(To Hernando.) Bend down and look through the keyhole
To see if her maids are around.

HERNANDO   She sure knows how to pull your chain!

LUCINDO   Better you should say to kill me.   985

HERNANDO   She won the old man's affections
Just to get you really ticked off.

LUCINDO   I know; she's heartless through and through.
Tell me, my exotic beauty,
Is there nothing your eyes can't do?   990

Enter the Captain.

CAPTAIN   I see you haven't moved at all.

LUCINDO   Why does that surprise you, father?
If with all your years you're planning
To marry the one I adore,
Is it strange that I wish to bid   995

	destas puertas y ventanas,	
	si mañana han de ser tuyas,	
	y hoy su dueño me llamaban?	
CAPITÁN	Pienso que te has vuelto loco.	
	Dijísteme mil infamias	1000
	de aquel ángel de Fenisa,	
	hija de Belisa honrada.	
	Voylas [a] hablar, y por poco	
	saliera, traidor, sin cara;	
	que caída de vergüenza,	1005
	no era menester cortarla.	
	Yo tengo mujer más noble	
	que tu madre.	
LUCINDO	¿De quién hablas?	
CAPITÁN	De Fenisa.	
LUCINDO	Pues, señor,	
	Fenisa es doncella, y basta;	1010
	que la que yo te decía,	
	es Gerarda, cortesana,	
	que vive en este balcón.	
CAPITÁN	¿Qué tiene que ver Gerarda	
	con Fenisa?	
LUCINDO	Yo, señor,	1015
	en aquesta calle estaba	
	cuando me reprehendiste	
	de que amaba aquella dama.	
CAPITÁN	Otro enredo habrás pensado	
	con aquella buena cara	1020
	de tu criado.	
HERNANDO	¿Yo enredo?	
	Siempre piensas que te engañan;	
	propia condición de viejos.	
CAPITÁN	Niega, Lucindo, que amas	
	a Fenisa.	
LUCINDO	¿Yo, señor?	1025
CAPITÁN	¿Luego tampoco la cansas	
	con papeles y alcahuetas?	
	Pues en este punto acaba	

Good-by to these windows and doors
That today are mine to possess
And that tomorrow will be yours?

CAPTAIN I think you've gone completely mad.
You told me a thousand wicked 1000
Things of that angel Fenisa,
Daughter of the good Belisa.
I went to speak to her, scoundrel,
And was mortally embarrassed.
It was clear from the shame she showed 1005
That my words had cut her deeply.
I tell you she is more noble
Than your mother herself.

LUCINDO Who is?
CAPTAIN Fenisa.
LUCINDO Of course. Fenisa
Is still a sheltered young lady. 1010
The one I was talking about
Was Gerarda, the courtesan,
Who lives in the house you see here.

CAPTAIN What does Gerarda have to do
With Fenisa?

LUCINDO Sir, I was here 1015
On this street when you came along
And gave me holy hell because
I was in love with that woman.

CAPTAIN That's just one more fabrication
That you and that no-good servant 1020
Of yours have invented.

HERNANDO I, sir?
You always suppose you're being
Tricked. That's typical of old men!

CAPTAIN Lucindo, deny if you can
That you love Fenisa.

LUCINDO I, sir? 1025
CAPTAIN Then you dispute you bombard her
With letters and base go-betweens?
She was telling me just moments

	de decirme que anteanoche,	
	por aquella reja baja,	1030
	enfrente de tu aposento,	
	muy tiern[o] llegaste a hablarla.	
LUCINDO	¿Yo papeles? ¿Yo alcahuetas?	
	Yo por reja ni ventanas?	
	Hernando…	
CAPITÁN	¡Qué buen testigo!	1035
	Falsos ojos, lengua falsa,	
	falsa la cara y la boca,	
	falso el pecho y falsa el alma.	
	Pues mira lo que te aviso:	
	¡Vive el cielo, que si pasas	1040
	por su puerta, ni la miras,	
	ni por la reja la llamas,	
	que para siempre jamás	
	has de salir de mi casa!	
LUCINDO	Escúchame.	
CAPITÁN	¿Para qué?	1045
LUCINDO	Escúchame una palabra.	
CAPITÁN	¿Qué palabra?	
LUCINDO	Que la digas	
	que si ha de ser mi madrastra,	
	no comience antes de serlo,	
	pues aun agora lo tratas,	1050
	a hacerme tan malas obras.	
CAPITÁN	Quita, necio.	
LUCINDO	Advierte…	
CAPITÁN	¡Guarda!	

Vase.

LUCINDO	¿Qué es esto, triste de mí?	
	¡Testimonios me levanta	
	antes que su rostro vea!	1055
HERNANDO	¿No es aquésta aquella dama	
	que te miró tiernamente	
	cuando el lienzo de las randas?	
LUCINDO	La misma.	

	Ago that the night before last	
	You came right up to her window,	1030
	The one that's across from your own,	
	And whispered tender words of love.	
LUCINDO	Letters you say, and go-betweens?	
	I came right up to her window?	
	Hernando…	
CAPTAIN	You want him to vouch	1035

CAPTAIN   You want him to vouch   1035
For you, Señor false eyes, false tongue,
False face, mouth, chest, soul, and every
Other part of the body too?
Well, listen to what I tell you.
I swear to God, if you pass by   1040
Her door, you are never to look
At her or knock on her window,
Because if you do, I'll throw you
Out of my house once and for all.

LUCINDO   Listen to me, please.

CAPTAIN   Why should I?   1045

LUCINDO   Listen to me. I've just one word.

CAPTAIN   What word?

LUCINDO   Please tell the young lady
If she's to be my step-mother
She shouldn't act like it until
You're married. For now I reject   1050
How each of you is treating me!

CAPTAIN   Get away, villain!

LUCINDO   Wait…

CAPTAIN   Enough!

Exit the Captain.

LUCINDO   What in hell is going on here?
She's accusing me of vile things
When I've just barely seen her face!   1055

HERNANDO   Isn't she that same young woman
Who looked at you so tenderly
When you picked up her handkerchief?

LUCINDO   She is.

HERNANDO	Pues que me maten
	si no es enredo que traza,
	enamorada de ti.
LUCINDO	¿Qué me cuentas?
HERNANDO	Lo que pasa.
	Yo leí cuatro renglones
	en sus ojos, de una carta,
	que al darte el lienzo escribió
	a tu ausente pecho y alma.
	Dejole caer adrede,
	si la vista no me engaña,
	y lo que a tu padre dice
	de que la escribes y cansas,
	es decirte que la escribas
	y que por las rejas bajas
	vengas a hablarla de noche.
LUCINDO	Cosas me dices extrañas.
HERNANDO	¿Qué se pierde en que las pruebes?
LUCINDO	No se pierde, Hernando, nada;
	que esa doncella podría,
	con su bellísima cara,
	con su rico entendimiento,
	con su voluntad esclava,
	desamartelarme el pecho,
	despicarme de Gerarda.
	Vámosla [a] hablar esta noche;
	que si es verdad que me llama
	con esta industria que dices,
	es la cosa más gallarda
	que ha sucedido en el mundo.
HERNANDO	Mucho importa enamoralla,
	así por dejar del todo
	esta fementida ingrata,
	como porque nos perdemos
	si el viejo otra vez se casa.
	Y si se quiere casar,
	¿qué cosa más acertada
	que con su madre Belisa,
	desta bellísima dama?

1060

1065

1070

1075

1080

1085

1090

1095

HERNANDO	Well, let them string me up	
	If this isn't some plot she's cooked	1060
	Up because she's in love with you.	
LUCINDO	What are you saying?	
HERNANDO	Just the truth.	

When she dropped the handkerchief, I
Could see in her eyes the message
She was sending straight to your soul; 1065
But, sad to say, you tuned it out.
If my eyes haven't deceived me
She dropped the hankie on purpose,
And that stuff your father mentioned
About letters and chasing her 1070
Was her way of telling you you
Should write and come to speak to her
At her window in the evening.

LUCINDO	All this is very peculiar.	
HERNANDO	What do you lose by testing it?	1075
LUCINDO	Nothing, Hernando not a thing.	

Because that young woman, with her
Innumerable virtues, her
Lovely, beautiful face, her keen
Intellect, her strength of purpose, 1080
Could erase my heart's obsession
With Gerarda and make me whole.
Let's go talk with her this evening.
If it's true she's signaling me
With that ploy you're describing, I'd 1085
Say it's among the sharpest schemes
This world of ours has ever seen.

HERNANDO It's important to woo her right,
So you can dump, once and for all,
That ungrateful hag, Gerarda; 1090
Also because if the old man
Marries again we're up the creek.
But if he should marry again,
It would be a much better match
If he got hitched to Belisa 1095
Rather than her gorgeous daughter.

LUCINDO	Si me quiere, Hernando mío,
	te mando ropilla y calzas.
HERNANDO	Bien puedes dármelas luego.
LUCINDO	Pues con discreción tan alta 1100
	supo engañar a dos viejos
	de edad y experiencia tanta;
	y enamorada de quien
	apenas le vio la cara,
	ha dicho su pensamiento, 1105
	y le han entendido el alma,
	bien la podemos llamar
	La discreta enamorada.

LUCINDO	Hernando, if all this works out	
	I'll send you a new set of clothes.	
HERNANDO	No need to wait; I'll take them now.	
LUCINDO	If with such wit and cleverness	1100
	She knew how to fool two old folks	
	Of much greater experience,	
	While finding a way to reveal	
	Her love, and manifest her thoughts	
	To one who's scarcely seen her face,	1105
	But whose soul she's truly captured,	
	Then she well deserves to be called	
	The Cleverest Girl in Madrid.	

JORNADA SEGUNDA

Salen Doristeo, Finardo en hábito de noche, Gerarda con rebociño y sombrero, Liseo, Fabio, y los músicos.

DORISTEO	Notable frescura.	
FINARDO	Extraña.	*redondillas*
GERARDA	Mucho de sus fuentes gusto.	1110
DORISTEO	No hay sitio de tanto gusto,	
	Gerarda bella, en España.	
GERARDA	¡Qué lindas tazas!	
DORISTEO	Famosas.	
GERARDA	Con perlas brindando están.	
DORISTEO	¡Qué liberales que dan	1115
	sus aguas claras y hermosas!	
	¿Haste holgado de venir?	
GERARDA	Basta venir a tu lado.	
DORISTEO	Sentémonos.	
FINARDO	Todo es Prado.	
DORISTEO	Así se suele decir.	1120
	¿Templaron vuesas mercedes?	
LISEO	La prima se me bajó.	
GERARDA	Subilla.	
DORISTEO	Eso digo yo.	
FABIO	¿Comienzo?	
DORISTEO	Comenzar [puedes].	
FABIO	¿Qué diremos?	
DORISTEO	La de Lope,	1125
	por vida del buen Liseo.	
LISEO	¿La del suspiro y deseo?	
FINARDO	A fe, que hay bien donde tope.	

Cantan.

	Cuando tan hermosa os miro,	*villancico*
	de amor suspiro,	1130
	y cuando no os veo,	

ACT TWO

The Prado. It is night.
Enter Doristeo and Finardo in evening wear, Gerarda, dressed in a shawl
and hat, and Liseo and Fabio, musicians.

DORISTEO	How cool it is.	
FINARDO	It's delightful.	
GERARDA	I've always loved the fountains here.	1110
DORISTEO	Charming Gerarda, in all Spain	
	There's no place so enjoyable.	
GERARDA	Look at the basins!	
DORISTEO	Exquisite!	
GERARDA	They seem to be bubbling with pearls.	
DORISTEO	Yes, they're filling with water so	1115
	Clear it's like the finest crystal.	
	Are you happy you've come tonight?	
GERARDA	My delight is to be with you.	
DORISTEO	Let's sit here.	
FINARDO	Unrivalled Prado!	
DORISTEO	I've heard many say the same thing.	1120
	Are your instruments all tuned up?	
LISEO	My top string seems to have gone flat.	
GERARDA	Well, fix it.	
DORISTEO	Yes, of course, fix it.	
FABIO	Should I begin?	
DORISTEO	When you're ready.	
FABIO	What should we sing?	
DORISTEO	The song by Lope;	1125
	The one Liseo knows so well.	
LISEO	The one about sighing and love?	
FINARDO	Yes, the evening's perfect for that.	

The musicians sing and play.

> When I behold you, chaste and fair,
> My love for you breaks out in sighs;   1130
> But sighs soon turn to deep despair,

suspira por mí el deseo.
Cuando mis ojos os ven,
van a gozar tanto bien;
mas como por su desdén   1135
de los vuestros me retiro,
de amor suspiro;
y cuando no os veo
suspiro por mi deseo.

Salen Lucindo y Hernando.

LUCINDO	Dijeron que llevarían	1140 *redondillas*
	quien cantase.	
HERNANDO	Ellos serán,	
	pues aquí cantando están.	
LUCINDO	Ni cantan mal ni porfían.	
HERNANDO	Cesaron, como las aves	
	luego que alguno se acerca.	1145
LUCINDO	Llega y míralos más cerca.	
HERNANDO	¡Plegue a Dios, señor, que acabes	
	de ser necio!	
LUCINDO	Si no es hora	
	para hablar con mi Fenisa,	
	¿que importa, pues todo es risa?	1150
HERNANDO	Celos ríen, y amor llora.	
	Yo paso a lo caballero	
	por delante; espera aquí.	
LUCINDO	Yo aguardo.	
FINARDO	¿Qué mira ansí	
	este necio majadero?	1155
DORISTEO	Algo debe de buscar	
	que de casa se le fue.	
GERARDA	Canta solo.	
LISEO	Cantaré.	
GERARDA	Sí, pero no has de templar.	
HERNANDO	En la voz la conocí.	1160

When you no longer fill my eyes.
My eyes can have no truer gain
Than seeing you cloaked all in charm;
But when you treat me with disdain, 1135
I then must flee in great alarm
And sigh again, now for love lost.
My heart sinks down and cannot rise
For you no longer fill my eyes.

Enter Lucindo and Hernando.

LUCINDO	They said they were going to bring	1140
	Someone who would sing.	
HERNANDO	There they are,	
	Then, because somebody's singing.	
LUCINDO	They're not bad, not straining at all.	
HERNANDO	Hang it! They've stopped, just like the birds	
	When they hear someone approaching.	1145
LUCINDO	Go up and get a better look.	
HERNANDO	For God's sake, would you stop being	
	So stupid!	
LUCINDO	Well, if it's not time	
	Yet to go speak with Fenisa,	
	What's the problem? It's all in fun.	1150
HERNANDO	Jealousy laughs, and love laments.	
	I'll stroll by in front of them like	
	A true gentleman. You stay here.	
LUCINDO	Fine. I won't move.	

His face half-hidden, Hernando walks in front of the seated group and returns to where his master is waiting.

FINARDO	What do you think	
	That asinine lout is doing?	1155
DORISTEO	Maybe he's looking for something	
	That he lost coming here tonight.	
GERARDA	Sing alone now.	
LISEO	With great pleasure.	
GERARDA	Good. Don't bother tuning again.	
HERNANDO	I recognized her by her voice.	1160

LUCINDO	Luego ¿es [Gerarda]?
HERNANDO	Sin duda.
LUCINDO	¡Ay!
HERNANDO	¿Es menester ayuda?
LUCINDO	Y el otro ¿es su galán?
HERNANDO	Sí.
LUCINDO	¡Triste de mí!
HERNANDO	¿Qué tenemos?

¿Date por ventura el parto?   1165

LUCINDO   Mientras más de ti me aparto,
            más me acerco.

HERNANDO   Sin extremos;
            que te podrá conocer.

LUCINDO   ¿Está en su regazo?

HERNANDO   ¡Y cómo!

LUCINDO   Celos por los ojos tomo;   1170
            ya el alma comienza a arder.
                ¡Oh, veneno, que desalmas
            la vida con tus enojos,
            siendo la copa los ojos
            donde le beben las almas!   1175
                ¡Nunca yo viniera acá!

HERNANDO   Vámonos de aquí, señor,
            ¿no es aquel ángel mejor,
            que esperándonos está?

LUCINDO   ¿Cuál ángel?

HERNANDO   Fenisa bella.   1180

LUCINDO   No estoy para hablar agora
            con ángeles.

HERNANDO   Si te adora,
            ¿no será justo querella?

LUCINDO   Ésa peligro no corre;
            que como es amor primero,   1185
            estará, como otr[a] Hero,
            aguardándome en la torre;
                pero ésta que está en los brazos
            deste venturoso amante,
            si me descuido un instante,   1190

LUCINDO	Then it's Gerarda?
HERNANDO	Without doubt.
LUCINDO	Ayyy!
HERNANDO	What's wrong? Should I call for help?
LUCINDO	The man with her? Her lover?
HERNANDO	Yes.
LUCINDO	I can't stand it!
HERNANDO	What's the matter?

You act like you're having a baby.   1165

LUCINDO	(*Speaking of Gerarda.*) The more apart from you I am

The closer I feel.

HERNANDO	Not so loud!

She's sure to recognize your voice.

LUCINDO	Was she in his lap?
HERNANDO	Was she ever!
LUCINDO	Seeing her I'm jealous again, 1170

And my heart is on fire once more.
Oh, poison, which destroys one's life
With a thousand doubts, created
By the eyes, and held as in a
Cup until the soul drinks it down.   1175
I just wish I'd never come here.

HERNANDO	Okay, sir. Let's get going then.

We're better off with that angel
Who's home waiting for us tonight.

LUCINDO	What angel?
HERNANDO	Fenisa, of course. 1180
LUCINDO	I'm not in the mood now to speak

With angels.

HERNANDO	If she adores you,

Shouldn't you show her that you care?

LUCINDO	I'm not concerned about that. Since

I'm no doubt the first man she's loved,   1185
Like Hero in her tower she's
Sure not to mind waiting a bit.
But this other one, all wrapped up
In the arms of her new lover,
If I'm not on guard every   1190

har[a]me el alma pedazos.
¿Traes el manto?

HERNANDO   ¿Pues no?
LUCINDO   Póntele.
HERNANDO   Gran mal recelo.
LUCINDO   Haz saya del herreruelo.
HERNANDO   ¡Yo mujer! ¡Tu dama yo!   1195
LUCINDO   A esos árboles te ve,
y de mujer te disfraza.
HERNANDO   Voy; mas temo que esta traza...
LUCINDO   Ve, majadero.
HERNANDO   Yo iré;
mas defenderme [te] toca,   1200
y si hacerlo no quisieres,
no te espantes si me vieres
con la barriga a la boca.

Éntrase.

LUCINDO   ¡Qué mal se cura amor con invenciones!   *soneto*
¡Qué vano error sobresanar la herida,   1205
si en las muertas cenizas [escondida],
la viva lumbre al corazón le pones!
    Celos, desdenes, iras, sinrazones
tienen el alma alguna vez dormida;
mas ¿qué letargo habrá que no despida   1210
la fuerza de celosas prevenciones?
    ¡Oh celos!, con razón os han llamado
mosquitos del amor, de amor desvelos:
el vivo de su fuego os ha engañado.
    ¿Qué importa que se duerma un hombre, ¡oh cielos!
de pesadumbres del amor cansado,
si con sus voces le despiertan celos?

Sale Hernando, el manto puesto y la capa por saya.

Second she'll rip my soul to shreds.
You have your cloak, don't you?

HERNANDO   Of course.
LUCINDO   Put in on.
HERNANDO   I think I smell a rat!
LUCINDO   And make a skirt out of your cape.
HERNANDO   Me, a woman! Me, your lady!   1195
LUCINDO   Go behind those trees over there
                   And get yourself up like a girl.
HERNANDO   I'm going; but I fear this plan ...
LUCINDO   Get going, you boob.
HERNANDO   I'm going;
                   But it's your job to defend me.   1200
                   And if you're not up to the job
                   Don't be surprised if you soon find
                   Me with my belly out to here!

Exit Hernando.
Lucindo remains standing, and at some distance from Gerarda, Doristeo,
Finardo, Liseo and Fabio, who are seated.

LUCINDO   How badly love is cured with fabrication;
                   How rash to think the wound is finally healed. 1205
                   Love's flames are always prone to restoration,
                   For in their coals lie sparks of life, there concealed.
                        The dozing mind can put off guilt and distrust,
                   Resentment, bother, annoyance, and despair;
                   But when beset by jealous thoughts it then must 1210
                   Awaken, all sleep destroyed beyond repair.
                        Jealousy! How rightly you've been called with scorn
                   Mosquito of love, the thief of needed sleep.
                   In the smoke of love's fire is where you were born,
                   Foul air that makes the lungs gasp and the eyes weep.
                        What repose is there for those by love oppressed
                   If fierce jealousy denies them any rest?

Enter Hernando, his cloak over his head and shoulders, and wearing his
cape for a skirt.

HERNANDO	¿Vengo bien?	*redondillas*
LUCINDO	Vienes tan bien,	
	que espero que bien me vaya.	
HERNANDO	¿Qué te parece la saya?	1220
LUCINDO	Muy bien.	
HERNANDO	¿Y el manto?	
LUCINDO	También.	
HERNANDO	¿No voy muy apetecible?	
LUCINDO	¿Cómo?	
HERNANDO	¿Llevo malos bajos?	
LUCINDO	Llega.	
HERNANDO	En notables trabajos	
	me pone tu amor terrible.	1225
DORISTEO	Un galán con cierta dama	
	hacia donde estamos viene.	
GERARDA	¡Gentil brío y arte tiene!	
	A fe que es ropa de fama.	
DORISTEO	¿Cómo?	
GERARDA	Diome el buen olor.	1230
DORISTEO	Tomó pastilla al salir.	
FINARDO	Pastilla y Prado es decir	
	que es dama…	
DORISTEO	De qué?	
FINARDO	…de amor.	
DORISTEO	A tu lado toma asiento.	
GERARDA	¡Qué de golpe se ha asentado!	1235
FINARDO	Debe de tener pesado	
	lo que es el quinto elemento.	
LUCINDO	Bella doña Estefanía,	
	¿qué os parece esta frescura?	
HERNANDO	Fue mucha descompostura	1240
	venir aquí sin mi tía;	

HERNANDO	*(To Lucindo.)* Well, how do I look?
LUCINDO	Quite fetching!
	My plan is off to a good start.
HERNANDO	So what do you think of the skirt? 1220
LUCINDO	Beautiful.
HERNANDO	And the cloak?
LUCINDO	The same.
HERNANDO	Would you say I'm desirable?
LUCINDO	Come again?
HERNANDO	Check the petticoat.
LUCINDO	Let's go!
HERNANDO	The things I do for you,
	Because of your mad, crazy love! 1225

The two of them approach the other five.

DORISTEO	A gentleman and his lady
	Seem to be coming over here.
GERARDA	She carries herself really well;
	And her clothes are ever so chic.
DORISTEO	What's that?
GERARDA	Don't you think she smells nice? 1230
DORISTEO	She must have taken a lozenge.
FINARDO	Lozenge plus Prado has to mean
	She's a lady…
DORISTEO	Of what?
FINARDO	The night.
DORISTEO	She's going to sit right next to you.

Hernando sits very heavily.

GERARDA	She plopped down like a ton of bricks! 1235
FINARDO	Just goes to show you the power
	Held by the force of gravity.
LUCINDO	*(To Hernando.)* Beautiful Estefanía,
	What do you think of the fresh air?

Hernando speaks with a girlish voice.

HERNANDO	It was a wicked thing to do, 1240
	Coming here without my dear aunt;

	pero el mucho amor que os tengo	
	a más me puede obligar.	
LUCINDO	Señores, ¿quieren cantar?	
HERNANDO	¿Déjanlo porque yo vengo?	1245
[GERARDA]	Lucindo es éste. ¡Ay de mí!	
	Verdad sin duda sería	
	que aquella dama quería	
	por quien preguntar le vi.	
	Celos que pensé fingidos	1250
	me han salido verdaderos.	
	¡Ay, amores lisonjeros,	
	de engaño y traición vestidos!	
	Entendídome ha la letra,	
	herido me ha por el filo,	1255
	vengose del mismo estilo.	
HERNANDO	Ya se altera [e] inquïeta.	
	¿Qué te parece el jarabe?	
LUCINDO	Que hace su operación.	
GERARDA	¡Qué bien sabe dar pasión!	1260
	¡Qué mal el tomarla sabe!	
	Por vida de Doristeo,	
	que un poco de agua traigáis.	
DORISTEO	Y traeré con qué bebáis;	
	que regalaros deseo.	1265
	Entreteneos aquí	
	mientras voy por colación.	

Vanse los dos.

GERARDA	Que vais solo no es razón.	
FINARDO	¿Acompañarele?	
GERARDA	Sí;	
	que aquí quedan los amigos.	1270
FINARDO	Pues vamos.	
DORISTEO	Venid.	
FINARDO	Adiós.	
GERARDA	Muérome porque las dos	
	quedásemos sin testigos.	

	But the deep love I have for you	
	Could make me do even worse things.	
LUCINDO	(*To Liseo and Fabio.*) Gentlemen, would you	
	sing more, please?	
HERNANDO	Have they stopped because I'm here too?	1245
GERARDA	(*Aside.*) (Oh, no! That man is Lucindo!	
	And the lady he's with must be	
	The one he was looking for when	
	He came by and asked about her.	
	I thought he was inventing her	1250
	To make me jealous… Well, now I am!	
	I never knew love was like this,	
	So two-faced, deceiving, and false.	
	He's learned all too well my lessons,	
	And now he's cut me to the quick,	1255
	Paying me with my own money.)	
HERNANDO	(*To Lucindo.*) What a change! She's fit to be tied!	
	How's that for a great love potion!	
LUCINDO	It's clear that it's working its spell.	
GERARDA	(*Aside.*) (How good he is at spurring love,	1260
	And how bad at taking it back.)	
	Dear Doristeo, could I please	
	Ask you to bring me some water?	
DORISTEO	I'll get it with pleasure, along	
	With some tidbits to go with it.	1265
	Please entertain yourself with the	
	Present company while I'm gone.	
GERARDA	It's not right you should go alone.	
FINARDO	Should I go along with him?	
GERARDA	Please.	
	There's no problem. We're all friends here.	1270
FINARDO	Let's go, then.	
DORISTEO	Come along.	
FINARDO	Good-bye.	

Exit Doristeo and Finardo.

GERARDA	(*Aside.*) (Now to get the others to leave
	So I can be alone with her.)

LISEO	¿Queréis que cantemos?
GERARDA	No.
	Antes merced recibiera 1275
	en quedar sola.
FABIO	Algo espera.
LISEO	Lindamente [nos echó.]
FABIO	Pues no estorbemos, Liseo.
LISEO	Fabio, venid por aquí.

Vanse los músicos.

GERARDA	¡Ah, mi señora!
HERNANDO	¿Es a mí? 1280
GERARDA	Veros y hablaros deseo.
HERNANDO	¡Verme y hablarme! ¿Por qué?
GERARDA	Porque soy vuestra vecina.
HERNANDO	¡Jesús, qué extraña mohína!
GERARDA	¿Desto sólo os enfadé? 1285
HERNANDO	Hace notable calor;
	vamos, Lucindo, de aquí.
LUCINDO	Mi bien, enfaldarse ansí
	parece mucho rigor.
	Descubríos a esa dama, 1290
	pues Dios os dio tal belleza,
	y esa hermosa gentileza
	tiene en la corte tal fama.
	Descubrid los ojos bellos,
	den envidia y den amor. 1295
HERNANDO	No estoy agora de humor,
	ni está enjuto el llanto en ellos;
	que los traéis hechos mar
	de celos de esa Gerarda,
	que me dicen que es gallarda. 1300
LUCINDO	¿Gerarda os los puede dar?
	No sé de qué los tenéis.
	¡Plegue a Dios que si la quiero,
	que para el mal de que muero
	nunca remedio me deis! 1305

LISEO	Would you like us to sing more?	
GERARDA	No.	
	At the moment I would prefer	1275
	To be left alone.	

Liseo starts to leave.

FABIO	*(To Liseo.)* Wait for me!	
LISEO	How nicely she showed us the door.	
FABIO	You can't stay if you're not wanted.	
LISEO	Right you are, Fabio. Let's go!	

Exit the musicians.

GERARDA	Hello!	
HERNANDO	Are you speaking to me?	1280
GERARDA	I'd like to see you and chat a bit.	
HERNANDO	See me and chat with me? What for?	
GERARDA	Because you and I are neighbors.	
HERNANDO	Well! You don't have to talk that way!	
GERARDA	Why is that upsetting to you?	1285
HERNANDO	It's become unbearably hot.	
	We'd better go now, Lucindo.	
LUCINDO	My dear, wrapping yourself up that	
	Way is hardly necessary.	
	Please do let this lady see you,	1290
	Since God gave you such great beauty,	
	As well as unbounded kindness	
	That's talked about throughout Madrid.	
	Uncover your two sparkling eyes;	
	Let them provoke envy and love!	1295
HERNANDO	I'm not in the mood for that now;	
	Besides, my eyes are not yet dry	
	From the sea of tears that filled them	
	When I learned you love Gerarda,	
	Who, I'm told, is very charming.	1300
LUCINDO	What? You're jealous of Gerarda?	
	There's nothing to be jealous of.	
	If I desire her, God grant that	
	You show me no pity when I	
	Gaze, helpless, upon your beauty.	1305

	¡Plegue a Dios que si la estimo,	
	nunca merezca estos brazos,	
	ni a mis amorosos lazos	
	den vuestros muros arrimo!	
	¡Plegue a Dios que si la amare,	1310
	nunca mi ventura poca	
	goce de esa dulce boca,	
	ni por mi bien se declare!	
	¡Plegue a Dios que si la viere,	
	jamás me vea con vos,	1315
	ni nos casemos los dos!	
GERARDA	¡Que esto sufra! ¡Que esto espe[re]!	
HERNANDO	¡Ay Dios!, ¡qué de maldiciones!	
GERARDA	Todas vengan sobre mí,	
	si más te sufriere aquí,	1320
	traidor, tantas sinrazones.	
HERNANDO	Dícenme que vais allá,	
	y estoy muy descolorida.	
LUCINDO	Pues tomad color, mi vida;	
	que a vos os adoro ya.	1325
GERARDA	No será, infame, en mis días.	
LUCINDO	¿Cómo ansí te has descompuesto?	
HERNANDO	¡A Estefanía! ¿Qué es esto?	
GERARDA	¡Y a cuarenta Estefanías!	
LUCINDO	Déjala, Gerarda.	
HERNANDO	¡Ay, cielo!	1330
	¡A una mujer como yo!	
GERARDA	¡Matarla tengo!	
LUCINDO	Eso no,	
	huye.	
HERNANDO	Mi muerte recelo.	

[Húyase Hernando.]

GERARDA	¿Qué mujer es ésta, perro?	
LUCINDO	Una mujer que me adora,	1335
	y eso que tú has hecho agora	

	If I esteem her, God grant that	
	You never hold me in your arms,	
	Nor allow me to clasp you to	
	My breast, as the vine grips the wall.	
	If I should love her, God grant that	1310
	I never again have the joy	
	Of kissing your sweet-tasting lips,	
	And hearing you say it's me you love.	
	If I visit her, God grant that	
	I never more am seen with you,	1315
	And you and I are never wed.	
GERARDA	Damn it! Do I have to take this?	
HERNANDO	Good Heavens! Such dreadful cursing!	
GERARDA	Let it be upon my own head,	
	Lucindo, you traitor, if I	1320
	Put up with more of this rubbish.	
HERNANDO	They tell me you go to see her,	
	Dear, and I turn pale from sadness.	
LUCINDO	Do regain your color, my pet;	
	I'll always give you all my love.	1325
GERARDA	As long as I'm alive, you won't!	

Gerarda throws herself on Hernando.

LUCINDO	Stop! What do you think you're doing?	
HERNANDO	Why attack me? What have I done?	
GERARDA	You've done more than enough, you witch!	
LUCINDO	Let her be, Gerarda.	
HERNANDO	Heavens!	1330
	Assaulting a lady like me!	
GERARDA	I'm going to kill her!	
LUCINDO	No you're not!	
	(To Hernando.) Run!	
HERNANDO	I think I'm going to die!	

Hernando runs off.

GERARDA	Who is that woman, you bastard?	
LUCINDO	She's a woman who adores me,	1335
	And what you're doing here tonight	

ha sido un notable yerro;
que es señora principal,
y te ha de costar la vida.

GERARDA   ¿Puede ser ya más perdida,   1340
que viéndome en tanto mal?
Déjame pasar.

LUCINDO   Detente;
que a quien me aborrece a mí,
nunca licencia le di
de hablarme tan libremente.   1345

GERARDA   ¿Yo te aborrezco, mi bien?
LUCINDO   ¿Tu bien soy?
GERARDA   ¡Ay, prenda mía!
Cuanto te dije fingía,
y cuanto hablaba también.
Aborrezco a Doristeo;   1350
sólo te adoro, Lucindo.
De nuevo el alma te rindo.

LUCINDO   ¡Cielos! ¿Qué es esto que veo?
GERARDA   En prenda de que tú eres
mi verdad, vente conmigo.   1355

LUCINDO   Mucho os alienta el castigo;
como bestias sois, mujeres.
Ahora bien, ya se acabó,
yo adoro en Estefanía.

GERARDA   ¿Por qué me dejas, luz mía?   1360
LUCINDO   Porque tu noche llegó.
GERARDA   Ven conmigo hasta mi casa.
LUCINDO   No hay remedio.
GERARDA   ¡Que esto veo!
LUCINDO   Presto vendrá Doristeo,
que es el que agora te abrasa.   1365

Híncase de rodillas Gerarda.

[GERARDA]   De rodillas, mi señor,
que vayas quiero pedirte,

	Is a most serious mistake.	
	Her family is well-placed at court	
	And can cause you a lot of harm.	
GERARDA	I don't care! Can my life be worse	1340
	Than it is right now? I'm leaving.	
	Move aside!	
LUCINDO	Now just a minute!	
	I've never allowed anyone	
	Who hates me as much as you do	
	To speak with such lack of respect.	1345
GERARDA	Hate? How could I hate you, my love?	
LUCINDO	You call me your love?	
GERARDA	Oh, my dear,	
	Everything I said to you was	
	A sham, I was only feigning.	
	I can't abide Doristeo.	1350
	It's you and you alone I love.	
	Once more I give my soul to you!	
LUCINDO	Can I be hearing correctly?	
GERARDA	As proof that only you hold a	
	Place in my heart, come with me now.	1355
LUCINDO	It's punishment that makes you speak.	
	Like unruly horses women	
	Need to feel the stick. But we're done.	
	I love Estefanía now.	

Lucindo turns to leave.

GERARDA	Why must you go, light of my life?	1360
LUCINDO	Because your night is falling fast.	
GERARDA	Don't you want to come home with me?	
LUCINDO	No longer.	
GERARDA	I can't believe that.	
LUCINDO	Soon Doristeo will be back;	
	He who now fills you with desire.	1365

Gerarda falls to her knees.

GERARDA	Look at me! On my knees, sir, I'm
	Asking that you come home with me,

porque allá quiero decirte
la causa de este rigor.
    Celos, por tu vida, han sido.   1370
No seas villano, ven;
ven, Lucindo; ven mi bien.

LUCINDO   En efeto, ¿me has querido?

GERARDA   Siempre te quise, mis ojos.

LUCINDO   Yo haré que sangre te cueste…   1375

Sale Hernando, ya desnudo.

HERNANDO   ¿Qué sacrificio es aquéste?

LUCINDO   El haberme dado enojos.

HERNANDO   Si Lucindo quiere hacer
una venganza gallarda,
y Gerarda el golpe aguarda,   1380
el ángel vengo yo a ser.
    ¿Qué es esto, señor?

LUCINDO   ¡Oh, Hernando!
Seas mil veces bien venido.

HERNANDO   Dos horas ando perdido,
todo este Prado buscando;   1385
    que en casa han echado menos
a esta dama.

LUCINDO   Otra sería.

HERNANDO   ¿Luego no es Estefanía?

LUCINDO   [Ha] habido rayos y truenos.

HERNANDO   ¿Es Gerarda?

LUCINDO   ¿No lo ves?   1390

HERNANDO   Déjala, ¡triste de mí!
Que te ponen culpa a ti.

LUCINDO   Gerarda, hablemos después.

GERARDA   Oye.

LUCINDO   No hay remedio.

GERARDA   Aguarda.

	So that I can explain to you	
	The reason for all this discord.	
	It was because of jealousy,	1370
	That's all. Please don't be cruel with me.	
	Come, Lucindo, my love, come now.	
LUCINDO	Then it's true? You really loved me?	
GERARDA	I always loved you, my darling.	

Lucindo pulls out his dagger.

| LUCINDO | I swear, you don't deserve to live! | 1375 |

Hernando enters, dressed in his normal ragged clothes.

HERNANDO	What unholy sacrifice is this?	
LUCINDO	She made me extremely angry.	
HERNANDO	*(Aside.)* (If Lucindo is determined	
	To play the vengeful lover, and	
	Gerarda the ready victim,	1380
	Then I must be the guardian angel.)	
	What's going on?	
LUCINDO	Oh, Hernando!	
	Thank God! You've arrived just in time.	
HERNANDO	I've been wandering in the Prado	
	For two hours, looking for you.	1385
	This lady's absence is causing	
	Worry at home.	
LUCINDO	It can't be her.	
HERNANDO	This is not Estefanía?	
LUCINDO	Not at all. It's the drama queen.	
HERNANDO	It's Gerarda?	
LUCINDO	Yes. Can't you see?	1390
HERNANDO	Oh, Lord! Leave her and come away.	
	You'll get the blame for everything.	
LUCINDO	Gerarda, we can speak later.	
GERARDA	Please listen.	
LUCINDO	No, it's over.	
GERARDA	Wait!	

HERNANDO	Grande valor has tenido.	1395
LUCINDO	El saber que soy querido	
	me ha despicado, Gerarda.	

Vanse los dos.
Salen Doristeo y Finardo.

DORISTEO	Desgracia ha sido, por Dios,	
	el no haber ya tienda abierta.	
FINARDO	Quebrada queda una puerta.	1400
GERARDA	Cansado os habéis los dos.	
DORISTEO	¿Sola estabas?	
GERARDA	Sola estaba.	
DORISTEO	¿Los músicos?	
GERARDA	Libres son.	
FINARDO	¡Que no hubiese colación!	
	¡Si en el verano se alaba	1405
	Madrid, para quien trasnoche	
	sin cotas ni sin broqueles,	
	que tiene nieve y pasteles,	
	vino y dulce a medianoche!	
GERARDA	Tarde llegará el favor;	1410
	que no estoy buena.	
DORISTEO	Sospecho	
	que este fresco mal te ha hecho.	
GERARDA	Más me ha dañado el calor.	
DORISTEO	¿Entiendes de estrellas?	
FINARDO	Sé	
	que el Carro ha de estar allí	1415
	para amanecer.	
DORISTEO	Ansí,	
	pues ya muy alto se ve.	
	Vamos, y descansarás.	
	¡Qué amigos!	
FINARDO	Pocos hay buenos.	
GERARDA	Cuando tú me quieres menos,	1420
	Lucindo, te quiero más.	

Vanse.

HERNANDO	*(Aside to Lucindo.)* (Way to go, sir.	
	You sure have guts!)	1395
LUCINDO	Just knowing that you love me has	
	Freed me, Gerarda, from your hook.	

Exit Lucindo and Hernando.
Enter Doristeo and Finardo.

DORISTEO	I'm sorry to have to report	
	Not a single shop was open.	
FINARDO	But we did leave one door bashed in.	1400
GERARDA	You must be completely worn-out.	
DORISTEO	Have you been alone?	
GERARDA	Yes, I have.	
DORISTEO	The musicians…?	
GERARDA	I sent them home.	
FINARDO	Can you believe there was nothing?	
	How can Madrid claim that in summer,	1405
	When people go out after dark,	
	With little fear, there are places	
	That offer pastries and ices,	
	wine and snacks, even at midnight?	
GERARDA	I appreciate your trying.	1410
	But now I don't feel well.	
DORISTEO	I fear	
	The cool air has quite done you in.	
GERARDA	It's more the heat that has done that.	
DORISTEO	*(To Finardo.)* Do you know about the stars?	
FINARDO	Well,	
	I know that Ursa Major can	1415
	Be seen just before dawn.	
DORISTEO	That's true.	
	And there it is, right above us.	
	Let's go then; now's the time to sleep.	
	Some friends they were!	
FINARDO	Hard to believe!	
GERARDA	*(Aside.)* (The less you love me, Lucindo,	1420
	The more my heart aches for you.)	

Exit Gerarda, Doristeo and Finardo.

Salen Lucindo y Hernando.

HERNANDO	Tan consolado vienes, que presumo	*versos sueltos*
	que no te acuerdas ya de aquella loca.	
LUCINDO	No lo digas de burlas.	
HERNANDO	¿Quién te ha hecho	
	milagro tan notable en su sentido?	1425
LUCINDO	La confïanza de que soy querido.	
	¡Bendiga el cielo la invención, la traza,	
	la hora, el movimiento, el manto, el Prado,	
	los celos, los disgustos!	
HERNANDO	¿Y no dices	
	que bendiga también a Estefanía?	1430
	Pues en verdad, que aún traigo las señales	
	de algunos mojicones de Gerarda.	
LUCINDO	La ventana han abierto; espera, aguarda.	

En la ventana, Fenisa.

FENISA	¡Ah, caballero!	
LUCINDO	¿Quién llama?	*redondillas*
FENISA	Llegad quedo. Una mujer.	1435
HERNANDO	Fenisa debe de ser,	
	que habrá [dejado] la cama.	
FENISA	Vuestro nombre me decid,	
	antes que os empiece [a] hablar.	
LUCINDO	Mira no echemos azar.	1440
HERNANDO	Todos duermen en Madrid,	
	hasta el viejo Arias Gonzalo.	
LUCINDO	Lucindo, señora, soy,	
	que de vos quejoso estoy,	
	si esta queja no es regalo.	1445
	¿Sabéis que del Capitán	
	Bernardo soy hijo?	
FENISA	Sí.	
LUCINDO	¿Sabéis que en mi vida os vi?	
	¿Cómo soy vuestro galán?	
	¿Yo, Fenisa, os solicito?	1450

The street in front of Belisa's house.
Enter Lucindo and Hernando.

HERNANDO	You seem so carefree I have to suppose that
	You've completely forgotten that mad woman.
LUCINDO	Don't mention her even in jest.
HERNANDO	What was it
	That caused such a miraculous change in you? 1425
LUCINDO	It was the realization I was loved.
	May the good Lord bless the hoax, the cooked-up tale,
	The hour, the song and dance, the cloak, the Prado,
	The jealousy, the quarrels.
HERNANDO	Don't you also
	Wish His blessing on sweet Estefanía? 1430
	Because I have to tell you she still bears the
	Bruises from the blows that Gerarda gave her.
LUCINDO	Someone just opened that window. Hush! Quiet!

Fenisa appears at the window.

FENISA	Oh, sir! sir!
LUCINDO	Who's that who's calling?
FENISA	Shh! A woman. Come over here. 1435
HERNANDO	It can only be Fenisa,
	Who heard us and got out of bed.
FENISA	Before I speak with you I must
	Ask you to tell me who you are.
LUCINDO	*(To Hernando.)* Keep watch. We don't want
	to tempt fate. 1440
HERNANDO	Don't worry. No one in Madrid
	Is awake at such a late hour.
LUCINDO	My lady, I am Lucindo,
	And I have a complaint to make
	Against you, if I may do so. 1445
	Are you aware that I'm the son
	Of Captain Bernardo?
FENISA	I am.
LUCINDO	And that I have scarcely seen you?
	Then how can I be your lover?
	How can I be pursuing you? 1450

¿Yo os escribo mil papeles?
¿Yo a estas rejas y vergeles
la casta defensa os quito?
    ¿Yo os desvelo con paseos
y terceras os envío?   1455

FENISA   No os enfaden, señor mío,
mis amorosos rodeos.
    Ni me habéis solicitado,
ni habéis cansado mis rejas,
ni son verdades mis quejas,   1460
supuesto que me he quejado.
    Jamás escrito me habéis,
ni por vos nadie me habló;
en lo que esto se fundó,
pues venís, vos lo entendéis.   1465
    No halló mi recogimiento
cómo decir mi pasión;
amor me dio la invención,
y vos el atrevimiento.
    Vuestro padre me ha pedido;   1470
mas yo nací para vos,
si algún día quiere Dios
que os merezca por marido.
    Y el hacerle mi tercero
no os parezca desatino;   1475
que es cuerdo, viejo y vecino,
y os quiere como yo os quiero.
    Este camino busqué
para que sepáis mi amor;
sólo os suplico, señor,   1480
que agradezcáis tanta fe.
    Y si mi hacienda y mi talle,
puesto que más [merecéis],
os obligaren...

LUCINDO   No echéis
más favores en la calle.   1485
    Sembrarla en almas quisiera
en esta buena fortuna,

I send you letters day and night?
I stand at your window trying
To overcome your resistance?
I keep you up late with nightly
Vigils and send bawds to your house?   1455

FENISA   Sir, please don't be upset by these
Little amorous tricks of mine.
Of course, you're not pursuing me,
And you don't stand at my window,
And my complaints about you aren't   1460
True, assuming I have complained.
You've never written to me, nor
Sent go-betweens to praise your charms.
The reason why I said those things
You must know, since you came tonight.   1465
Shut up, as I was, in my room,
I couldn't tell you my feelings;
But love revealed the way to me,
And gave you the wits to follow.
Your father has asked for my hand;   1470
But I was born for you alone,
If it's God's desire that someday
I should deserve to marry you.
Please don't think that it's madness to
Make your father our go-between,   1475
For he's a neighbor, old and wise,
And he loves you as I love you.
This is the pathway that I've found
To make my feelings known to you.
In response I only ask, sir,   1480
That you respect my trust in you.
And if my wealth and appearance
Should seem acceptable to you,
Although not worthy…

LUCINDO   Please don't throw
Your favors to the barren street.   1485
Had I the power I'd fill it
With loving souls, because only

porque palabra ninguna
menos que en alma cayera.
  A mi ventura agradezco   1490
saber, mi bien, que os agrado;
que bien sé que no he llegado
a pensar que lo merezco.
  El día, mi bien, que os vi
de aquel santo jubileo,   1495
[despertasteis] el deseo;
nunca más con él dormí.
  Mi poco merecimiento
que entendiese me impedía
lo que mi padre decía,   1500
y era justo pensamiento;
  mas viéndole porfïar,
vine a ver lo que ya veo.

FENISA   Conocéis mi buen deseo.
LUCINDO   El conocerle es pagar;   1505
  que tras el conocimiento
de una deuda, pagar sobra.
Pero si se pone en obra
de mi padre el casamiento,
  ¿qué tal vendré yo a quedar?   1510
FENISA   No creáis que ellos lo puedan;
que los dos que los heredan
son los que se han de casar.
  Mal conocéis lo sutil
de una rendida mujer.   1515
LUCINDO   Discreta debéis de ser
y de ánimo varonil.
  Bien se ha visto en la invención.
FENISA   Pues hasta agora no es nada.
LUCINDO   *La discreta enamorada*   1520
llamaros será razón.
FENISA   Perdóneme vuestro padre;
que dél me pienso valer,
para daros a entender
lo que no quiere mi madre.   1525

	Upon such fertile ground should your	
	Gracious words be allowed to fall.	
	I thank my good fortune that I	1490
	Now know that I'm pleasing to you,	
	Although I'm aware that in no	
	Way do I deserve such reward.	
	During the festivities when	
	I first beheld you, precious one,	1495
	You awakened my deep desire.	
	Since then I'm not able to sleep.	
	My lack of wits has prevented	
	Me from understanding what it	
	Was that my father was saying,	1500
	Although it wasn't so obscure.	
	But when he kept on insisting,	
	I came to glimpse what now is clear.	
FENISA	Then you know of the love I bear?	
LUCINDO	To know it is to return it.	1505
	Because when one is made aware	
	Of a debt, one must pay it back.	
	But if my father's wedding plans	
	Are already well underway,	
	What role is there for me to play?	1510
FENISA	Please don't suppose it's preordained,	
	For as the heirs of our parents	
	We are the ones who should marry.	
	You have yet to see how keen is	
	The mind of a woman in love.	1515
LUCINDO	I bow to your sharp wits and your	
	Bravery, worthy of a man.	
	All that's clear in the tricks you've played.	
FENISA	Just you wait. There's much more to come!	
LUCINDO	You richly deserve to be called	1520
	The cleverest girl in Madrid.	
FENISA	May your dear father forgive me,	
	For I plan to make use of him	
	To let you know all those things that	
	My mother would be shocked to hear.	1525

Cuánto deciros quisiere,
será quejarme de vos,
y verémonos los dos
por donde posible fuere.
    Cuando os riña, estad atento; 1530
que son recaudos que os doy.

LUCINDO Digo, señora, que estoy
en el mismo pensamiento.

FENISA   Así sabréis lo que pasa
desta puerta adentro vos, 1535
casándonos a los dos
cuando él piensa que se casa;
    que ya estaremos casados
el día que se descubra.

LUCINDO Quiera el amor que se encubra 1540
el fin de nuestros cuidados.
    Y dad orden cómo os vea,
pues no os falta discreción.

FENISA He pensado otra invención
para que el remedio sea; 1545
    y es que diré a vuestro padre
que os envíe a que toméis
mi bendición, y vendréis
sin que se enoje mi madre.
    Pero tratadme verdad 1550
o [desengañadme] aquí.

LUCINDO El alma, señora, os di
por fe de mi voluntad.
    Preguntadla allá si os quiero.

HERNANDO Señor, advertid que al alba 1555
hacen las calandrias salva,
y está muy alto el lucero.
    En cas deste mercader
una codorniz cantó,
con que a tu amor avisó 1560
de que quiere amanecer.

FENISA   Vete, mi amor, que amanece;
no me eche menos mi madre.

	Everything I'll convey to you	
	Will take the form of a grievance,	
	And then we can see each other	
	As frequently as possible.	
	When he rebukes you, listen well,	1530
	For it's a message I'm sending.	
LUCINDO	I can only say, my lady,	
	That that's a truly brilliant scheme.	
FENISA	That way you'll know every single	
	Thing that's taking place in this house.	1535
	We'll get married and your father	
	Will think it's he who's marrying.	
	By the time what we've done is known,	
	We'll already be man and wife.	
LUCINDO	May love have the power to hide	1540
	The purpose of our stratagems	
	Work it out all out so I'll see you,	
	Since your cleverness knows no bounds.	
FENISA	All right; I've just thought of something	
	That should allow you to do so.	1545
	What I'll do is ask your father	
	To send you to me to receive	
	My blessing; that way you can come	
	Without angering my mother.	
	But now you must tell me the truth;	1550
	I couldn't bear to be deceived.	
LUCINDO	I swear to you, precious lady,	
	That my heart is yours forever.	
	Ask my servant if I love you!	
HERNANDO	Sir, take heed that the meadowlark	1555
	Has already greeted the dawn,	
	And Venus is high in the sky.	
	Listen up! In the merchant's house	
	Over there the quail are stirring,	
	Sending a signal to your love	1560
	That day is soon to be breaking.	
FENISA	You should go, my love; dawn is here;	
	Mother mustn't notice I'm gone.	

LUCINDO	Pide licencia a mi padre
	para verte.
HERNANDO	La luz crece.

1565

LUCINDO	Dame alguna prenda tuya
	con que me vaya acostar.
FENISA	A mí me quisiera dar.
HERNANDO	Dile, señor, que concluya.
FENISA	Truécame esa cinta.

Echa un listón.

LUCINDO	¿A qué?
FENISA	A deseos.
HERNANDO	¡Bueno está!
LUCINDO	Todos los tienes allá.
FENISA	Adiós.

1570

[Vase Fenisa.]

LUCINDO	¿Fuese?
HERNANDO	Ya se fue.
LUCINDO	¡Gran ventura!
HERNANDO	Di que estás
	enamorado.
LUCINDO	Pues ¿no?
HERNANDO	¿Y Gerarda?
LUCINDO	Ya pasó.
HERNANDO	¿Cómo?
LUCINDO	Lo que oyendo estás.
	Es bella, es noble, es gallarda.
HERNANDO	¡Brava cólera española!
LUCINDO	Más precio esta cinta sola
	que mil almas de Gerarda.

1575

1580

Vanse.
Salen Doristeo y Gerarda.

DORISTEO	¿Para qué es tanto desdén,	*quintillas*
	sino decirme verdad?	
	Hombre soy, y hombre de bien;	

LUCINDO   Ask permission of my father
             For me to see you.
HERNANDO   It's daybreak.   1565
LUCINDO   Give me some remembrance of you
             That I can take to bed with me.
FENISA   If only that could be myself.
HERNANDO   Sir, it's late. Tell her to finish.
FENISA   I'll trade you this ribbon.

Fenisa throws him a ribbon.

LUCINDO   For what?   1570
FENISA   All your love.
HERNANDO   Come on, sir! Let's go!
LUCINDO   I give it now and forever!
FENISA   Good-by.

Exit Fenisa.

LUCINDO   Is she gone?
HERNANDO   Yes, she's gone.
LUCINDO   I can't believe my luck!
HERNANDO   Admit
             You're in love.
LUCINDO   I do so gladly.   1575
HERNANDO   And Gerarda?
LUCINDO   That's all over.
HERNANDO   So soon?
LUCINDO   Why not? Fenisa is
             Noble, clever, and beautiful!
HERNANDO   Long live the fair ladies of Spain!
LUCINDO   This ribbon means more to me than   1580
             All of Gerarda's endearments.

Exit Lucindo and Hernando.
The entrance to the house of Gerarda.
Enter Doristeo and Gerarda.

DORISTEO   What is the point of this coldness
             If it's not to tell me something?
             I'm a man and a gentleman;

	háblame con libertad.	1585
	¿Quieres a Lucindo bien?	
GERARDA	Pensé que no le quería,	
	y anoche...	
DORISTEO	Pasa adelante.	
GERARDA	Quiso la desdicha mía	
	que fuese un desdén bastante	1590
	a encender nieve tan fría.	
	¿No viste aquella mujer	
	que se sentó junto a mí?	
DORISTEO	Lucindo debió de ser	
	el que la trujo.	
GERARDA	Es ansí.	1595
DORISTEO	Eso me basta saber.	
	¡Ay, Gerarda, cuánto pueden	
	unos celos!	
GERARDA	Muerta estoy.	
	En fuerza al amor exceden;	
	no hay desdén, mi fe te doy,	1600
	de que triunfando no queden.	
	Estudiado parecía	
	lo que Lucindo decía,	
	y lo que ella preguntaba;	
	supe al fin que se llamaba	1605
	esta dama Estefanía,	
	y que es mujer principal,	
	que un crïado, a un rayo igual,	
	vino a decir que en su casa	
	la echaron menos.	
DORISTEO	¡Que pasa	1610
	por mí una desdicha igual!	
	Pero es dicha. ¿Cómo dices	
	que esa dama se llamaba?	
GERARDA	¿Hay de qué te escandalices?	
DORISTEO	Pensando en el nombre estaba	1615
	de esa mujer que maldices.	
GERARDA	Estefanía decía.	
DORISTEO	¿Estefanía?	

	Please speak to me with honesty.	1585
	You love Lucindo, do you not?	
GERARDA	I thought that I didn't love him,	
	But then last evening…	
DORISTEO	Yes? Go on.	
GERARDA	It was my unhappy fortune	
	To be treated with so much scorn	1590
	It would set snow itself on fire.	
	You remember that woman who	
	Came up and sat down next to me.	
DORISTEO	You're speaking of the one who came	
	With Lucindo, I suppose.	
GERARDA	Yes.	1595
DORISTEO	Then there's no more I need to know.	
	Oh, Gerarda, the power that	
	Jealousy has!	
GERARDA	It's destroyed me!	
	Its strength is far greater than love.	
	I swear to you that not even	1600
	Disdain can withstand its command.	
	Everything that Lucindo was	
	Saying seemed to have been rehearsed,	
	And all that she was saying too.	
	I found out subsequently that	1605
	Her name is Estefanía.	
	She must be a high-born lady	
	Because a servant rushed up to	
	Say that her absence was causing	
	No end of concern at her home.	
DORISTEO	That I	1610
	Should have to bear such misfortune!	
	But so it is. What did you say	
	Was the name of that young lady?	
GERARDA	What's the matter? You seem perturbed.	
DORISTEO	I was thinking of the name of	1615
	That young woman you're maligning.	
GERARDA	Estefanía, she had said.	
DORISTEO	Estefanía?	

GERARDA	Esto pasa.
DORISTEO	¡Buena venganza sería
	si porque he entrado en su casa, 1620
	diese Lucindo en la mía!
GERARDA	¿Cómo?
DORISTEO	Una hermana que tengo,
	Estefanía se llama.
GERARDA	¡Ella es!
DORISTEO	¿Cómo detengo
	la defensa de mi fama, 1625
	y del traidor no me vengo?
GERARDA	Él la sirve, porque un día
	dijo que se vengaría
	deste agravio.
DORISTEO	Y lo cumplió;
	porque anoche me contó 1630
	que fue al Prado Estefanía.
	¡Alto, mi honor es perdido!
	Vete en buen hora, Gerarda...
GERARDA	Más que quisiera he sabido.
DORISTEO	Que si mi deshonra aguarda, 1635
	hoy ha de ser su marido.
GERARDA	¡Su marido! Mayor daño
	es el que me viene agora.
DORISTEO	Pues ¿hay otro desengaño?
GERARDA	¡Bien vivirá quien le adora, 1640
	si le casas!
DORISTEO	¡Caso extraño!
	Pues ¿puede ser de otra suerte?
GERARDA	Dame primero la muerte.
DORISTEO	Vete de aquí.
GERARDA	¡Nunca hablara!
DORISTEO	¿Con mi hermana? ¿Quién pensara 1645
	una venganza tan fuerte?
	Buscar a Finardo quiero
	para que a Lucindo saque
	donde, pues es caballero,
	o saquemos el acero, 1650

GERARDA	Yes, that's it.
DORISTEO	What true vengeance for Lucindo
	If he's managed to enter my 1620
	House just as I have entered yours!
GERARDA	What do you mean?
DORISTEO	I have a sister
	Whose name is Estefanía.
GERARDA	Then she's the one!
DORISTEO	What's preventing
	Me from defending my honor, 1625
	And avenging myself on him?
GERARDA	It's clear that he's pursuing her,
	Since he'd said earlier that he'd
	Take vengeance on you.
DORISTEO	And he has;
	Because my sister told me last 1630
	Night that she'd gone to the Prado.
	That's it, then! My honor is lost!
	You'd better go in, Gerarda.
GERARDA	I've learned more than I intended.
DORISTEO	I'll face up to my dishonor, 1635
	And compel him to marry her!
GERARDA	Marry her! That would be far worse
	Than what I've already suffered.
DORISTEO	Is there another solution?
GERARDA	How can I live if you marry 1640
	Him off to her?
DORISTEO	What a huge mess!
	But what other way can there be?
GERARDA	Have you thought of killing me first?
DORISTEO	Please go.
GERARDA	Why did I ever speak?
DORISTEO	With my sister? Who would have thought 1645
	Of such a terrible vengeance?
	I must find Finardo and have
	Him bring Lucindo here so we
	Can settle this like gentlemen;
	Either he marries my sister, 1650

o casándose me aplaque.
Hoy muere si no se casa.
¡Oh, vil hermana! ¿Esto pasa?
Mas, justa ley me condena;
que no anda bien en la ajena 1655
quien ha de guardar su casa.

Vanse.
Salen Belisa, el Capitán, Fenisa, y Fulminato, criado.

FENISA	Hacedme aqueste placer,	*redondillas*
	para mayor regocijo;	
	que vea yo vuestro hijo,	
	pues su madre vengo a ser.	1660
CAPITÁN	Digo que tenéis razón.	
FENISA	Pues todo queda tan llano,	
	venga a besarme la mano	
	y a tomar mi bendición.	
BELISA	Ya sois dueño desta casa;	1665
	venga vuestro hijo acá.	
CAPITÁN	Digo que a veros vendrá;	
	que ya sabe lo que pasa.	
	Fulminato.	
FULMINATO	Señor.	
CAPITÁN	Corre,	
	llama al alférez, mi hijo.	1670
FULMINATO	¡Voy!	

Vase.

FENISA	Que le llamasen dijo.	
	Todo el cielo me socorre.	
	Hoy te verán estos ojos	
	en esta casa, mi bien.	
CAPITÁN	Aunque le muestre desdén,	1675
	me ha dado el llamarle enojos.	
	Es galán, mozo y discreto,	
	y dirá acaso entre sí	
	que no le caso, y que a mí	
	me caso, viejo en efeto.	1680

              Or we draw our swords on the spot.
              It's his choice: he weds or he dies.
              Oh, vile sister! What have you done?
              But it's my fault too; it's foolish
              To set foot in another's house   1655
              While your own remains unguarded.

Exit Gerarda and Doristeo.
Belisa's House.
Enter Belisa, the Captain, Fenisa, and Fulminato, a servant.

FENISA   I would be grateful and receive
              Much pleasure if you would send your
              Son to speak to me. After all,
              I am soon to be his mother.   1660
CAPTAIN   A most excellent idea!
FENISA   If, then, we're in agreement here
              Please bid him come to kiss my hand
              And receive my heartfelt blessing.
BELISA   Since you're now master of this house,   1665
              Do ask the dear boy to come by.
CAPTAIN   I promise he'll arrive shortly;
              He's quite aware of what we've planned.
              Fulminato…
FULMINATO   Sire.
CAPTAIN   Go tell my
              Son, the lieutenant, to come here.   1670
FULMINATO I'm off!

Exit Fulminato.

FENISA   *(Aside.)* (To think he'll soon be here!
              Heaven's granting all my wishes.
              Today, at last, my beloved,
              My eyes will see you in this house.)
CAPTAIN   *(Aside.)* (She might treat him with disdain; still   1675
              I'm uneasy to have called him.
              He's young, handsome, and quite bright too.
              Maybe she'll wonder why I don't
              Find a wife for him, while I, old,
              Well-worn, take a wife for myself.   1680

¿Quién duda que le parezca
mejor, y que le [dé pena]
ver que a mi edad le condena
donde sin gusto [padezca]?
    Fuera de eso, es mal consejo   1685
que venir aquí le mande;
que a vista de un hijo grande
parece un hombre más viejo.
    Ya comienzo a estar celoso;
no entrará otra vez acá.   1690

Salen Fulminato y Lucindo.

FULMINATO	Aquí el alférez está.
LUCINDO	¡Cielos, que fui tan dichoso!
	Aquí mis ojos están.
	Señor…
CAPITÁN	De enojo estoy lleno.
	Para danzar eras bueno. 1695
LUCINDO	¿Cómo?
CAPITÁN	Eres cierto y galán.
LUCINDO	¿No me mandaste venir?
CAPITÁN	Besa la mano a tu madre.
LUCINDO	Yo voy.
CAPITÁN	¡Qué presto!
LUCINDO	Mi padre…
FENISA	Ya me comienzo a reír. 1700
LUCINDO	…como a madre, que sois mía,
	me manda, ¡oh bien soberano!,
	que os bese esa hermosa mano.
CAPITÁN	¡Qué superflua cortesía!
	La mano basta decir; 1705
	¿para qué es decir hermosa?
LUCINDO	Quiere mi boca dichosa
	este epíteto añadir.
FENISA	Hablan ansí los discretos.
BELISA	¿De eso recibís disgusto? 1710

Who can doubt that he'd seem to her
A better match, or that she'd think
That being wed to one like me
Would be all pain and no pleasure.
I see now that it wasn't wise   1685
To have ordered him to come here.
Next to a fit, robust young man
Any other will seem older.
I'm beginning to feel jealous.
He is not to come here again.)   1690

Enter Lucindo and Fulminato.

FULMINATO The young lieutenant has arrived!
LUCINDO *(Aside.)* (Dear God, How lucky can I be!
Here she is: my heart's desire.)
Sir …
CAPTAIN *(Aside.)* (I mustn't show the rage I feel.)
I see you've come dressed for dancing.   1695
LUCINDO Sir?
CAPTAIN Look at you, all gallant and proud.
LUCINDO But you're the one who bid me come.
CAPTAIN No more! Go kiss your mother's hand.
LUCINDO Gladly!

He kneels down.

CAPTAIN Not so fast!
LUCINDO My father…
FENISA *(Aside.)* (I can scarcely keep from laughing.)   1700
LUCINDO Has asked me… *(Aside.)* (Oh, consummate joy!)
To show respect, my dear mother,
By kissing this beautiful hand.
CAPTAIN Come now, you don't need extra words!
It's enough to say 'hand' alone;   1705
You don't need to add 'beautiful'.
LUCINDO Pardon. My lips were so thrilled they
Had to throw in the adjective.
FENISA For my part, I love courtly speech.
BELISA Why does that annoy you so much?   1710

CAPITÁN	Levántate; que no gusto
	que beses con epitetos.
BELISA	Dejadle, no seáis extraño;
	bese la mano a su madre.
LUCINDO	Señor, siendo vos mi padre,
	no resulta en vuestro daño.
CAPITÁN	No me llames padre aquí.
LUCINDO	Llamo madre a una señora
	tan moza, y ¡a vos agora
	os pesa que os llame ansí?
CAPITÁN	Adonde la edad no sobre,
	padre, dulces letras son;
	mas a un viejo, no es razón,
	no siendo ermitaño o pobre.
	Acaba, besa la mano.
FENISA	¡Que me veo en tanto bien!
LUCINDO	Dadme esa mano, por quien
	de mano esta suerte gano.
	Ten, mi vida, este papel.

Métele un papel en la mano.

FENISA	Ya le tengo.
LUCINDO	Y dadme aquí
	vuestra bendición, que en mí
	tendréis un hijo fïel.
CAPITÁN	¡Hijo fïel! Mas ¿qué quiere?
	¿comprar algún regimiento?
LUCINDO	¡Qué gloria en los labios siento!

Bendígale.

FENISA	Dios te bendiga y prospere;
	Dios te dé mujer que sea
	tal como la has menester;
	en efeto, venga a ser

Números de línea:
1715
1720
1725
1730
1735

CAPTAIN	Get off your knees; it's not right to
	Kiss a person with epithets.
BELISA	Leave him be; don't be so cranky.
	He's just kissing his mother's hand.

Lucindo gets up.

LUCINDO	Sir, since you're my father, nothing	1715
	I've done can possibly harm you.	
CAPTAIN	Don't you 'father' me in this house!	
LUCINDO	I'm confused; I'm to call this young	
	Lady 'Mother', but it bothers	
	You that I should call you 'Father'?	1720
CAPTAIN	If and when age is not involved	
	'Father' is a beautiful word.	
	But with an old man who's neither	
	Poor nor a hermit, it's ugly.	
	Finish up quickly. Kiss her hand.	1725
FENISA	*(Aside.)* (I'm so happy I can't stand it!)	
LUCINDO	Give me your hand, for it is with	
	That hand that I gain great fortune.	
	(Aside to Fenisa.) (Here, my love, take this paper, quick.)	

He puts a paper in her hand.

FENISA	(I've got it.)

Lucindo kisses Fenisa's hand.

LUCINDO	I also ask for	1730
	Your blessing, for I pledge to give	
	To you my most loyal service.	
CAPTAIN	Loyal service? What's he after?	
	A command in the king's army?	
LUCINDO	*(Aside.)* (Now my lips have tasted glory!)	1735

Fenisa blesses Lucindo.

FENISA	May God bless you and keep you well;
	May he provide you with a wife
	Who meets all your needs and desires,
	That is to say, a wife who is

como tu madre desea. 1740
   Dios te dé lo que a este punto
tienes en el corazón;
quien te da su bendición,
todo el bien te diera junto.
   Dios te haga, y sí serás, 1745
tan obediente a mi gusto,
que jamás me des disgusto,
y que a nadie quieras más.
   Dios te haga tan modesto,
que queriendo estos envites, 1750
a tu señor padre quites

Señala en el pecho.

esta pesadumbre presto.
   Y te dé tanto sentido
en querer y obedecer,
que te pueda yo tener, 1755
como en lugar de marido.

CAPITÁN   ¿Qué libro matrimonial
te enseñó estas bendiciones?
Acaba, abrevia razones.

FENISA   Celos [tiene].

LUCINDO   ¿Hay cosa igual? 1760

FENISA   Una palabra, madre de mis ojos.   *versos sueltos*

BELISA   ¿Qué quieres?

FENISA   ¿Ves este papel?

BELISA   Sí veo.

FENISA   Pues es memoria de vestidos míos,
que el Capitán me ha dado; yo querría
leerle, y no quisiera que él lo viese 1765
porque no me tuviese por tan loca,
que pensase que estimo en más las galas
que no el marido. Por tu vida, madre,
que le entretengas.

BELISA   Que me place.

	Everything your mother could wish.	1740
	May He also give you those things	
	That are now hidden in your heart.	
	The one who blesses you today	
	Would certainly wish you the same.	
	May God in his wisdom make you	1745
	So compliant to my desires	
	That you never cause me dismay,	
	And never turn your love away.	
	May God make you so devoted	
	That, accepting these entreaties,	1750
	You relieve your reverend father	

She makes the sign of the cross on Lucindo's chest.

	Of all his preoccupation.	
	And may God give you such good sense	
	In matters of love and duty,	
	That you would almost seem to me	1755
	More a husband than a son.	
CAPTAIN	From which marriage manual did	
	You learn these ludicrous blessings?	
	Enough! No more of this nonsense!	
FENISA	*(Aside.)* (He's jealous.)	
LUCINDO	*(Aside.)* (Lord, is he ever!)	1760
FENISA	Mother, dear, could I have a brief word with you?	

Fenisa and Belisa speak together, as do the Captain and Lucindo.

BELISA	What is it?	
FENISA	Do you see this paper?	
BELISA	Of course.	
FENISA	It's a listing of the clothes the Captain is	
	Giving me for our marriage. I do want to	
	Read it, but I prefer that he not see me,	1765
	So he won't think I'm a senseless young woman	
	Who cares more for fine clothes than for my husband.	
	On your life, then, dear mother, would you help me	
	By keeping him busy?	
BELISA	All right.	

FENISA	¡Ay cielo!	
	¡Qué industria hallé para leer agora	1770
	el papel que me dio Lucindo, al tiempo	
	que me besó la mano, por si es cosa	
	que importa darle luego la respuesta!	
BELISA	[Escuchadme] a esta parte dos palabras.	

Lee Fenisa.

FENISA	«Mi bien, mi padre tiene concertado,	1775
	de celos de que has dicho que te quiero,	
	enviarme a Portugal; remedia, amores,	
	esta locura, o cuéntame por muerto.	
	Esto escribí, sabiendo que venía	
	a besarte la mano. A Diós te queda	1780
	y quiera el mismo que gozarte pueda.»	
	¿Hay desdicha semejante?	*redondillas*
	¿Hay celos con tal locura?	
	Así Dios me dé ventura,	
	que he de hablarle aquí delante.	1785
	Lucindo, el papel leí;	
	no me haga el cielo este mal,	
	que vayas a Portugal,	
	ni que una hora estés sin mí;	
	y si dicen que mejor	1790
	vive en él su desvarío,	
	vive en mí, Lucindo mío,	
	que soy Portugal de amor.	
LUCINDO	¡Ay Dios! ¡Quién pudiera hablarte!	
	¡Quién abrazarte pudiera!	1795
FENISA	Yo sabré hacer de manera	
	que me abraces.	
LUCINDO	¿En qué parte?	
FENISA	Fingir quiero que caí;	
	tú me irás a levantar,	
	y me podrás abrazar.	1800
LUCINDO	Tropieza.	

FENISA	*(Aside.)*	(Thank heavens
	I managed to find a way to read the note	1770
	That Lucindo gave me when he kissed my hand,	
	Since it's quite possible that it has to do	
	With something that calls for an instant reply.)	
BELISA	Captain, might you and I have a word alone?	

Belisa and the Captain move to one side while Fenisa reads.

FENISA	*(Reading.)* "Darling, filled with jealousy because you said	1775
	That I love you, my father is proposing	
	To send me to Portugal. Dear one, you must	
	Find a way to prevent this, or I shall die.	
	I wrote this knowing I was shortly to kiss	
	Your hand. May God bless and preserve you and may	1780
	He so will it that we'll soon be together."	
	(Aside.) (Can there be a worse misfortune?	
	Can jealousy breed more madness?	
	Lord, come to my aid, for I must	
	Speak to Lucindo right away.)	1785
	(To Lucindo.) I read your note. May heaven not	
	Permit so great an evil as	
	Your leaving for Portugal or	
	Our parting for even an hour.	
	If it's true that Portugal is	1790
	Where fantasies are best fulfilled,	
	Fulfill yours in me, Lucindo,	
	For I'm the Portugal of love.	
LUCINDO	Dear God! If only we could talk,	
	If only I could hold you tight.	1795
FENISA	I've thought of a way for you to	
	Embrace me right here.	
LUCINDO	What is that?	
FENISA	I'll pretend that I tripped and fell;	
	Then you can come to my aid, lift	
	Me up and hold me in your arms.	1800
LUCINDO	Perfect! Do it!	

Cayga.

FENISA	Caigo, ¡ay de mí!

Abrázanse.

CAPITÁN   ¿Qué es aquesto?
LUCINDO   Tropezó
mi señora madre aquí,
y yo levántola ansí.
CAPITÁN   Y levántola ansí yo.   1805
      Salte de aquí, noramala.
LUCINDO   Pues cayendo, es cortesía.
BELISA   ¿Haste hecho mal, hija mía?
CAPITÁN   Despeja luego la sala.
LUCINDO   Yo me iré.
CAPITÁN   Vete al momento.   1810
LUCINDO   ¿Ansí me arrojas?
CAPITÁN   ¡Camina!
LUCINDO   ¡Ay, mi Fenisa divina!
¡Ay, divino entendimiento!
      ¡Ay, discreción extremada!
Por vos se puede entender   1815
lo que puede una mujer
discreta y enamorada.

Vase.

FENISA   No tengo mal ninguno, por tu vida.   *versos sueltos*
CAPITÁN   ¡Así lo creo yo!
FENISA   ¿Fuese mi hijo?
CAPITÁN   Tu hijo se fue ya.
FENISA   Mil males tengo.   1820
BELISA   ¿Quieres verle? ¡Hola, Beatriz, de presto!
FENISA   No quiero, por tu vida.
CAPITÁN   Aquel grosero
debió de daros causa a la caída.
No ha de estar en mi casa un punto solo,
ni entrar en ésta mientras tengo vida.   1825

She falls.

FENISA   Oh, I'm falling!

Lucindo embraces her to raise her up.

CAPTAIN   What's going on here?
LUCINDO   My honored
                 Mother tripped and fell, and now I'm
                 Helping her get back on her feet.

The Captain separates them, and holds Fenisa.

CAPTAIN   Your help is not necessary.   1805
                 Get away from here, you scoundrel!
LUCINDO   But isn't it just courteous...?
BELISA   Did you hurt yourself, my daughter?
CAPTAIN   I order you to leave this room.
LUCINDO   I'll leave shortly.
CAPTAIN   No, you'll leave now!   1810
LUCINDO   Are you throwing me out?
CAPTAIN   Yes! Go!
LUCINDO   *(Aside.)* (Oh, my heavenly Fenisa!
                 What unrivalled intelligence!
                 What discretion beyond compare!
                 Because of you one can see what   1815
                 A woman who is clever and
                 In love can attain in this world.)

Exit Lucindo.

FENISA   Don't worry, Mother; I'm perfectly fine now.
CAPTAIN   That seems more than evident.
FENISA   Has my son left?
CAPTAIN   Yes, your son has left.
FENISA   That makes me very sad.   1820
BELISA   You wish to see him? Beatriz, come quickly.
FENISA   It's all right; let him be.
CAPTAIN   That ill-mannered boy
                 Must have done something to provoke such a fall.
                 He's no longer welcome in my house and while
                 I'm still alive he's not to come here either.   1825

BELISA	¡Qué poco amor tenéis a vuestro hijo!
	Que os prometo que es gentil mancebo,
	y que le miro yo con tales ojos,
	que si en mis mocedades me cogiera,
	holgara de tenerle por marido.

1830

FENISA	Asite la ocasión por el copete.
CAPITÁN	¿Este loco os agrada?
FENISA	Escucha madre.
BELISA	Como sois Capitán, la casa es guerra.
	¡Todo es escusa!
CAPITÁN	Tal me la dan celos.
FENISA	El papel que te dije, no es vestidos,

1835

	ni me le dio Bernardo.
BELISA	¿Qué me cuentas?
FENISA	Lucindo me le dio.
BELISA	Pues ¿qué te escribe?
FENISA	Una cosa que a risa ha de moverte.
BELISA	No me tengas suspensa.
FENISA	Al fin, me dice
	que se quiere casar.
BELISA	¿Con quién?
FENISA	Contigo.

1840

BELISA	¡Conmigo! ¿Qué me cuentas?
FENISA	Lo que pasa.
	Dice que le pareces en extremo,
	y que esa gravedad, esa cordura
	le agrada más que yo a su padre agrado.
	Dice más: que con este casamiento

1845

	se juntan las haciendas, de manera
	que los hijos de entrambos quedan ricos.
	Si supieras leer, mil cosas vieras;
	mas dice que le pidas que no trate
	enviarle a Portugal, que antes le mate.

1850

BELISA	¿Qué es ir a Portugal? Hija, las hijas
	cuerdas y honradas, todo el gusto suyo
	ponen en sólo dársele a sus padres.

BELISA	How little affection you have for your son.
	I assure you he's an excellent young man,
	And I look upon him with such tenderness
	That had I known him in my youth I'm sure I
	Would have been overjoyed to have married him. 1830
FENISA	*(Aside.)* (Now is the time to take the bull by the horns.)
CAPTAIN	You like that foolish young man?
FENISA	Mother, listen.
BELISA	You're a captain, always wanting to make war.
	Everything provokes you.
CAPTAIN	Blame it on jealousy.

Fenisa and her mother speak apart.

FENISA	The note I mentioned was not about clothes and 1835
	It wasn't from the Captain.
BELISA	From whom was it?
FENISA	It was from Lucindo.
BELISA	Well, what did he write?
FENISA	Something that I know will give you a good laugh.
BELISA	Don't keep me in suspense.
FENISA	What he said was that
	He wants to get married.
BELISA	Yes? To whom?
FENISA	To you. 1840
BELISA	To me? Are you serious?
FENISA	Yes, it's quite true.
	He says that he finds you very attractive,
	And that your maturity and wisdom please
	Him more than I can ever please his father.
	He says in addition that with this marriage 1845
	Our two households will be joined, ensuring that
	The children of each couple will be well-off.
	If you could read, you'd see much more; the crucial
	Thing is that you must prevent his being sent
	To Portugal. If you can't, he says he'll die. 1850
BELISA	What's this about Portugal? Fenisa, you
	Know that daughters who are honest and wise have
	But one desire, which is to please their parents.

	Ya sabes que soy moza, y que en efecto
	estaré más honrada con marido,
	y marido que así te logres, hija,
	que me lleva los ojos en mirándole.
	¡Qué cortés,! ¡Qué galán! ¡Qué lindo talle!
FENISA	Si esto pasa, ¿qué hará quien andar puede?
BELISA	¿Qué dices?
FENISA	Que le estorbes la partida.
BELISA	¡Partida! ¿Qué partida? Haz que esta noche
	me venga a hablar Lucindo de secreto.
FENISA	Vete, y déjame hablar con mi marido.
BELISA	Que me cogió a descuido. Mas no importa;
	ponerme quiero menos largas tocas.
	Consultaré el espejo. ¡Ay mi Lucindo!
	Si tú me quieres, cuanto soy te rindo.

1855

1860

1865

Vase.

CAPITÁN	Milagro, Fenisa, fue	*quintillas*
	dejarnos solos Belisa;	
	y pues que nadie nos ve,	1870
	dame, gallarda Fenisa,	
	tus manos.	
FENISA	¡Bien por mi fe!	
	Mucho os preciáis de galán.	
CAPITÁN	Si celos enojo dan,	
	dame la mano de amigos.	1875
FENISA	No me atrevo sin testigos.	
CAPITÁN	Presentes, señora, están	
	celos, amor y deseo.	
FENISA	Con justos celos, señor,	
	de vuestro Lucindo os veo.	1880
CAPITÁN	¿Prosigue en tenerte amor?	
FENISA	Y aun me cansa.	
CAPITÁN	Yo lo creo.	
FENISA	Anoche sentí rüido	
	a la reja, y diome un miedo,	
	que me privó del sentido.	1885
	Levántome como puedo,	

	You also know that I'm still youthful, and that	
	I'd get more respect if I took a husband,	1855
	A husband like the young man you've found for me,	
	One whom my eyes would never tire of seeing.	
	How polite he is! How gallant! How noble!	
FENISA	If he goes what will be the end of all this?	
BELISA	What are you saying?	
FENISA	You must prevent his leaving.	1860
BELISA	Leaving! What leaving? Do something so that he	
	And I can speak in secrecy this evening.	
FENISA	Then go now, and let me talk with my husband.	
BELISA	(*Aside.*) (He took me quite by surprise. But no matter.	
	I'll change my headdress for one more becoming	1865
	And consult with my mirror. Oh, Lucindo!	
	If you love me truly, all I have is yours.)	

Exit Belisa.

CAPTAIN	It's a miracle, Fenisa,	
	That Belisa left us alone.	
	And now that no one can see us	1870
	Give me your hand, my enchanting	
	Bride.	
FENISA	My word! What a bold request!	
	You must think you're quite a gallant!	
CAPTAIN	If my ardor is upsetting	
	You, give me the hand of friendship.	1875
FENISA	Without witnesses, I don't dare.	
CAPTAIN	Three of them are here, my lady:	
	Love, jealousy, and true desire.	
FENISA	I see, sir, that you're still jealous	
	Of your son – and with good reason.	1880
CAPTAIN	Then, he is still pursuing you?	
FENISA	More than ever.	
CAPTAIN	I believe it.	
FENISA	Last evening I heard a racket	
	At the window that gave me such	
	A fright that I nearly passed out.	1885
	I got out of bed, but without	

	sin luz no acierto el vestido,	
	topo el manteo en efeto,	
	salgo a la reja, y en ella...	
	¿De qué estás tan inquïeto?	1890
CAPITÁN	Es cólera, esposa bella,	
	de ese rapaz indiscreto.	
FENISA	Y entre la reja y ventana	
	hallo en lo hueco un papel.	
CAPITÁN	Eso ya es cosa inhumana;	1895
	hoy seré un león con él.	
FENISA	Ser padre os dará cuartana.	
	Sosegaos.	
CAPITÁN	No puede ser.	
	Yo le tengo de buscar.	

Vase.

FENISA	¡Qué bien le he dado a entender	1900
	dónde el papel ha de hallar!	
	Que le quiero responder,	
	para que quede advertido	
	que con mi madre he trazado	
	que diga que es su marido,	1905
	para que quede estorbado	
	el camino prevenido.	
	Que mi madre hará por él	
	que se impida la tormenta	
	desta partida crüel;	1910
	porque si mi bien se ausenta,	
	todo se pierde con él.	

Vase.
Sale[n] Hernando y Lucindo.

HERNANDO	¿Que todo eso ha pasado?	*octavas reales*
LUCINDO	Si me vieras	
	de rodillas, Hernando, a mi Fenisa,	
	que era imagen bellísima dijeras.	1915
HERNANDO	No lo dudes, muriérame de risa.	

	A light I couldn't find my dress	
	And had only a wrap to wear.	
	Then I crept to the window where …	
	Are you all right? You don't look well.	1890
CAPTAIN	My dear wife, I'm absolutely	
	Furious with that rash young man.	
FENISA	Right between the window and the	
	Grillwork someone had left a note.	
CAPTAIN	That's it! This is unbearable!	1895
	My wrath will roar like a lion!	
FENISA	Being a father will be the	
	End of you. Calm down.	
CAPTAIN	I cannot.	
	Excuse me. I must go find him.	

Exit the Captain.

FENISA	Well done! Now Lucindo will know	1900
	Where to find the note I'll leave him,	
	In answer to his note to me.	
	I need to inform him that I've	
	Arranged things so my mother will	
	Say that they're to be married, thus	1905
	Creating an impediment	
	To his going to Portugal.	
	I'm certain she'll do all she can	
	To prevent the cruel suffering	
	That his leaving would occasion.	1910
	Dear God, if my love goes away,	
	I have no more reason to live.	

Exit Fenisa.
The Street.
Enter Lucindo and Hernando.

HERNANDO	All that really happened?	
LUCINDO	If you had seen me,	
	Hernando, kneeling to my dear Fenisa,	
	You would say that she was beauty incarnate.	1915
HERNANDO	It's more likely I would have died of laughter.	

LUCINDO	Si a Tántalo en el agua consideras,
	verás que ya le tengo por divisa;
	porque si aquél, ni fruta ni agua toca,
	yo vi su boca y no llegué a su boca.

1920

HERNANDO	¿No te bastó la mano?
LUCINDO	Templó el fuego
	arrimando la nieve de su mano,
	porque salió a la boca el alma luego,
	hecha un volcán de amor, por agua en vano.
	¿Qué me dirás cuando a la boca llego?

1925

HERNANDO	¿Mordístela?
LUCINDO	No sé; ¿mármol indiano,
	cristal de roca, quieres que mordiese?
	¿No basta, si es imagen, que le bese?

....   [1929]

....   [1930]

....   [1931]

HERNANDO	¡Tu padre!
LUCINDO	Calla, y déjale que pase.

Sale el Capitán.

CAPITÁN	¡Qué cabizbajo en viéndome te pones!
	Como si no me vieses.
LUCINDO	Si pensase
	que contigo ese crédito tenía,

1935

no a Portugal, hasta el Japón me iría.

CAPITÁN	Pues no te admires; que peor le tienes.	*versos sueltos*
	¿No te avisé que es mi mujer Fenisa?	
LUCINDO	¿No me mandaste tú que la besase	
	la [mano] como a madre? ¿Es, por ventura,	

1940

porque llamé su blanca mano hermosa?

CAPITÁN	¡Hermosa entonces, y ahora hermosa y blanca!
	¡Qué lindo bellacón te vas haciendo!
LUCINDO	Cosas te enfadan de tan poco tomo,
	que es ponerte a la sombra de un cabello.

1945

¡Válgame Dios! ¿En qué te ofendo tanto?

CAPITÁN	¿No es nada, si Fenisa me ha contado
	que anoche hiciste en su ventana ruido,

LUCINDO	Think of Tantalus in his pool of water,
	And you'll see why I take him as my emblem;
	He couldn't drink or touch the nearby fruit; I
	Was inches from her lips but couldn't kiss them. 1920
HERNANDO	Her hand wasn't enough?
LUCINDO	The fire in me was
	At first cooled by the nearness of her snowy hand;
	But as her hand drew closer, my soul blazed up
	Like a volcano, vainly seeking water.
	What do you think happened when my mouth 1925
	touched her hand?
HERNANDO	Did you bite it?
LUCINDO	No, of course not, you blockhead.
	Would you want me to bite the finest crystal?
	Such divine images should only be kissed.
	 1930
HERNANDO	Your father!
LUCINDO	Keep quiet, and let him go by.

Enter the Captain.

CAPTAIN	So you turn away when you see me coming?
	As if you hadn't seen me?
LUCINDO	If I had known
	That was how you thought of me, I would go not 1935
	Just to Portugal, but as far as Japan.
CAPTAIN	Well, don't be surprised. I've had even worse thoughts.
	Didn't I tell you Fenisa is my wife?
LUCINDO	And didn't you order me to kiss her hand
	As my mother-to-be? Are you not angry 1940
	Just because I called her white hand beautiful?
CAPTAIN	First beautiful, and now beautiful *and white*.
	What a sly, pretentious rogue you're becoming!
LUCINDO	These days the smallest things get you all upset;
	Talk about making mountains out of molehills! 1945
	God help me! What have I done to offend you?
CAPTAIN	Is it nothing, then, that Fenisa told me
	You made a racket last night at her window,

y que entre el suelo della y de la reja
le pusiste un papel?

LUCINDO					¿Yo?

CAPITÁN						Tú, villano.					1950

LUCINDO		Pues di que te le dé; que si mi letra
tuviere ese papel...

CAPITÁN						Detente un poco;
que si es ajena, mayor mal sería.

LUCINDO		Hernando.

HERNANDO				¿Señor?

LUCINDO					¿Oyes?

HERNANDO						Ya lo entiendo.

Sin duda que papel quiere escribirte,					1955
y que te avisa que a buscarle vayas
entre la reja y la ventana.

CAPITÁN							Escucha;
que pasa alguna gente, y no querría
se dijese en Madrid mi casamiento.

Sale[n] Doristeo y Finardo.

DORISTEO			Hablando está con su padre.		1960		*romance o-a*

FINARDO		Pues apártale, que importa.

DORISTEO		Una palabra os quisiera.

LUCINDO		Estoy con mi padre agora;
pero sepamos lo que es
buscarme con tanta cólera;					1965
que después habrá lugar
de responderos a [solas].

CAPITÁN		¿Qué quieren éstos, Hernando?

HERNANDO		Amigos son.

CAPITÁN					Serán cosas
del juego.

HERNANDO					Así lo sospecho.		1970

CAPITÁN		Nunca dél resultan pocas.

DORISTEO		Sin tener obligación,
ni conoceros (que sobra

	And that you left her a message between the	
	Window and the grille?	
LUCINDO	I?	
CAPTAIN	Yes, you, you blackguard!	1950
LUCINDO	Well, ask her to show it to you; if it has	
	My handwriting…	
CAPTAIN	Stop! Hold it there a minute.	
	If it's someone else's, then so much the worse.	
LUCINDO	*(Aside.)* (Hernando.	
HERNANDO	Sir?	
LUCINDO	Did you get that?	
HERNANDO	Yes, of course.	
	Fenisa's going to leave you a message,	1955
	And she's telling you that you should look for it	
	Stuck between the window and the grille.)	
CAPTAIN	Quiet;	
	People are approaching and I don't want them	
	To turn my marriage into spiteful gossip.	

They speak softly.
Enter Doristeo and Finardo.

DORISTEO	There he is, talking to his father.	1960
FINARDO	Then take him aside. It's urgent.	
DORISTEO	*(To Lucindo.)* Sir, I demand a word with you.	
LUCINDO	You can see I'm with my father.	
	Do tell us, please, why it is that	
	You seek me out with such anger.	1965
	But let us move aside where we	
	Can speak in greater privacy.	

Lucindo, Doristeo and Finardo withdraw.

CAPTAIN	What do those men want, Hernando?	
HERNANDO	They're old friends.	
CAPTAIN	Does it relate to	
	Gambling?	
HERNANDO	I wouldn't be surprised.	1970
CAPTAIN	Nothing good ever comes of that.	
DORISTEO	Not being obliged to you, or	
	Even knowing you – and thus free	

para no guardar la cara,
que un hidalgo no os conozca), 1975
puse en Gerarda los ojos.

LUCINDO Si es ésa la queja sola,
yo os doy desde aquí a Gerarda.

DORISTEO No es ésa.

LUCINDO Pues ¿cómo? ¿Hay otra?

DORISTEO Otra tan grande, que creo 1980
que sólo el [ver me] reporta
aquí vuestro anciano padre.

LUCINDO Engaños son de esa loca.

DORISTEO Vos, de picado de ver
que a vuestro amor me anteponga, 1985
habéis pensado vengaros
quitándome a mí la honra.
Servido habéis a mi hermana;
y ella, mal sabia y bien moza,
fue anoche con vos al Prado. 1990

LUCINDO ¡Extraña invención de historia!
Ni conozco a vuestra hermana,
ni trato vuestra deshonra,
ni sé, ¡por Dios!, vuestra casa.

FINARDO La tercera es sospechosa. 1995
¡Vive Dios, que os ha engañado!

DORISTEO ¿Cómo engañado, si nombra
a Estefanía, mi hermana,
de un indiano muerto esposa?

LUCINDO Ya entiendo todo el engaño. 2000
La dama, señor, fue otra,
con quien me pienso casar;
que porque aquesta celosa
por el nombre no supiese
quién era antes de las bodas, 2005
la puse el nombre primero
que me vino a la memoria,
que lo mismo fuera Inés,
Francisca, Juana o Antonia.
Esto es la verdad, por Dios. 2010

	Of the need to hide my face when	
	We chanced to meet on the street – I	1975
	Fixed my desire on Gerarda.	
LUCINDO	If that's your sole quarrel with me,	
	She's entirely yours from now on.	
DORISTEO	That's not it.	
LUCINDO	It's not? What is it?	
DORISTEO	Something so offensive I swear	1980
	That only seeing you here with	
	Your father is holding me back.	
LUCINDO	That mad woman is telling lies.	
DORISTEO	You, stung by seeing that I have	
	Replaced you in Gerarda's heart,	1985
	Have decided to take vengeance	
	By robbing me of my honor.	
	You're chasing after my sister;	
	And she, young and not very smart,	
	Went with you last night to the Prado.	1990
LUCINDO	That's complete and utter nonsense!	
	I have never met your sister;	
	I've no designs on your honor;	
	I don't even know where you live.	
FINARDO	Your informant can't be trusted.	1995
	By God, I think you've been deceived.	
DORISTEO	How is that possible? She named	
	Estefanía, my sister,	
	Whose late husband came from the Indies.	
LUCINDO	Now I understand the mix-up.	2000
	The woman I'm pursuing, sir,	
	Is the one I plan to marry.	
	So that Gerarda, as jealous	
	As she is, wouldn't discover	
	Who she is before the wedding,	2005
	I gave her the first name that came	
	To mind; I could just as well have	
	Said Inés, or Francisca, or	
	Juana, or Sancha, or Ana.	
	I swear to God, that's what happened.	2010

DORISTEO	Pues siendo verdad notoria,	
	para satisfacción mía,	
	aunque decirlo vos sobra,	
	holgaré que me digáis	
	el nombre de esa señora.	2015
LUCINDO	Porque habéis de ver muy presto	
	que conmigo se desposa,	
	Fenisa, señor, se llama.	
	Ésta quiero, ella me adora;	
	la calle de los Jardines	2020
	es la esfera donde posa,	
	y yo soy vecino suyo.	
	Recelo mi padre toma,	
	y yo querría dejarle;	
	dadme licencia.	
DORISTEO	Estas cosas	2025
	hace el honor. Perdonad.	
	Mil años gocéis la novia.	

Váyase Lucindo.

CAPITÁN	¿Dónde va aquél?	
HERNANDO	No sé.	
CAPITÁN	¿Si es desafío?	*octavas reales*
HERNANDO	Habla [a] esos hombres.	
CAPITÁN	¡Ah, señores! Creo,	
	si no me engaña de mi sangre el brío,	2030
	que de reñir los dos tenéis deseo.	
	Sabed que aquel hidalgo es hijo mío;	
	y pues va solo, y dos con armas veo,	
	yo iré con él, y dos a dos podremos	
	probar los corazones que tenemos.	2035
	Soldados fuimos ya los dos en Flandes;	
	fui capitán, y él fue mi alférez. ¡Vamos!	
FINARDO	Los dos irán a que servir los mandes,	
	que es bien que de soldados te sirvamos.	
	De hoy más serán, señor, amigos grandes;	2040
	que aunque por unos celos le buscamos,	
	él nos aseguró que no servía	

DORISTEO	Now that you've divulged what occurred,
	For my greater satisfaction –
	Though it may seem trifling to you –
	I'd be most obliged if you would
	Tell me the name of that lady. 2015
LUCINDO	Since it will soon be made known that
	She and I are to be married,
	Her name, sir, is Fenisa.
	I love her, and she adores me.
	The street you may know called Garden 2020
	Is where her home is located,
	And I am one of her neighbors.
	My father's getting suspicious.
	It's best that I be on my way.
	Please excuse me.
DORISTEO	Honor requires 2025
	These quarrels. My apologies.
	I wish you immense happiness.

Exit Lucindo.

CAPTAIN	Where's he going?
HERNANDO	I don't know.
CAPTAIN	Is there a duel?
HERNANDO	Speak to those men.
CAPTAIN	Gentlemen, I do believe,
	If I'm not deceived by the fire in my blood, 2030
	That the two of you are looking for a fight.
	Know, then, that that young man who left is my son;
	And since he's alone, and you both carry arms,
	I will go with him, and two against two we
	Will prove the courage we carry in our hearts. 2035
	The two of us were both soldiers in Flanders;
	I was captain, he, my lieutenant. Onward!
FINARDO	We will happily go wherever you wish,
	Since as brave soldiers you deserve to be served.
	But from today forward we and he are friends, 2040
	Because, although we sought him on a matter
	Of honor, he assured us that he was not

la dama que este hidalgo presumía.
Ya sabemos quién es a quien pasea
y Fenisa nos dijo que se llama.   2045

CAPITÁN   ¿Cómo? ¡Fenisa!
FINARDO   En fin, cómo desea
casarse, y que a ésta sola adora y ama.

CAPITÁN   Antes su muerte a vuestras plantas vea.
DORISTEO   ¿Mandaisnos otra cosa?
CAPITÁN   Que esa dama
tengáis por mujer mía; que no suya.   2050

DORISTEO   El cobarde mintió.
FINARDO   La culpa es tuya.
DORISTEO   ¡Vive el cielo, que sirve a Estefanía!
FINARDO   Disimula y busquémosle.
DORISTEO   El soldado
se fue de aquí de pura cobardía.

FINARDO   ¡Qué éste es hijo de un padre tan honrado!   2055

Vanse los dos.

CAPITÁN   ¡Que sirva este traidor la esposa mía,
con quien casarme tengo concertado,
y que se alabe que ha de ser su esposa!
HERNANDO   ¿Posible es que lo dijo? ¡Extraña cosa!
CAPITÁN   Alto, ponle su ropa en la maleta.   2060
No ha de quedar aquí ni sólo un día.
Camine a Portugal.
HERNANDO   No fue discreta
la industria de Lucindo.
CAPITÁN   ¿Hay tal porfía?
De noche por las rejas la inquïeta;
besó su mano, y dijo: «Madre mía»,   2065
y quizá dijo «esposa» entre los labios
¡No se pueden sufrir tantos agravios!
Notifícale luego la partida.
Cálzate botas.
HERNANDO   Cásate primero.
CAPITÁN   No quiero dar lugar a que lo impida;   2070

Pursuing the young lady we had supposed.
Now we know who it is he's paying court to;
Her name, he has informed us, is Fenisa.   2045

CAPTAIN   Did you say Fenisa?
FINARDO   Yes, and he intends
To marry her, for he loves and worships her.

CAPTAIN   *(Aside.)* (I would sooner see the knave dead at your feet!)
DORISTEO   How else may we serve you?
CAPTAIN   By acknowledging
That the young lady is not his wife, but mine!   2050

DORISTEO   *(To Finardo.)* The coward lied!
FINARDO   Yes, but you must share the blame
DORISTEO   By God, he *is* after Estefanía!
FINARDO   Show nothing. We'll hunt him down.
DORISTEO   He's no valiant
Soldier but a miserable, spineless wretch!

FINARDO   To think he's the son of a man of honor!   2055

Exit Doristeo and Finardo.

CAPTAIN   How is it possible my faithless son is
After my wife, the woman I'm to marry,
And that he brags she's going to be *his* wife!

HERNANDO   How could he have said that? What a strange affair!
CAPTAIN   Enough! Go pack up his clothes and belongings.   2060
He's not to remain in Madrid one more day.
He leaves for Portugal at once.

HERNANDO   *(Aside)*   (Lucindo's
Sure messed this up!)

CAPTAIN   Such infamous behavior!
At night he harasses her at her window;
Then, he kisses her hand and calls her 'Mother',   2065
While no doubt whispering 'wife' under his breath.
Such insults are not to be tolerated!
Tell him he's to leave Madrid without delay.
Put on your boots!

HERNANDO   Shouldn't you be married first?
CAPTAIN   No; if he were there he'd try to prevent it.   2070

que sirva al Rey, y no a Fenisa, quiero.
No ha de entrar en Madrid más en mi vida.

HERNANDO Que templarás aquese enojo espero.

CAPITÁN Darete, ¡vive Dios!, con la de Juanes.
¡Oh, qué lindo soy yo para truhanes!   2075

I wish him to serve the king, not Fenisa.
While I'm alive he's not to set foot in Madrid.

HERNANDO *My* wish is that you'll get over your fury.
CAPTAIN By God, Lucindo, I swear if you dare come
Near I'll thrash you within an inch of your life. 2075

JORNADA TERCERA

[Calle en que vive Belisa. Es de noche.]
Salen Lucindo y Hernando, Lucindo con capa con oro y plumas.

LUCINDO	¿Que mi padre les contó	*redondillas*
	que era su esposa y no mía?	
HERNANDO	¿Que siendo yo Estefanía,	
	ande con estos cuentos yo?	
LUCINDO	El nombre ha dado a entender	2080
	que es su hermana a Doristeo.	
HERNANDO	Tan ciego a tu padre veo,	
	que te ha de echar a perder.	
	Pienso que van a buscarte;	
	que de Fenisa el amor,	2085
	dirán que ha sido temor	
	y término de escaparte.	
	¿Para qué se lo decías?	
LUCINDO	Para asegurar un hombre,	
	no entendiendo que aquel nombre	2090
	se le acordara en sus días.	
HERNANDO	¿Piensas ir a Portugal?	
LUCINDO	¿Cómo, si mi bien me avisa	
	de que su madre Belisa	
	ha de remediar mi mal?	2095
HERNANDO	¿Fuiste a la reja?	
LUCINDO	Pues ¿no?	
HERNANDO	Y ¿hallaste el papel?	
LUCINDO	Estaba	
	donde a mi padre avisaba,	
	cuando a mi padre engañó.	
	Hallele, al fin, en la reja;	2100
	leíle, y dice que luego	
	me finja de amores ciego	
	de su madre.	

ACT THREE

The street on which Belisa lives.
Nighttime.
Enter Lucindò, dressed in a gold-embroidered cape and plumed hat, and
Hernando.

LUCINDO	You say that my father told them	
	That she was his wife and not mine?	
HERNANDO	Being sweet Estefanía,	
	Do you think I'd make these things up?	
LUCINDO	Don't mention that name! Christ, it's the	2080
	Same as Doristeo's sister!	
HERNANDO	Your father is so blinded by	
	Anger he's going to ruin your life.	
	They're coming now to look for you;	
	They're certain you named 'Fenisa'	2085
	As your love simply out of fear,	
	Hoping to avoid their vengeance.	
	Why in the hell did you say that?	
LUCINDO	Well, to reassure the fellow,	
	Not supposing he'd remember	2090
	The name for even five seconds.	
HERNANDO	Are you going to Portugal?	
LUCINDO	How can I, if my love tells me	
	That her mother, Belisa, is	
	Going to fix all my problems?	2095
HERNANDO	You went to her window?	
LUCINDO	Of course.	
HERNANDO	Did you find the paper?	
LUCINDO	It was	
	Exactly where my father said,	
	After she had tricked him once more.	
	She'd put it in the window grille.	2100
	I read it, and what she said was	
	I should pretend to be madly	
	In love with her mother.	

HERNANDO	¿De la vieja?
LUCINDO	De la misma.
HERNANDO	¡Extraño caso!
LUCINDO	Pues más me ha mandado hacer.

2105

HERNANDO	¿Y es?
LUCINDO	Pedirla por mujer.
HERNANDO	¿Por mujer?
LUCINDO	Habla más paso;

que ha de salir al balcón,
y acaso te puede oír.

HERNANDO Sólo pudiera impedir   2110
tu partida esta invención.
    ¡Discreta mujer!

LUCINDO   Notable.

HERNANDO Y ¿piensas con ella hablar?

LUCINDO Tú has de estar en mi lugar,
para que contigo hable.   2115
    Fíngete Lucindo, y yo,
mientras hablas a Belisa,
estaré con mi Fenisa;
que así el papel me avisó.

HERNANDO   ¿Qué hablaré?

LUCINDO   Cosas de amor.   2120

HERNANDO Mucho sabe esta doncella;
mil veces pienso si es ella...

LUCINDO ¿Quién?

HERNANDO   La doncella Teodor.

LUCINDO Hoy quiero probar tu seso.
Veamos cómo requiebras   2125
esta vieja.

HERNANDO   Hoy me celebras
por único.

LUCINDO   Yo confieso
que por inferior me nombre
a tu ingenio, si la engañas.

HERNANDO Mis telas son telarañas.   2130
¿Qué importa ser gentilhombre
si faltan galas?

HERNANDO	Belisa?	
LUCINDO	Well, who else!	
HERNANDO	This is getting weird!	
LUCINDO	There's another thing I'm to do.	2105
HERNANDO	What's that?	
LUCINDO	Ask her to be my wife.	
HERNANDO	Your wife!	
LUCINDO	Yes, but don't speak so loud.	

           She'll come out on her balcony
           And hear every word you're saying.

HERNANDO	A perfect scheme for preventing	2110

           Your departure for Portugal.
           Fenisa's got brains!

LUCINDO	Does she ever!	
HERNANDO	You're going to speak with Belisa?	
LUCINDO	Well, no. You're going to take my place,	
	And it's *you* who will speak with her.	2115

           You'll pretend to be me; and then
           While you're talking to Belisa
           I'll be speaking with Fenisa.
           That's what her message instructed.

HERNANDO	What should I say?	
LUCINDO	You know. Words of love.	2120
HERNANDO	That young woman is so clever	

           I sometimes wonder if she's not…

LUCINDO	What?	
HERNANDO	Scheherazade come to life.	
LUCINDO	Tonight's to be a test of your wits.	
	We'll see how well you make love to	2125

           That old woman.

HERNANDO	Never you fear.	

           I'll do myself proud.

LUCINDO	I swear to	

           God, if you fool her, I'll admit
           You're even smarter than I am.

HERNANDO	But look; my clothes are in tatters.	2130

           How can I be a gentleman
           If I look like a bum?

LUCINDO	Pues bien...
HERNANDO	Dame esa capa con oro.
LUCINDO	Diérate, Hernando, un tesoro.
	Toma el sombrero también. 2135
HERNANDO	Tú podrás ponerte el mío.

[Cambian de capa y sombrero.]

LUCINDO	A fe que quedo galán.
HERNANDO	¡Ah, Lucindo, cómo dan
	los vestidos talle y brío!
LUCINDO	Quedo, al balcón han salido. 2140

Sale[n] Fenisa y Belisa en alto.

BELISA	Dame, Fenisa, lugar;
	que quiero a Lucindo hablar.
FENISA	¿De qué sabes que ha venido?
BELISA	Veo dos hombres parados
	mirando nuestro balcón. 2145
FENISA	Bien conoces, ellos son;
	que hacen señas embozados.
	Voyme, y Dios te dé ventura.
	Mas dame licencia un poco
	de hablar a Hernando.
BELISA	Es un loco. 2150
FENISA	Agrádame su locura,
	y téngole que decir
	un recado al Capitán.
BELISA	Ve a esotra reja.
HERNANDO	Ya están
	donde nos pueden oír. 2155
LUCINDO	Fenisa se fue de allí.
HERNANDO	Su madre la despidió.
BELISA	¿Sois Lucindo?
HERNANDO	No soy yo,
	después que [vivís] en mí;
	pero soy el que os adora 2160

LUCINDO	Well, I…
HERNANDO	Give me your gold-embroidered cape.
LUCINDO	You deserve that and more, my friend.
	I'll give you my plumed hat also.

2135

HERNANDO	Good! I'll wear your clothes, you wear mine.

They exchange capes and hats.

LUCINDO	Voila! Now I'm really in style!
HERNANDO	You know how the old saying goes,
	Lucindo, it's clothes make the man!
LUCINDO	Shush! They've come to the balcony.

2140

Fenisa and Belisa appear at a high window.

BELISA	Fenisa, do move aside, please.
	I want to speak to Lucindo.
FENISA	But how do you know that he's come?
BELISA	I see two men down in the street,
	Looking up at our balcony.

2145

FENISA	You're right. Lucindo and his man,
	And they're making gestures our way.
	I'm going; God bring you good luck.
	But first give me leave to have a
	Word with Hernando.
BELISA	He's quite mad!

2150

FENISA	He is, but he amuses me.
	Also, I have a message for
	Him to convey to the Captain.
BELISA	Go to the other window.

Fenisa withdraws.

HERNANDO	I'm
	Sure that they can hear us from here.

2155

LUCINDO	Fenisa has left the window.
HERNANDO	Probably she was told to go.
BELISA	Lucindo?
HERNANDO	I am no longer
	I, since you became my whole life.
	Rather, I'm he who adores you,

2160

con el alma que le dais,
pues mi humildad levantáis
a vuestro valor, señora.
    ¿No va bueno?

LUCINDO   ¡Pesia tal,
que hablas con gran discreción!   2165

HERNANDO Estoy hecho un Cicerón.

BELISA Puesto que parece mal,
    Lucindo, que una mujer,
que en fin de Fenisa es madre,
la case con vuestro padre   2170
y a vos os venga a querer,
    que en efecto sois su hijo;
llegado a que me [queráis],
yo confieso que me dais
un juvenil regocijo.   2175
    ¿Es posible que os agrado
y que os parezco tan bien?

Fenisa, en otra ventana, al otro lado del teatro.

FENISA ¡Ce, Lucindo!

LUCINDO   ¿Quién es?

FENISA   Quien
el alma y vida te ha dado.
    Llega, mientras entretiene   2180
a la loca de mi madre
tu crïado.

HERNANDO   Si mi padre,
como viejo, a querer viene
    la tierna edad de Fenisa,
yo, como mozo, os adoro   2185
por ese grave decoro.

FENISA Muriéndome estoy de risa.

HERNANDO Esas tocas reverendas,
Ese estupendo mongil
ese pecho varonil   2190
testigo de tantas prendas,
    ese chapín enlutado

With the soul you've bestowed on him.
You've raised my humble self so high
I now truly see your great worth.
(Aside to Lucindo.) (How'm I doing?)

LUCINDO (I'll be damned if
You don't have a real way with words!) 2165

HERNANDO (Cicero has nothing on me!)

BELISA I realize, Lucindo, that
It might seem wrong that a woman
Who is the mother of the girl
Who is to marry your father 2170
Has developed an affection
For you, who are, of course, his son;
But if you do indeed love me,
I confess that you give me such
Joy that I feel I'm young once more. 2175
Is it really possible you
Find me pleasing and attractive?

Fenisa appears at the other window.

FENISA Psst, Lucindo.

LUCINDO Who is it?

FENISA One
Who gives to you her heart and soul.
Come over here while your servant 2180
Distracts the attention of my
Silly mother.

HERNANDO If my father,
The old man, can fall in love with
Fenisa, still tender in years,
Then why can't I, young as I am, 2185
Adore your great maturity?

FENISA Oh, Lord, I'm dying of laughter.

HERNANDO I sing hymns to your honored cap,
Your most excellent nun-like dress,
Your celebrated, virile chest 2190
Adorned with medals and bright gems;
Your hefty clogs, bedecked in black,

que del pie los puntos sabe,
que pisa el suelo, más grave
que un frisón recién herrado,   2195
    esa bien compuesta voz,
ese olor de amor espuela,
que es azúcar y canela
de aquestas tocas de arroz,
    esos antojos al lado   2200
para encubrir los de enfrente,
ese manto en que consiente
ser el amor manteado,
    esa encarnada nariz
donde amor destila y saca   2205
ámbar, mirra y tacamaca
más que el Arabia feliz;
    en fin, tocas, pies, frisón,
nariz, monjil, manto, antojos,
voz, chapín, son a mis ojos   2210
selvas de varia lición.

LUCINDO   ¿Escuchástelo?

FENISA   Sospecho
que ha de entender el engaño.

LUCINDO   En que yerre está mi daño,
y en que acierte mi provecho.   2215
    Pero dime, prenda mía,
¿qué ha de ser de nuestro amor,
si de ti con tal rigor
este padre me desvía?
    No te descuides, mi bien;   2220
que apresura mi partida.

FENISA   No tengas pena, mi vida,
ni esos miedos te la den;
    que mi madre, loca y vana
está por tu amor de modo   2225
que pondrá remedio en todo.

LUCINDO   Sí, mas la boda cercana
    me amenaza, como ves;
y si él se llega a casar,

	That take the measure of your feet,	
	Treading the ground as lightly as	
	The hooves of a newly-shod horse;	2195
	Your sweet and melodious voice,	
	Your aroma, the spur of love,	
	That hints of sugar and spices	
	And comes from your newly-starched toque;	
	Blinders on the side of your face	2200
	That divert the gaze from whims in front;	
	Your outsized cloak in which Cupid	
	Consents to be snuggled and tossed;	
	Your glowing nose, where love distills	
	And secretes liquids more precious	2205
	Than the amber, myrrh, and poplar	
	Resin of fair Arabia.	
	In short, starched white cap, feet, and horse,	
	Nose, cloak, birthmarks, and widow's weeds	
	Voice, chest and clogs are to my eyes	2210
	A miscellany of desire.	
LUCINDO	Did you hear all that?	
FENISA	I suspect	
	She'll soon see through all his nonsense.	
LUCINDO	If he overplays it, I'll lose;	
	But if he keeps his wits, I'll win.	2215
	So tell me, my dearest treasure,	
	What is to become of our love	
	If my father is determined	
	To banish me to Portugal.	
	Think well, my love, for as we speak,	2220
	He's arranging my departure.	
FENISA	Please don't worry, love of my life,	
	And don't give in to all your fears.	
	For my crazy and vain mother	
	Is so smitten by you she'll find	2225
	A solution for everything.	
LUCINDO	Good; but the approaching wedding	
	Is a terrible threat to us.	
	If my father should marry you,	

¿cómo podrás remediar   2230
mi ausencia, y muerte después?
　　A la fe, que aunque es tan cierto
que eres discreta y sutil,
que no halles modo entre mil
para dar la vida a un muerto.   2235

FENISA　　Si soy tuya, si nací
para ti sola, y si estoy
cierta que como yo soy
tuya, tú lo eres de mí,
　　da traza cómo salgamos   2240
destos padres enemigos;
hacienda tienes y amigos.
Adonde quisieres vamos.
　　Discreta y enamorada
me sueles, Lucindo, hacer,   2245
mas ya sólo quiero ser
mujer y determinada.

LUCINDO　　Si tienes resolución
de que te saque de aquí,
ánimo me sobra a mí   2250
para igual ejecución.
　　Esta noche, gloria mía,
joyas y vestidos coge,
y aunque tu madre se enoje,
te sacaré a mediodía;   2255
　　que no temo de mi padre
el mal que me pueda hacer.

FENISA　Si voy a ser tu mujer,
máteme después mi madre.

BELISA　　¿Que tiene determinado   2260
envïarte a Portugal?

HERNANDO　No he visto locura igual
como en la que el viejo ha dado.
　　Dice que adoro a Fenisa,
que la sirvo y solicito,   2265
que el sueño y quietud le quito,
y sigo en saliendo a misa;

	What remedy can you find for	2230
	My exile and quite certain death?	
	Although I'm the last to deny	
	That you're clever and resourceful,	
	I doubt that you have the power	
	To bring a dead man back to life.	2235
FENISA	If I am yours, if I was born	
	For you alone, and if I know	
	That as I belong to you, so	
	You belong to me, then we must	
	Come up with a plan to escape	2240
	From our tyrannical parents.	
	You have both property and friends.	
	We can go wherever you wish.	
	You have made me all that I am:	
	Smart, clever, and deeply in love.	2245
	But now I must become something	
	More, a strong, determined woman.	
LUCINDO	If you're firmly resolved to flee	
	With me from this place, I promise	
	You I have the courage needed	2250
	To carry out our getaway.	
	Dearest one, this evening gather	
	Up your garments and your jewels.	
	Tomorrow at noon, I'll rescue	
	You from here, your mother be damned.	2255
	As for my father, I have no	
	Fear of what he may do to me.	
FENISA	Once I'm your wife, my mother can	
	Kill me if that's what she desires.	
BELISA	You say that your father insists	2260
	On sending you to Portugal?	
HERNANDO	I've never seen a worse madness	
	Than the one that's come over him.	
	He says I adore Fenisa,	
	Chase after her and pester her,	2265
	Rob her of peace and of sleep and	
	Follow her when she goes to mass.	

	y de celos me destierra.	
BELISA	Mi bien, y ¿quereisla vos?	
HERNANDO	¡Yo a Fenisa! ¡Plegue a Dios	2270
	que aquí me trague la tierra,	
	que me maten seis villanos	
	en su heredad o su aldea	
	porque no hay muerte que sea	
	más infame que [a] sus manos,	2275
	plegue a Dios que un arcabuz	
	probándole me traspase,	
	o que una espada me pase	
	desde la punta a la cruz	
	si en mi vida tuve intento	2280
	de amalla ni pretendella,	
	ni jamás hablé con ella	
	de amor ni de casamiento!	
LUCINDO	Muy bien lo puede jurar.	
BELISA	Satisfecha estoy, mi bien.	2285
HERNANDO	Dejando aquesto también,	
	¿tienes algo que me dar?	
	Porque en dándome un enojo,	
	o en jurando alguna cosa,	
	me da una hambre espantosa;	2290
	soy preñada con antojo.	
BELISA	¿Gana tienes de comer?	
HERNANDO	Rabio, ¡por Dios!	
BELISA	Todo es malo	
	cuanto hay en casa; un regalo	
	mañana te quiero hacer.	2295
	¿Qué conserva comes bien?	
	Que soy en dulces notable;	
	de guindas es razonable,	
	y de perada también.	
	Duraznos es extremada.	2300
	¿Qué conserva haré?	
HERNANDO	Un menudo	
	con su perejil; que dudo	
	que la haya tal, bien lavada.	

	He's jealous, and so I'm banished.	
BELISA	And do you love her, my precious?	
HERNANDO	I love Fenisa? If ever	2270
	In my whole life I thought about	
	Loving or wooing her; or if	
	Ever in my life I spoke with	
	Her about love or marriage, then	
	God grant that the earth swallow me up;	2275
	That six low-born rogues strike me dead	
	In town or in their very house,	
	Since there's no more infamous death	
	Than to be killed in such a way.	
	God grant too, that I shoot myself	2280
	By mistake with my own long gun,	
	Or that a sword runs me through all	
	The way from the point to the hilt.	
LUCINDO	He's a genius at making vows!	
BELISA	I do believe you, my dear one.	2285
HERNANDO	Now to change the subject a bit,	
	Is there anything to eat here?	
	I ask because when I get riled	
	Up or swear a couple of oaths	
	I get hungrier than a bear;	2290
	It's like I was half-way pregnant.	
BELISA	You're hungry this very moment?	
HERNANDO	You bet I am!	
BELISA	I've nothing now	
	Fit to eat. Come back tomorrow	
	And I'll make you a special treat.	2295
	Do you have a liking for sweets?	
	I'm quite noted for my preserves;	
	My cherry glacé is good, too,	
	And so is my grated pear jam.	
	Best of all is my peach jelly.	2300
	But what should I make?	
HERNANDO	How about	
	Tripe with parsley? When it's clean and	
	Well-seasoned there's nothing like it.	

BELISA	¿Deso gustas? Pues hallaste
	la limpieza, la sazón 2305
	y el buen gusto.
HERNANDO	Cosas son
	en que el tuyo conformaste.
	Envíamele mañana.
LUCINDO	¿Hay villano tan grosero?
BELISA	¡Qué menudo hacerte espero! 2310
HERNANDO	No será peor la gana.
BELISA	¿Menudo comes?
HERNANDO	No pudo
	ponerse [ese] gusto en [duda],
	porque quien sirve a vïuda,
	se obliga a comer menudo. 2315
LUCINDO	Gente pasa. ¡Ce!
BELISA	¿Quién llama?
HERNANDO	Hernandillo, mi crïado,
	que allá con Fenisa [ha] hablado.
BELISA	¡Lindo pícaro!
HERNANDO	De fama.
	Díceme que pasa gente. 2320
	¡Adiós!
BELISA	Él, mi bien, os guarde.
LUCINDO	Pues pasa gente y es tarde,
	adiós.
FENISA	¡Ay mi gloria ausente!
	¡Qué bien que la has divertido!
HERNANDO	¡Famosamente la hablé! 2325
LUCINDO	Ven tras mí. Pero ¿qué fue
	aquello que le has pedido?
HERNANDO	Un menudo.
LUCINDO	Y ¿eso pudo
	pedir tu lengua, grosero?
HERNANDO	Tú negocias por entero, 2330
	yo negocio por menudo.

BELISA	That's what you'd like? Then I'm certain	
	You'll find mine to be not just clean	2305
	But quite tasty too.	
HERNANDO	I'm sure that	
	In matters of taste we agree.	
	I'll come by for some tomorrow.	
LUCINDO	What an ill-born peasant he is!	
BELISA	What tripe you'll get when you return!	2310
HERNANDO	That would just about make my day!	
BELISA	You really like tripe?	
HERNANDO	(*Aside*) (I couldn't	
	Leave that weakness in any doubt.	
	Those who woo widows know they'll be	
	Eating scraps and warm left-overs.)	2315
LUCINDO	Psst! Someone's coming.	
BELISA	Who's calling?	
HERNANDO	It's my servant Hernandillo.	
	He's talking there with Fenisa.	
BELISA	He's a sly fellow.	
HERNANDO	A scoundrel!	
	He's says that people are coming.	2320
	Good-by!	
BELISA	God be with you, my love.	

Exit Belisa.

LUCINDO	People are coming and it's late.	
	Good-by!	
FENISA	(*To Lucindo.*) I can't bear your leaving!	
	(*To Hernando.*) How well you kept her occupied!	
HERNANDO	Just call me a wizard with words!	2325

Exit Fenisa.

LUCINDO	Quick. Come along. But what was it	
	That you asked her to make for you?	
HERNANDO	A plate of tripe.	
LUCINDO	You had the nerve	
	To ask for that, you nincompoop?	
HERNANDO	You always expect the whole cow.	2330
	I'm happy with the remainders.	

Vanse.
Salen Doristeo y Gerarda.

GERARDA	Sosiega el pecho celoso;	*quintillas*
	que yo sabré si es verdad.	
DORISTEO	Sospecho que, temeroso,	
	de alguna temeridad,	2335
	a que obliga un caso honroso,	
	dijo que el nombre fingía,	
	y fue a tiento Estefanía,	
	porque su padre, en mi daño,	
	me dijo por desengaño	2340
	cómo a Fenisa servía.	
GERARDA	El padre acaso pensó	
	que a Fenisa amabas.	
DORISTEO	¿Yo?	
GERARDA	Y para en paz os poner,	
	dijo que era su mujer.	2345
DORISTEO	No lo entiendo.	
GERARDA	¿Cómo no?	
	Si pensó que la cuestión	
	era por Fenisa allí,	
	¿no fue sutil invención	
	hacerla su mujer?	
DORISTEO	Sí,	2350
	tienes, Gerarda razón;	
	pero mi celoso honor	
	aún quiere desto más prueba.	
GERARDA	También la pide mi amor.	
DORISTEO	Esta sospecha me lleva	2355
	de un temor a otro mayor.	
GERARDA	¿Quieres que los dos sepamos	
	si es verdad que ama a Fenisa?	
DORISTEO	Sí quiero.	
GERARDA	A su casa vamos.	
DORISTEO	¿Cuál ignorancia te avisa	2360
	que si le quiere digamos?	
GERARDA	¿Digo yo que sea ansí?	

Exit both.
A room in Gerarda's house.
Enter Doristeo and Gerarda.

GERARDA	Please try to calm your jealousy.
	I'll soon find out what's true or not.
DORISTEO	What I think is that fearing that
	Something dangerous was afoot,
	As happens when honor's at stake,
	He said he invented a name,
	Just by chance Estefanía.
	Then, later, his father told me,
	To my shock, it's not his son who's
	Courting Fenisa, but himself.
GERARDA	Well, perhaps the father thought that
	You, also, loved Fenisa.
DORISTEO	I?
GERARDA	And to defuse your anger said
	That she was going to be his wife.
DORISTEO	I don't understand.
GERARDA	It's simple.
	If he thought your quarrel was all
	About Fenisa, wasn't it
	Smart to say that he intended
	To make her *his* wife?
DORISTEO	Yes, I do
	Suppose that you're right, Gerarda.
	But my jealousy and honor
	Demand more proof of the matter.
GERARDA	I know they do. So does my love.
DORISTEO	But this suspicion leads me from
	One fear to another that's worse.
GERARDA	Of course. But do you want to learn
	If it's Fenisa whom he loves?
DORISTEO	I do.
GERARDA	Then we'll go to her house.
DORISTEO	That's absurd! We just go there and
	Ask her if Lucindo loves her?
GERARDA	That's not what I was suggesting.

Line numbers: 2335, 2340, 2345, 2350, 2355, 2360

DORISTEO	Pues ¿cómo?
GERARDA	Yo entraré huyendo.
DORISTEO	¿De quién has de huír?
GERARDA	De ti,

que eras mi esposo diciendo, 2365
....
sacarás la daga.

DORISTEO	Bien.

GERARDA Pondrános en paz su gente;
quedaréme allí también,
donde a Fenisa le cuente 2370
que quiero a Lucindo bien,
  y que por él me matabas;
que te llame, y en secreto
te diga lo que dudabas.

DORISTEO ¡Gentil industria, en efeto, 2375
de mujer!

GERARDA	¿Su ingenio alabas?
DORISTEO	¡Oh mujeres!
GERARDA	¡Y españolas!
DORISTEO	Camina.
GERARDA	Si estamos solas,

ella dirá la verdad.

DORISTEO Mujeres con voluntad 2380
son como la mar con olas.

Vanse.
Salen el Capitán, Fenisa y Belisa.

CAPITÁN Si supiera vuestro intento, *redondillas*
no le echara de mi casa.

BELISA Yo os he dicho lo que pasa.

CAPITÁN Huélgome del casamiento; 2385
  daros quiero el parabién.

BELISA Si mi bien camino va,
el paramal me dará
quien me ha dado el parabién.

CAPITÁN Si [yo] estuviera avisado 2390

DORISTEO	Well, what, then?
GERARDA	I'll burst in, fleeing.
DORISTEO	Yes? Fleeing from whom?
GERARDA	From you. I'll
	Be crying you're my husband, and 2365
	....
	You'll pull out your dagger.
DORISTEO	And then?
GERARDA	The people there will calm us down.
	You'll leave and I'll stay behind. When
	We're alone, I'll tell Fenisa 2370
	That I'm in love with Lucindo,
	And that's why you wished to kill me.
	Then I'll ask her to speak to you,
	And privately clear up your doubts.
DORISTEO	An ingenious plan, worthy of 2375
	A woman!
GERARDA	You praise women's minds?
DORISTEO	I do.
GERARDA	Then take care they're Spanish!
DORISTEO	Let's get going.
GERARDA	Once we're alone
	She's certain to tell me the truth.
DORISTEO	Not even the ocean waves have 2380
	The force of a strong-willed woman.

Exit Gerarda and Doristeo.
A room in Belisa's house.
Enter the Captain, Fenisa and Belisa.

CAPTAIN	Had I learned of your intent, I
	Wouldn't have thrown him from the house.
BELISA	Well, now you know what's happening.
CAPTAIN	I'm most pleased about the wedding. 2385
	Permit me to wish you both well.
BELISA	If my loved one had been exiled,
	The one who now wishes me well
	Would have wished me quite ill instead.
CAPTAIN	If I had only been told that 2390

de que Lucindo os quería,
que en opinión le tenía
de hombre menos asentado,
   yo propio tratara aquí,
Belisa, del casamiento;   2395
que es dar a mi bien aumento
que nos troquemos ansí.
   Casado con quien es madre
de mi bien, como confío
de vos misma, el hijo mío   2400
vengo yo a tener por padre;
   y Fenisa, mi mujer
y vuestra hija, tendrá
padre en Lucindo; y dará
a todo el mundo placer   2405
   la discreción del trocar
las edades por los gustos.

BELISA   Dado me habéis mil disgustos
en pretenderle ausentar;
   y no os descuidéis en ir   2410
donde el camino estorbéis.

FENISA   Gran rigor usado habéis.

CAPITÁN   No me supe resistir.

FENISA   ¿Fue celos, por vida mía,
del destierro la ocasión?   2415

CAPITÁN   Celos de su vida son,
que una cierta Estefanía
   le trae de manera ciego,
que le han querido matar
dos hombres deste lugar.   2420
   Y le matan si no llego.

BELISA   Pues ¿quiere a alguna mujer?

FENISA   (¿Qué es lo que escucho? ¡Ay de mí!)

CAPITÁN   Así entonces lo entendí;
mentira debe de ser.   2425
   No me acordé que le [amáis].
Perdonad; que por él voy.

Vase.

                    Lucindo was in love with you –
                    And in truth I always took him
                    For someone much less sensible –
                    Then I myself would have been glad
                    To make the marriage arrangements, 2395
                    Since an exchange among us can
                    Only increase my happiness.
                    If my son marries the one who
                    Is the mother of my own bride,
                    As you now say he plans to do, 2400
                    Then he'll be both my son and my
                    Father-in-law. And Fenisa,
                    My wife and your daughter, will gain
                    In him a second father. Then
                    The whole world will have the pleasure 2405
                    of witnessing how wise it is
                    To choose true fondness over age.

BELISA   Your intention to banish him
                    Has caused me a great deal of concern.
                    You must go to him at once and 2410
                    Prevent him from leaving Madrid.

FENISA   You've been very severe with him.

CAPTAIN   I could act in no other way.

FENISA   Really! Was it jealousy, then,
                    That occasioned his banishment? 2415

CAPTAIN   No; it was concern for his life.
                    A certain Estefanía
                    Has him so infatuated
                    That two men of this city were
                    Determined to kill him. And they 2420
                    Would have if I hadn't been there.

BELISA   Then he loves another woman?

FENISA   *(Aside.)* (What's this I hear? Can it be true?)

CAPTAIN   That's what I understood from their
                    Words. It must be a complete lie. 2425
                    I wasn't aware of your love.
                    Please excuse me. I must find him.

Exit the Captain.

BELISA	Confusa, Fenisa, estoy.
FENISA	Mi pensamiento imitáis.
BELISA	Si tiene alguna mujer,

2430

¡buen lance habemos echado!

FENISA	A ti poco te ha burlado, *Aparte*

si burla te quiso hacer;

pero a mí, que me engañó

fingiendo amarme de veras.

2435

BELISA	¿Qué dices?
FENISA	Que no creyeras

lo que este viejo contó;

que con los celos que tiene

finge dos mil desatinos.

BELISA	¡Por qué notables caminos

2440

a darnos enojo viene!

     Gente se nos entra [acá.]

FENISA	Dejose abierta la puerta.
BELISA	¡Bien hará lo que concierta

si otra mujer tiene ya!

2445

Sale Gerarda huyendo, y Doristeo, la daga desnuda.

GERARDA	¡Favor, señores! Socorredme presto,	*versos sueltos*

que me mata este bárbaro tirano.

DORISTEO	¿Quién te ha de dar favor, infame adúltera?
BELISA	Tened, señor; no la matéis os ruego.
FENISA	Paso, señor. ¿Por qué le dais la muerte?

2450

GERARDA	¡Yo adúltera, señor!
BELISA	Tened la mano.

Respetad esas tocas norabuena.

DORISTEO	Si no mirara esa presencia noble,

de vuestra calidad notorio indicio,

el corazón le hubiera atravesado.

2455

GERARDA	Y matáraste en él, que en él te tengo.
DORISTEO	¡Ahora amores, falsa, vil perjura!

¡Ahora hechicerías! ¡Vive el cielo!

FENISA	Acabad, si queréis; que venís loco,

y algún demonio revestido en celos

2460

os debe de mover la lengua y manos.

BELISA	I'm very confused, Fenisa.
FENISA	I'm just as confused as you are.
BELISA	If he really loves another 2430
	Woman, what a fine fix we're in!
FENISA	(*Aside.*) (Having misled you is one thing,
	Since he made clear he would do that;
	But to deceive me is something
	Else. He said he truly loved me.) 2435
BELISA	What's that you say?
FENISA	That you shouldn't
	Believe what you just heard. The old
	Man is so jealous he's apt to
	Make up just about anything.
BELISA	How strange that he would tell such tales 2440
	Knowing it would make us upset.
	Good Lord! People are coming in.
FENISA	He must have left the door open.
BELISA	Can it be there's still another
	Woman we've not yet heard about? 2445

Enter Gerarda, fleeing, and Doristeo, with dagger drawn.

GERARDA	Help me, ladies, for the love of God, help me!
	This tyrannical monster wants to kill me.
DORISTEO	There's no help here, you shameless adulteress!
BELISA	Sir, hold your hand! Don't harm her, I beg of you!
FENISA	Yes, calm down. Why are you trying to kill her? 2450
GERARDA	I'm no adulteress, sir!
BELISA	Do hold your hand
	I ask you to show respect for these gray hairs.
DORISTEO	If I could not see by your august presence
	That you are a person of great quality,
	I would have run this base woman through the heart!
GERARDA	And killed yourself, because that's where you have life!
DORISTEO	So now you speak of love, false, vile, perjurer!
	Now you pronounce endearments! Great God above!
FENISA	That's enough! You're talking like a crazy man.
	Some devil all wrapped up in vile jealousy 2460
	Must be working your mouth and moving your hands.

BELISA	No habéis de estar aquí, por vida mía.
	Venid; que os quiero hablar en mi aposento.
	Descansaréis de vuestro mal conmigo.
DORISTEO	Yo os quiero obedecer, y referirle,
	aunque traiga mi infamia a la memoria.
BELISA	Pues con mi hija quedará esta dama.
	¿Qué nombre tiene?
DORISTEO	Estefanía se llama.

2465

Vanse los dos.

FENISA	De gran peligro os ha librado el cielo.
GERARDA	¡Ay, señora, que estoy temblando toda!
	¿Dónde me podré ir?
FENISA	No tengáis miedo.
	Contadme vuestro mal.
GERARDA	Sí haré, si puedo.

2470

	Yo soy, gallarda señora,
	una mujer desdichada;
	aunque esto ya lo sabéis,
	pues lo veis en mi desgracia.
	Nací en Burgos, ciudad noble,
	y mis padres, que Dios haya,
	me trajeron a la corte,
	niña, en los brazos del ama.
	Criáronme en su regalo,
	y de mi talle o mis galas
	rendido el hombre que veis,
	me pide con grandes ansias.
	Casáronme a mi disgusto;
	en fin, sobre estar casada
	de la manera que digo,
	carga el peso de esta infamia.
	Vime sin gusto con él,
	mil veces determinada
	para quitarme la vida.

romance a-a

2475

2480

2485

2490

FENISA	No digáis tal.
GERARDA	Esto pasa.

BELISA	*(To Doristeo.)* On my life, it's best that you
	don't remain here.
	Come now. I'd like to speak with you in my room.
	Alone with me you'll get over your anger.
DORISTEO	I'd like to obey and tell you everything, 2465
	Even if it brings back how defamed I am.
BELISA	Meanwhile, this lady will stay with my daughter.
	What is her name?
DORISTEO	She's called Estefanía.

Exit Belisa and Doristeo.

FENISA	Heaven has rescued you from frightful danger.
GERARDA	Dear lady, you can see how I'm still trembling. 2470
	But where am I to go?
FENISA	Please don't be afraid.
	Tell me what's happened.
GERARDA	I'll do so, if I can.
	I am, kind and gracious lady,
	A most unfortunate woman,
	Although you already know that, 2475
	Having seen what has just happened.
	I was born in the noble town
	Of Burgos, and my parents, God
	Rest them, brought me here to Madrid,
	Still a babe in my nurse's arms. 2480
	I was raised in great luxury.
	Later, attracted by my looks,
	Or by my wealth, the man you've seen
	Requested my hand in marriage.
	I was wed against my wishes; 2485
	Now, I'm not just unhappily
	Married, but I must bear the weight
	Of the infamy you've just seen.
	I live without love or pleasure,
	Over and over determined 2490
	To take my life, once and for all.
FENISA	Don't say that!
GERARDA	Such things do happen.

FENISA	Pues, ¿por desdicha ninguna,	
	dice una mujer cristiana	
	que se ha de quitar la vida?	2495
GERARDA	Señora, experiencia os falta.	

No sabéis lo que es tener
en la mesa y en la cama
un enemigo de día
y de noche una fantasma. 2500
Mas mi desesperación
fue en este medio templada
con la vista de un mancebo,
soldado y sol dado al alma.
Era un alférez galán, 2505
por quien por puntos les daba
a las niñas de mis ojos
alferecía sin causa,
que en la mala compañía
del marido que me daban, 2510
pensé que con un alférez
[pudiera] sufrir las faltas.
Pagome la voluntad,
y con obras y palabras
marchamos diez y seis meses, 2515
llevándose amor las armas.
Mas como en marchando amor
toca la envidia las cajas,
oyó el bando mi marido
y los tiros a su fama. 2520
Comenzó a tener sospechas;
puso un espantajo en casa,
para que el pájaro viese
que el hortelano velaba.
Busqué medios por vecinos, 2525
hubo puertas y ventanas,
porque cuando quieren dos,
fácilmente se baraja.
Mas para abreviar, señora,
con mi amor y mi esperanza, 2530

FENISA	Whatever the circumstances,
	Should a Christian woman declare
	She wishes to take her own life? 2495
GERARDA	It's clear you lack experience.
	You have no idea what it
	Is like to have at your table,
	In your bed, an enemy by
	Day, and a phantom at night. 2500
	But while this was happening my
	Despair was somewhat abated
	By the sight of a young man, a
	Soldier, who was sun for my soul.
	He was a gallant lieutenant, 2505
	So handsome that in a short while
	He took command not only of
	My eyes, but of my heart as well.
	It seemed to me that his manly
	Virtues could make up for the faults 2510
	I bore in the bad company
	Of the husband they'd forced on me.
	My feelings for the young man were
	Soon returned, and thus with words here
	And actions there, sixteen months passed, 2515
	The arms of war now arms of love.
	Sadly, love, when glimpsed by others,
	Seems to stir the drums of envy;
	My husband heard their beat and knew
	That his honor was in danger. 2520
	He became extremely watchful
	And installed a kind of living
	Scarecrow in the house, and thus the
	Thieving bird knew to be on guard.
	I sought the help of our neighbors, 2525
	We made use of windows and doors,
	For where there's a will there's a way,
	And truth is cast into grave doubt.
	But to conclude, dear lady, this
	Story of my love and fond hopes, 2530

no ha faltado quien me ha dicho
que el ver mi marido en arma
hizo a Lucindo mudar,
que así el alférez se llama,
el alma y el pensamiento,   2535
adonde agora se casa
con una Fenisa, dicen,
a quien de discreta alaban;
que quien la alaba de hermosa,
dicen que a su rostro agravia.   2540
He perdido tanto el seso,
que he salido de mi casa,
y buscado de tal suerte
este ingrato que me agravia,
que hoy, como veis, mi marido   2545
me ha topado disfrazada;
que pensaba hallarle aquí,
que aquí vive quien me mata.
¿Conocéis en esta calle
esta dama, hermosa dama?   2550
¿Sabéis quién es, por ventura,
la que mis desdichas causa?
Que ya que de mi marido
tomé puerto en vuestra casa,
tras el remedio del cuerpo,   2555
de vos espero el del alma.

FENISA   ¿Que Lucindo os quiere bien?   *redondillas*
GERARDA   ¿Conocéisle?
FENISA   ¡A Dios pluguiera
                que ni yo le conociera,
                ni él a mí!

GERARDA   ¡Ni a vos también!   2560
                ¡Cosa que a tiento haya dado
                con la causa de mi mal!

FENISA   El vuestro no ha sido igual
                al mal que me habéis causado.
                    Yo soy Fenisa, ¡ay de mí!,   2565
                engañada de ese ingrato,

People say that it was seeing
That my husband was on to us
That caused Lucindo – for that's the
Name of the lieutenant – to shift
His heart and soul to another,   2535
Whom he soon intends to marry.
I'm told her name is Fenisa,
And she's known for her discretion.
I've heard that those who would praise her
Beauty instead much offend her.   2540
All of this has so driven me
Mad that I abandoned my house
And went in search of that ingrate
Who has so clearly done me wrong;
Then, just now, my husband happened   2545
Across me in the street, face veiled,
And assumed that the one for whom
I'm dying resides in this house.
Might you know, beautiful lady,
If Fenisa's home is nearby?   2550
Do you possibly know her, the
One who's causing me such distress?
Now that I've burst into your home,
Seeking bodily refuge from
My husband, I can only ask   2555
For refuge for my soul as well.

FENISA	You say that Lucindo loves you?
GERARDA	Do you know him?
FENISA	I wish that I

Had never met him, or that he
Had met me!

GERARDA   Then you do know him!   2560
How strange that just by chance I should
Find the cause of all my despair.

FENISA The woe that you're suffering can't
Compare to what you've brought on me!
Oh, dear God! I am Fenisa!   2565
Deceived by that ungrateful man,

que no sabiendo su trato,
mucho del alma le di.
   Yo soy con quien de secreto
su casamiento trató,   2570
porque no pensaba yo
tanto mal en tal sujeto.
   Pero pues a tiempo estoy,
y mi honor salvo, creed
que agradezco la merced   2575
y que de mano le doy.
   Hoy con su padre me caso
por sólo hacerle pesar;
que le tengo de abrasar
con el fuego en que me abraso.   2580
   Y pues que vos le queréis,
gozadle por largos años.

GERARDA   ¿Que vos me hacéis tantos daños,
y que vos muerto me habéis?
   ¿Que vos os llamáis Fenisa?   2585

FENISA   Estad segura que ya
Lucindo vuestro será.

GERARDA   Mi desengaño os avisa.
   Es el hombre más traidor,
más mudable y lisonjero   2590
que ha visto el mundo.

FENISA   No quiero
más desengaños, amor.
   Adiós, gustos atrevidos.
¿Vuestro nombre?

GERARDA   Estefanía.

FENISA   Bien su padre me decía: 2595
no eran sus celos fingidos.
   Ya sabía vuestro nombre,
ya sé todo lo que pasa.

GERARDA   No admitáis en vuestra casa,
pues que sois cuerda, tal hombre. 2600
   Mirad que os ha de quitar
el honor.

	I gave my entire soul to him,	
	Knowing nothing of his vile ways.	
	I'm the one with whom in secret	
	He was contriving to marry,	2570
	Because I never imagined	
	That a man could be so evil.	
	Luckily I found out in time,	
	And my honor is intact. I	
	Thank you for your favor to me,	2575
	And I gladly give him to you.	
	Today I'll marry his father,	
	If only to make him suffer,	
	For I want him to burn with the	
	Fire that has been consuming me.	2580
	And now, since you love him so much,	
	I wish you years of happiness.	
GERARDA	You're the one who brought me such harm?	
	The one who almost caused my death?	
	Can you really be Fenisa?	2585
FENISA	Be assured that from this day on	
	Lucindo will be yours alone.	
GERARDA	Be forewarned by my deception.	
	He is the most unfaithful man,	
	The most fickle and flattering	2590
	The world has ever seen.	
FENISA	*(Aside.)* (I wish	
	No more foul dishonesty, Love.	
	Good-by, all daring thoughts and deeds.)	
	And your name?	
GERARDA	Estefanía.	
FENISA	*(Aside.)* (That's the one his father mentioned.	2595
	His jealousy was not put on.)	
	Then I know your name very well,	
	And everything that has happened.	
GERARDA	Since you are sensible, never	
	Admit that man into your house.	2600
	Look well, that he does not steal your	
	Virtue.	

FENISA	[Perded] el miedo.
GERARDA	Ya, señora, que me puedo
	de mi marido librar,
	dadme licencia; que quiero 2605
	irme en casa de una hermana.
FENISA	¿Querréis verme?
GERARDA	Cosa es llana.
	Ser muy vuestra amiga espero.
	¿Hay puerta falsa?
FENISA	Sí habrá,
	si por Lucindo salís. 2610
GERARDA	¡Qué bien, señora, decís!
	Adiós.
FENISA	Presto, que os verá.
GERARDA	Famosamente he sabido
	de Lucindo el pensamiento
	y su gusto y casamiento 2615
	por notable estilo impido.
	¡Bella mujer, lindo talle!
	Muriéndome voy de celos.
	Guardad a Lucindo, cielos;
	que he de matarle en la calle. 2620

Vase.

FENISA	Salga del alma aquel violento rayo	*soneto*
	que la dejó como ceniza fría,	
	porque parezca la esperanza mía	
	palma sobre las nieves de Moncayo.	
	Ya estaba en flor, cuando en mitad de mayo	2625
	el hielo derribó su lozanía;	
	que [cuando] muda el tiempo, basta un día	
	para que su verdor trueque en desmayo.	
	No más gustos de amor, que sois engaños,	
	que llevan la razón por los cabellos;	2630
	no sufra el alma tan injustos daños.	
	No quiero bienes ya, por no perdellos;	
	mas ¿cómo olvidaré con desengaños,	
	si dice[n] que se aumenta amor con ellos?	

FENISA	There's no danger of that.
GERARDA	Now that I'm free of my husband,
	Dear lady, please give me leave to
	Depart. My plan is to go to 2605
	The house of a sister of mine.
FENISA	Will you come again?
GERARDA	I'd like that.
	I hope to become your good friend.
	Is there a false door?
FENISA	Yes. It's the
	Door to the heart of Lucindo. 2610
GERARDA	How well you put that, dear lady.
	Good-by.
FENISA	Go now, or you'll be seen!
GERARDA	*(Aside, as she leaves.)* (How cunningly I was able
	To find out Lucindo's intents
	And devise a way to prevent 2615
	His marriage and thwart his pleasure.
	How pretty she is, how noble!
	I'm burning up with jealousy.
	May heaven preserve Lucindo,
	For if I catch him, I'll kill him! 2620

Exit Gerarda.

FENISA

Like the palm that stood upon Moncayo's slope,
Turned to gray ashes by lightning's sudden blow,
My soul too was once alive with strength and hope;
Before it stretched upward, but now it lies low.

    The palm was in flower that bright month of May
When a harsh storm killed what the heavens had made.
Once the weather turns it takes only a day
For all of God's beauty to shrivel and fade.

    Away, all love's pleasures, they're only deceit
That cause one's best judgment to stumble and fall;   2630
So let my soul bear not such grievous defeat.
I wish no more gains lest I then lose them all.

    But how will bitterness then help me forget
When they say it makes love more long-lasting yet?

Sale Lucindo.

LUCINDO	Con la determinación,	2635 *quintillas*
	bella Fenisa, de ser	
	en tan dichosa ocasión	
	tu esposo, y tú mi mujer,	
	que nombres seguros son,	
	he tenido atrevimiento	2640
	de llegar a tu aposento,	
	y dejo un coche en la calle,	
	que de ese gallardo talle	
	viene a ser alojamiento.	
	Ven sin poner dilación	2645
	al coche, fénix divina,	
	porque en aquesta ocasión	
	te quiero hacer Proserpina	
	deste abrasado Plutón.	
	¿Qué te suspendes? ¿Qué miras?	2650
FENISA	¿No quieres que me suspenda?	
	¿Qué dices? ¿Burlas? ¿Deliras?	
	¿Con quién hablas?	
LUCINDO	Dulce prenda	
	del alma, ¿a qué blanco tiras?	
	¿Hay alguien con quien cumplir?	2655
	¿No es hora ya de salir,	
	como anoche concerté?	
FENISA	¿Con quién el concierto fue?	
	Eso me vuelve a decir.	
LUCINDO	¿No me hablaste anoche?	
FENISA	Sí.	2660
LUCINDO	Lo que concertamos di.	
FENISA	Que te cases con mi madre,	
	pues yo lo estoy con tu padre.	
LUCINDO	¿Con tu madre? Eso fingí.	
FENISA	Ya no puede ser fingido.	2665
	Testigos hay que has tratado	
	ser de mi madre marido.	
LUCINDO	Luego ¿tú me has engañado?	

Enter Lucindo.

LUCINDO	Beautiful Fenisa, filled with	2635
	High resolve to become your most	
	Faithful husband and, so doing,	
	To make you my beloved wife,	
	Two names we can now proudly bear,	
	I have dared on this most happy	2640
	Occasion to come to your room.	
	My carriage awaits in the street,	
	Desirous of giving welcome	
	To your ever-gracious person.	
	Without further ado, come, then,	2645
	Divine Phoenix, to the carriage,	
	That richly appointed abode,	
	Where you'll become Proserpina	
	To my most passionate Pluto.	
	Why do you pause? Is something wrong?	2650
FENISA	You think it odd that I should pause?	
	Are you mad? Surely you're joking!	
	Do you know who I am?	
LUCINDO	Dear love	
	Of my life, I don't understand.	
	Is there someone you must speak to?	2655
	Is it not the time to leave here	
	As I had agreed to last night?	
FENISA	And with whom was your agreement?	
	Be so kind as to tell me that.	
LUCINDO	Did you not speak with me?	
FENISA	I did.	2660
LUCINDO	Then tell me what we had settled.	
FENISA	That you would marry my mother,	
	Just as I will wed your father.	
LUCINDO	Your mother? That was all pretense.	
FENISA	It can hardly be pretense now.	2665
	Witnesses say that you've arranged	
	To become my mother's husband.	
LUCINDO	Are you saying you've deceived me?	

FENISA   El engaño tuyo ha sido.

De mí no hay que pretender; 2670
que soy mujer de tu padre,
y mi madre es tu mujer.

LUCINDO   ¿Cómo mi mujer tu madre?
Demonio debes de ser.

¿No te acuerdas que tú fuiste 2675
la que primero me quiso?
Tercero a mi padre hiciste,
mi padre me dio el aviso
y te hablé donde quisiste.

En orden a nuestro intento 2680
fingimos el casamiento.
¿Qué me dices de tu madre?

FENISA   Yo soy mujer de tu padre,
esto es verdad y esto siento.

Si mi madre no te agrada, 2685
más señora, más honrada
que tu dama Estefanía,
vete a buscarla y porfía;
que es dulce la fruta hurtada.

Mas guarda; que su marido 2690
te busca.

LUCINDO   En lo que has hablado,
celosa te he conocido.
Sin duda te han engañado
con ese nombre fingido.

Mi lacayo Hernando fue 2695
una noche Estefanía;
que así al Prado le llevé.
No dilates, fénix mía,
el galardón de mi fe;

que si he visto a Estefanía, 2700
la vida me quite el cielo,
fálteme el sol, falte el día,
sepúlteme vivo el suelo
y pierda tu luz, luz mía.

Mira que te han engañado 2705

FENISA	The deceit has been yours alone.
	There's nothing further to be said. 2670
	I am the wife of your father,
	And my mother is now your wife.
LUCINDO	How's that? Your mother is my wife?
	What the devil are you saying!
	Don't you remember that it was 2675
	You who first fell in love with me?
	You made my father into a
	Go-between; I got your message
	And came to speak where you asked me to.
	It was in accordance with your 2680
	Plan that we feigned the whole marriage.
	What's all this about your mother?
FENISA	I am the wife of your father;
	I'm sorry, but that is now so.
	If you no longer care for my 2685
	Mother, who's far more worthy than
	Estefanía, go look for
	Your dearest and pursue your love.
	I'm sure that stolen fruit is sweet.
	But be on guard; her husband is 2690
	Looking for you.
LUCINDO	I see now what
	The problem is; it's jealousy.
	How cleverly they've deceived you
	With a name that I invented.
	It was my man. Hernando,who 2695
	Pretended to be that lady
	And went with me to the Prado.
	Please don't waver now, dear Phoenix,
	Prized reward of my constancy.
	May heaven strike me dead if I 2700
	Ever saw Estefanía;
	May there be no more sun, or day;
	May I be buried alive and
	Lose all your light, light of my life.
	Don't you see how they've misled you? 2705

porque Hernando, disfrazado,
ha sido la Estefanía.

FENISA   Conozco tu alevosía;
tarde, Lucindo, has llegado.
 Y no me hagas perder   2710
el respeto; que has de ser
antes de un hora mi padre,
que al marido de mi madre
debo por padre tener.

LUCINDO   ¿Qué dices?

FENISA   Lo que has oído.   2715

LUCINDO   ¿Tienes seso?

FENISA   El que te falta.

LUCINDO   O tú o yo le hemos perdido.

FENISA   Eso sí, da voces falsas,
que ya vendrá mi marido.

LUCINDO   ¡Válgame Dios!

FENISA   Valga, pues.   2720

LUCINDO   ¿Matareme?

FENISA   Necedad.

LUCINDO   Pues ¿qué haré?

FENISA   Casarte.

LUCINDO   ¿Ves
cómo fue mi amor verdad,
y tu liviandad lo es?
 ¿Ves cómo vine por ti   2725
y que como hombre cumplí
lo que anoche concerté?
¿Ves cómo mujer te hallé,
y no mujer para mí?
 ¿Ves cómo es bien empleado 2730
todo cuanto mal decimos
de vosotras? ¿Ves que he estado,
conforme el concierto hicimos,
prevenido y confïado?
 Pues ¡plegue a Dios que te veas, 2735
y tan presto, arrepentida,
que tú mi venganza seas!

	It was Hernando in disguise	
	Who play-acted Estefanía.	
FENISA	Your treachery is crystal clear.	
	You've arrived too late, Lucindo.	
	Please don't make me lose all respect	2710
	For you, since in less than an hour	
	You'll be my father, having wed	
	My mother and, as her husband,	
	Acquire that rank and that title.	
LUCINDO	What are you saying?	
FENISA	What you've heard.	2715
LUCINDO	Have you lost your mind?	
FENISA	Not at all.	
LUCINDO	Well, one of the two of us has.	
FENISA	Go ahead; create a scandal.	
	My husband will be here shortly.	
LUCINDO	God help me!	
FENISA	Fine; no one else will.	2720
LUCINDO	Should I kill myself?	
FENISA	How puerile!	
LUCINDO	Then what should I do?	
FENISA	Get married.	
LUCINDO	But	
	Don't you see that my love has been	
	Genuine, and yours just a game?	
	Don't you see that I came for you,	2725
	And that like a man I fulfilled	
	What I had agreed to last night?	
	Don't you see I chose you as my	
	Wife, little though that interests you?	
	Don't you see how justified it	2730
	Is when we men speak ill of you	
	Ladies? Don't you see how I've been	
	Ready and willing, honoring	
	What we had said before we'd do?	
	I hope to God you see what you	2735
	Have done and then seek repentance;	
	That would be my perfect revenge.	

Que en lo que toca a mi vida,
será lo que tú deseas.
   Goza a mi padre, que es padre,   2740
y es mejor que yo en efeto,
puesto que menos te cuadre;
que yo seré tan discreto,
que la mujer trueque en madre;
   que pues mi padre me envía   2745
a Portugal, porque tal
delito en quererte hacía,
me pasaré a Portugal
por la libertad, que es mía.

Vase.

FENISA   Ay, Dios!, detente señor...   2750
[aguarda mi lindo amor,
suspende, querido esposo.]
Pero no, que es cauteloso.
Vaya esta vez el traidor.

Sale Hernando.

HERNANDO   Oye, escucha.
FENISA   ¿Qué haces señas?   2755
HERNANDO   ¡Tan tibia en esta ocasión!
¿Cómo ese rigor me enseñas?
   ....
   ....
   ¿No vino Lucindo aquí,   2760
según me dijo, por ti?
FENISA   Ya estamos desconcertados.
HERNANDO   ¿Cómo?
FENISA   Hay amores casados;
no era bueno para mí.
   ¿Quién es una Estefanía   2765
a quien Lucindo quería?
HERNANDO   ¿Hasta acá llega el enredo?
FENISA   ¿Qué enredo?
HERNANDO   Decirte puedo

As for my life in the future,
It's sure to be what you would want.
I wish you joy with my father;   2740
He's a real one, and more fitting
For you as father than husband.
I will be discreet, exchanging
The wife I sought for a mother.
And now, since my father exiles   2745
Me to Portugal for the crime
Of having loved you, I'll go to
Portugal and there find the peace
And liberty that is my right.

Exit Lucindo.

FENISA   Oh, dear God! Sir, don't go! Come back!   2750
Don't leave me now my darling one.
Wait, wait, my one and only love!
But, no. No. I have to be strong.
It's best to let the traitor go.

Enter Hernando.

HERNANDO   Psst, Fenisa!
FENISA   What do you want?   2755
HERNANDO   Whoa, there! What's the matter with you?
Why so cold and unwelcoming?
....
....
Didn't Lucindo come for you,   2760
As he earlier said he would?
FENISA   He did, but I've broken with him.
HERNANDO   Why?
FENISA   He's involved with a married
Woman, and that I can't accept.
Who is that Estefanía   2765
With whom Lucindo is in love?
HERNANDO   My God! The plot has come to this?
FENISA   What plot?
HERNANDO   Listen to what I tell

que fui yo esa dama un día.

FENISA   ¿Tú esa dama?

HERNANDO   Disfrazado   2770
con un manto, estuve al lado
de cierta dama. En efeto
di celos; y esto secreto,
no sepa que lo he contado.
    Que mi señor la quería   2775
antes que os viese; y después
os juro, señora mía,
que un tigre a sus ojos es,
aunque se cansa y porfía;
    que anda perdida y celosa.   2780

FENISA Sin duda me han engañado.

HERNANDO Yo sé que no hay otra cosa
que le dé en Madrid cuidado
sino vos, Fenisa hermosa.
    Mas ¿qué le diré?

FENISA   No sé;   2785
que viene mi madre aquí.
Huye.

HERNANDO   Por allí me iré.

Vase.
Sale Belisa.

BELISA Ya, Fenisa, despedí
aquel hombre.

FENISA   Y ¿cómo fue?

BELISA   No sé si podré, de risa,   2790
contarte lo que ha pasado.

FENISA De todo, madre, me avisa.

BELISA De verte se ha enamorado.

FENISA ¿Tan presto?

BELISA   Escucha, Fenisa;
que te quiere por mujer.   2795

FENISA ¿Siendo casado?

BELISA   Es enredo
que esta mujer quiso hacer.

	You. I myself was that woman.	
FENISA	You were the woman?	
HERNANDO	Yes. Disguised	2770

In a cloak, I sat next to a
Certain lady, and she became
Jealous. Keep this as a secret;
No one must know that I've told you.
My master loved her before he   2775
Set eyes on you. And then later,
I swear to you, dear lady, she
Became like an enraged tigress,
Scratching, scheming for all she's worth;
That's how envious she was then.   2780

FENISA   I can see now I've been deceived.
HERNANDO   I know, beautiful Fenisa,
You are the only thing in all
Madrid he truly cares about.
What should I tell him?

FENISA   I don't know;   2785
But I hear my mother coming.
Leave quickly now.

HERNANDO   I'll go through here.

Exit Hernando.
Enter Belisa.

BELISA   At long last, Fenisa, I'm free
Of that man.

FENISA   Well, how did it go?

BELISA   I'm not sure I can tell you what   2790
Happened, I've been laughing so much.

FENISA   So I see, but try anyway.
BELISA   He saw you and he fell in love!
FENISA   What? That fast?
BELISA   That's not all, my dear;
He says he wants to marry you.   2795

FENISA   But he *is* married!
BELISA   That's a ploy
Fabricated by that woman.

FENISA	Que son celos tengo miedo.	
BELISA	Celos debieron de ser.	
	Contome que concertaron	2800
	que se hiciese su marido,	
	porque los dos sospecharon,	
	él que su hermana ha servido	
	y ella que aquí le engañaron.	
FENISA	¿A quién?	
BELISA	A Lucindo.	
FENISA	¡Bien!	2805
	¿Que de Lucindo son celos?	
BELISA	Y a mí me los dan también	
FENISA	Pusieron en paz los celos	
	su verdad y mi desdén.	
	Perdí gallarda ocasión	2810
	de gozarle a mi contento;	
	mas no faltará invención.	
	Hoy será mi casamiento	
	en casa y con bendición.	
	Madre, no estés divertida.	2815
	Después que esta cautelosa	
	mujer, falsa y atrevida,	
	vino sin vida, celosa,	
	para quitarnos la vida,	
	ha estado Lucindo aquí	2820
	y me ha dicho que [te] adora.	
BELISA	¿Es cierto?	
FENISA	Esto pasa ansí.	
	Pero díceme, señora,	
	que hablando a su padre en ti	
	le halla muy desabrido	2825
	en que sea tu marido,	
	y que es forzoso, en [efeto],	
	el [casaros] de secreto.	
BELISA	Siempre lo tuve entendido.	
	No quisiera el Capitán	2830
	que su hijo se casara	
	donde m[u]rmurar podrán	

FENISA	I presume jealousy's to blame.
BELISA	I've no doubt you're right about that.
	He said they had devised the scheme 2800
	To confirm what each suspected:
	He, that a certain fellow was
	After his sister; she, that the
	Same man was betraying her here.
FENISA	Who's the man?
BELISA	Lucindo.
FENISA	So then 2805
	It's Lucindo they're jealous of?
BELISA	And not only them; I am too.
FENISA	Her jealousy was tempered when she
	Heard the truth and witnessed my scorn.
	(Aside.) (Have I lost my one chance to share 2810
	A life of happiness with him?
	No! Once more I'll think my way through!
	Today I'll marry in this house,
	And with everybody's blessing.)
	Mother, please pay close attention. 2815
	After that conniving, brazen,
	And false-hearted woman came here,
	Half dead and filled with jealousy,
	Just to destroy your life and mine,
	Lucindo also arrived and 2820
	Told me how much he adored you.
BELISA	Can that be true?
FENISA	That's what he said.
	But he also mentioned, Mother,
	That when he spoke to his father
	About you, the Captain opposed 2825
	His plan to become your husband;
	Therefore it's necessary for
	You two to marry in secret.
BELISA	I had always suspected that.
	The Captain would never have wished 2830
	His son to be married to me,
	Because people would gossip that

	que el viejo goza esa cara,	
	y que a Lucindo me dan,	
	pues mi marido ha de ser.	2835
FENISA	Él dice que en tu aposento	
	te quiere esta noche ver.	
BELISA	¿Qué sientes de eso?	
FENISA	¿Qué siento?	
	¡Que allí serás su mujer!	
BELISA	Trázalo, pues anochece.	2840
FENISA	Vete a prevenir y calla.	
BELISA	Mi ventura me enloquece;	
	por no darte que envidialla,	
	no digo lo que me [ofrece].	
	Voy a perfumarlo todo	2845
	y que esté con grande aseo.	

Vase.

FENISA	Hazlo, madre, de ese modo.	
	¡Qué bien mis bodas rodeo,	
	y el nuevo engaño acomodo!	

Sale el Capitán.

CAPITÁN	¿Es mi Fenisa?	
FENISA	Soy quien te desea.	2850 *versos sueltos*
	¿Adónde está Lucindo? que mi madre	
	ya quiere efectuar el casamiento.	
CAPITÁN	¿Qué casamiento?	
FENISA	El suyo con el mío.	
CAPITÁN	Bien dice, y no aguardemos a más términos;	
	que ya los dos tenemos corta vida.	2855
FENISA	Yo estoy, señor, también desengañada	
	de que no era Lucindo el que venía	
	de noche a mi ventana.	
CAPITÁN	¿Qué me cuentas?	
FENISA	Hoy supe que era un cierto amigo suyo;	
	y así, quiero que vayas a buscarle,	2860
	y le digas que ronde aquesta noche	
	la puerta desta casa con Hernando;	

	Your pretty face would go to an	
	Old man, and mine to Lucindo.	
	But he will become my husband!	2835
FENISA	He says that this very evening	
	He'll come to you in your bedroom.	
BELISA	To my bedroom? What for?	
FENISA	Isn't	
	It clear? There you'll become his wife.	
BELISA	Then make it happen! Night is near!	2840
FENISA	Hush, now, and go prepare yourself.	
BELISA	I simply can't believe my good	
	Fortune. So you won't be jealous	
	I won't speak of what awaits me.	
	I'm going to perfume the whole room,	2845
	And make it warm and inviting.	

Exit Belisa.

FENISA	That's a good idea. Do so.	
	My marriage now is all but set;	
	My wits have never failed me yet	

Enter the Captain.

CAPTAIN	Fenisa?	
FENISA	Yes, I've been waiting for you here.	2850
	But where is Lucindo? My mother has said	
	That she's ready for the marriage to take place.	
CAPTAIN	What marriage?	
FENISA	Both of them. Hers, but mine also.	
CAPTAIN	She's quite right. There's no point in further delay.	
	Neither of us is getting any younger.	2855
FENISA	But now it's my duty to inform you, sir,	
	That it was not Lucindo who came to my	
	Window last night.	
CAPTAIN	It wasn't? Who was it then?	
FENISA	I found out today it was a friend of his.	
	So I must ask you to go seek him out and	2860
	Tell him that he and Hernando are to stand	

porque anoche a las diez, por la ventana
del huerto entró el amigo que te digo,
y a la puerta llamó de mi aposento.
Levanteme, pensando que mi madre   2865
venía a visitarme, y si no cierro,
no dudes que sucede una desgracia.

CAPITÁN   ¡Hay maldad semejante! ¡Vive el cielo,
que he de ser yo quien ronde!

FENISA   No, mis ojos;   2870
que en ese tiempo habéis de estar conmigo.

CAPITÁN   ¿Adónde?

FENISA   En mi aposento, de secreto.

CAPITÁN   Dadme esas manos.

FENISA   Advertid que quiero
que vengáis muy galán y rebozado,   2875
y que os hagáis la barba; que no gusto
de verla de esa hechura; que en efeto
pareceréis mejor más atusado.

CAPITÁN   Quien para tanta gloria se previene,
no dudéis que vendrá galán del todo.
La barba haré cortar a vuestro gusto,
pues hacerse la barba es muy de novios;   2880
y yo lo he de ser vuestro.

FENISA   Ya es muy tarde,
hablad a vuestro hijo.

CAPITÁN   El cielo os guarde.

Vanse.
[Salen Lucindo y Hernando.]

LUCINDO   Arrepintiose.

HERNANDO   ¿Qué dices?   *redondillas*

LUCINDO   Lo que oyes.

HERNANDO   No lo creas.   2885

LUCINDO   Ni tú mudanzas que veas.

HERNANDO Son retóricos matices

	Guard this evening by the front door of the house,	
	Because last night, around ten, the friend whom I	
	Mentioned climbed over the gate of the garden,	
	Got inside, and knocked right on my bedroom door.	2865
	I got up, thinking that it was my mother	
	Who had come to see me, and if I hadn't	
	Slammed the door shut who knows what	
	might have happened!	

CAPTAIN Who ever heard of such iniquity! By
God, tonight I myself will guard the door.

FENISA   No,   2870
My dear one; tonight you are to be with me.

CAPTAIN Yes; where?

FENISA   In my bedroom, unbeknownst to all.

CAPTAIN How I've longed for this. Give me your hand.

FENISA   But you
Must appear as a true gallant, covered up,
And with your beard clipped. I don't like to see you
With all that hair, and you'll look far better and
Certainly more youthful when you've been trimmed up.

CAPTAIN Have no fear. The one who awaits a night of
Glory will take pains with every detail.
I'll cut my beard exactly as you desire,   2880
Since that is what the groom – a title I bear
Proudly – does for his bride.

FENISA   But it's getting late.
Go speak to your son.

CAPTAIN   May heaven preserve you.

Exit Fenisa and the Captain.
The house of the Captain.
Enter Lucindo and Hernando.

LUCINDO She changed her mind.

HERNANDO   What did you say?

LUCINDO You heard me.

HERNANDO   Don't you believe it.   2885

LUCINDO I'm telling you, she's not the same.

HERNANDO You're making that up so I'll be

	para encarecerme el bien.	
	¿Hasla por dicha gozado?	
	Que te veo muy mirlado.	2890
LUCINDO	Y aun muerto me ves también.	
HERNANDO	¿Hablas de veras?	
LUCINDO	Llegué	
	para sacalla de allí,	
	y de manera la vi,	
	que dando voces bajé.	2895
	Volví el coche, y los amigos	
	se volvieron [a su casa].	
HERNANDO	[Pues ella] toda se abrasa,	
	y estos ojos son testigos...	
LUCINDO	¿Cómo?	
HERNANDO	...de celos crüeles.	2900
LUCINDO	Pues ¿de quién?	
HERNANDO	De Estefanía.	
LUCINDO	¡Que esto dure todavía!	
	No me aflijas, como sueles;	
	que todo nace de amor.	
HERNANDO	¡Tu padre!	
LUCINDO	No importa nada.	2905

Sale el Capitán.

CAPITÁN	Bien aprestas la jornada.	
LUCINDO	Mañana me voy, señor.	
CAPITÁN	¡Bueno es eso! Estás casado	
	con Belisa, y ¿vaste luego?	
LUCINDO	Eso ha sido burla y juego.	2910
CAPITÁN	Yo sé que tomas estado;	
	pero que sea o no sea,	
	ya te quedarás aquí.	
LUCINDO	¿Por qué?	
CAPITÁN	Porque ya entendí	
	quién a Fenisa desea,	2915
	y aún es grande amigo [tuyo.]	
LUCINDO	También te habrán engañado.	
CAPITÁN	Ya Fenisa me ha contado	

	More impressed by your great triumph.	
	You got her in bed, didn't you?	
	You're looking pretty grim and grave.	2890
LUCINDO	Grave, indeed! Fit for a dead man.	
HERNANDO	Are you telling the truth?	
LUCINDO	I went	

To her house to take her away,
But found her in such a state that,
With harsh words, I soon turned and left.   2895
I dismissed the coach, and the friends
With me all returned to their homes.

HERNANDO   I tell you she's madly in love,
And these eyes of mine bear witness...

LUCINDO   To what?

HERNANDO   ...To cruel jealousy.   2900

LUCINDO   Of whom?

HERNANDO   Of Estefanía.

LUCINDO   Is that rubbish still going on?
Don't ever mention it again.
Love is the cause of everything.

HERNANDO   Your father!

LUCINDO   It doesn't matter.   2905

Enter the Captain.

CAPTAIN   I see you're all set to travel.

LUCINDO   I'll be going tomorrow, sir.

CAPTAIN   That's really something. You marry
Belisa, and then off you go.

LUCINDO   That was all a game and a joke.   2910

CAPTAIN   You said you were getting married
But whether you do or you don't
You're staying here at least for now.

LUCINDO   Why?

CAPTAIN   Because I've learned who it is
Who's chasing Fenisa, and it   2915
Turns out to be a friend of yours.

LUCINDO   It seems that you've been duped, also.

CAPTAIN   No. Fenisa has explained that

que fue todo engaño suyo.
 Dice que anoche pasó   2920
por la pared de la huerta
cierta persona, o incïerta,
y a su aposento llegó:
 llamó, salió [a] abrir y viendo
el engaño, cerró.

LUCINDO   Extraño   2925
hubiera sido el engaño.

CAPITÁN Dio voces, y fuese huyendo.
 Hame dicho que te diga
rondes esta noche allí.
Haraslo ansí?

LUCINDO   [Señor, sí;]   2930
mandármelo tú me obliga.

CAPITÁN Pues yo vengo muy de prisa.
Ármate, y guárdete Dios.

Vase.

LUCINDO Hoy nos casamos los dos.
HERNANDO ¿Cómo?
LUCINDO   Ya entiendo a Fenisa,   2935
 quiere que entre a su aposento
por el huerto.

HERNANDO   Dices bien,
y que ella estará también
allí con el mismo intento.
 Mas los celos le han picado;   2940
hoy se cumplen tus deseos.

LUCINDO ¡Por qué notables rodeos
a mi remedio he llegado!
 Vente a armar, porque has de entrar
al huerto y guardar la puerta.   2945

HERNANDO Beatriz es dama encubierta;
pero allá la pienso hablar.

Vanse.
Salen Doristeo y Finardo.

	She was the one who was deceived.	
	She says that last night someone or	2920
	Other tiptoed into the house	
	After scaling the garden gate,	
	And got as far as her bedroom	
	Door. He knocked, she opened, and seeing	
	The perfidy slammed the door.	
LUCINDO	Who	2925
	Knows what the outcome might have been!	
CAPTAIN	She screamed and he took off running.	
	She told me to tell you that she	
	Wishes you to stand guard tonight.	
	Will you do it?	
LUCINDO	Yes, sir. Of course.	2930
	Your order is my sworn duty.	
CAPTAIN	I've much to do right now, but arm	
	Yourself well and God preserve you.	

Exit the Captain.

LUCINDO	Tonight our marriage will take place.	
HERNANDO	Yes? How so?	
LUCINDO	I know Fenisa.	2935
	She wants me to come to her room	
	Through the garden.	
HERNANDO	That's it for sure.	
	And you can bet she'll be there too	
	With the same idea as you.	
	It's jealousy that spurred her on.	2940
	Tonight all your wishes come true!	
LUCINDO	I can't believe all the detours	
	It's taken to get to this point.	
	Go get armed; tonight you're to slip	
	Into the garden and stand guard.	2945
HERNANDO	Beatriz is a proper lady,	
	But I bet I'll find her there too.	

Exit Lucindo and Hernando.
The street.
Enter Doristeo and Finardo.

FINARDO	Yo no sé si le llame desengaño	*octavas reales*
	el que de vuestra hermana habéis tenido,	
	pues veo que resulta en vuestro daño,	2950
	viniendo de Fenisa tan rendido.	
DORISTEO	Hizo Gerarda aquel enredo extraño.	
	Entré fingiendo que era su marido;	
	pero en viendo a Fenisa, quedé luego	
	ciego del rayo de su ardiente fuego.	2955
	Estuve con su madre en su aposento;	
	y si verdad os digo, dije el caso,	
	y pedile a Fenisa [en] casamiento.	
FINARDO	Éstas son sus ventanas; hablad paso.	
DORISTEO	¡Ay divino y dichoso alojamiento	2960
	de la décima musa del Parnaso,	
	de la mujer más bella, y fénix solo	
	que en la dama del Toro ha visto Apolo!	
FINARDO	Y qué, ¿os pensáis casar?	
DORISTEO	¡Si ella me quiere!	
FINARDO	¿Es gente principal?	
DORISTEO	De virtud tanta,	2965
	que la doncella a las demás prefiere,	
	y la madre, Finardo, es una santa.	
FINARDO	¿Qué hacienda tiene?	
DORISTEO	Sea la que fuere,	
	virtud en dote a todos se adelanta.	
	De su recogimiento y virtud quiero	2970
	hacer, Finardo, el dote verdadero.	

[Salen] el Capitán, con barba diferente, muy hecha, en hábito de noche; y Fulminato.

CAPITÁN	Ya puedes volverte a casa.	*redondillas*
FINARDO	Gente pasa.	
DORISTEO	Y encubierta.	
FINARDO	Creo que para a la puerta;	
	que de la puerta no pasa.	2975
FULMINATO	¿Mandas que te aguarde aquí,	
	o que llame otros criados?	
CAPITÁN	No, que aquellos embozados	

FINARDO	I'm not certain that clearing up the matter
	Of your sister was such a constructive thing,
	Because I see that the consequence has been 2950
	That you're now madly in love with Fenisa.
DORISTEO	It was Gerarda who dreamed up that little play.
	I burst in pretending to be her husband,
	But once I saw Fenisa her beauty struck
	Me blind, just as if I'd been hit by lightning. 2955
	I withdrew with her mother into her room;
	There I explained the subterfuge to her and
	Asked for the hand of Fenisa in marriage.
FINARDO	Aren't those her windows over there? Speak softly.
DORISTEO	Oh, most divine, happy, and blessed dwelling 2960
	Of the unrivalled tenth muse of Parnassus,
	The most beautiful woman ever, lovely
	As Europa, who was adored by Zeus.
FINARDO	So you plan to marry her?
DORISTEO	If she'll have me.
FINARDO	Is her family a good one?
DORISTEO	Of high regard. 2965
	Fenisa outshines all other young women,
	And her mother, Finardo, is a real saint.
FINARDO	Are they rich?
DORISTEO	I don't have any idea.
	But a good name is more important than wealth.
	I intend to make their reputation and 2970
	Their well-recognized virtue my true dowry.

Enter the Captain, dressed in formal evening clothes with his beard trimmed, and Fulminato.

CAPTAIN	*(To Fulminato.)* That's all for now. You may go home.
FINARDO	Someone's coming.
DORISTEO	All covered up.
FINARDO	He's pausing there at the door, and
	It seems he's not going farther. 2975
FULMINATO	Are you certain you don't need me?
	Should I go to call for more help?
CAPTAIN	Those two fellows there, with their cloaks

vienen a guardarme a mí.
[Entro], vuélvete.

FULMINATO   ¿Quién son?   2980
CAPITÁN   Lucindo y Hernando.

[Vase el Capitán.]

FULMINATO   Quiero
hablarlos.
FINARDO   Entró.
DORISTEO   ¿Qué espero?
FINARDO   ¡Gran virtud! ¡Gran religión!
FULMINATO   ¿Es menester compañía?
FINARDO   Pase adelante, galán.   2985
FULMINATO Perdonen.
DORISTEO   Perdón le dan.
FULMINATO Que por otros los tenía.

Vase.

DORISTEO   ¡Corrido estoy, vive Dios!
FINARDO   ¡Qué gran dote es la virtud!
DORISTEO   Tal les dé Dios la salud.   2990
FINARDO   Pues quedo.
DORISTEO   ¿Cómo?
FINARDO   ¡Otros dos!

Salen Lucindo y Hernando.

LUCINDO   Pies, en mi amor os tened.
            [Por la escala se llegará.]
DORISTEO   ¿Echó escala?
FINARDO   ¡Y suben ya,
            [traspasando la pared!]   2995
DORISTEO   ¿Qué casa es ésta?
FINARDO   No sé.
            Que es fuerza es lo más seguro,
            pues por la puerta y el muro
            tanto enemigo se ve.

Pulled up, are here to protect me.
I'm going in. Leave.

FULMINATO   Who are they?   2980
CAPTAIN   Lucindo and his man.

Exit the Captain.

FULMINATO   I'll speak
With them.
FINARDO   He's gone.
DORISTEO   *(Aside.)*   (Why am I waiting?)
FINARDO   *(Aside.)* (Such forbearance! Such trust in God!)
FULMINATO May I have a word?
FINARDO   Be gone, sir!   2985
FULMINATO I beg your pardon.
DORISTEO   You have it.
FULMINATO I thought you were some men I know.

Exit Fulminato.

DORISTEO   I tell you, I'm so embarrassed.
FINARDO   Self-control is a sacred gift!
DORISTEO   Then may God grant it to them too!   2990
FINARDO   Quiet!
DORISTEO   Why?
FINARDO   Two more are coming.

Enter Lucindo and Hernando with a ladder.

LUCINDO   Feet, my love depends on you now.
This ladder will get me over.
DORISTEO   They've got a ladder!
FINARDO   They're climbing
Over the gate next to that house.   2995

Exit Lucindo and Hernando.

DORISTEO   Whose house is it?
FINARDO   I can't be sure.
But it sure looks like a fortress,
One that's besieged by enemies,
All of them trying to break in.

DORISTEO	¿Suben los dos?
FINARDO	Así pasa.
DORISTEO	Muchas mujeres habrá.
FINARDO	Pues más gente viene ya;

que aún no está llena la casa.   3000

Sale Gerarda, en hábito de hombre.

GERARDA   Por ver si aquel mi enemigo
viene a rondar por aquí,   3005
salgo de mi casa ansí,
con mi amor y sin testigo.
    No creo que me he engañado;
él y su Hernando serán
los que en esta esquina están.   3010
¡A qué buen tiempo he llegado!
    ¿Eres tú, crüel?

DORISTEO   ¿Quién va?

GERARDA   Yo soy, Lucindo.

DORISTEO   ¿Quién?

GERARDA   Yo.

DORISTEO   ¿[Mi] Gerarda?

GERARDA   Tuya, no;
de Doristeo soy ya.   3015

DORISTEO   Yo soy ese Doristeo.

GERARDA   ¡Tú! Pues ¿qué buscas aquí?

DORISTEO   A ti te busco.

GERARDA   ¡Tú a mí!

FINARDO   Con un mismo intento os veo;
    tú por Fenisa venías,   3020
y tú por Lucindo vienes.

DORISTEO   Es sin duda.

GERARDA   Razón tienes.

DORISTEO   Hoy habemos sido espías;
    mas mira ¡qué cosa aquésta!
Tres hombres tienen allá.   3025

GERARDA   ¿Tres hombres?

FINARDO   Y aun treinta habrá.

DORISTEO	Are they both over?	
FINARDO	I think so.	3000
DORISTEO	There must be a lot of women in	
	There.	
FINARDO	More people are arriving.	
	I guess the house isn't full yet.	

Enter Gerarda in the clothes of a man.

GERARDA	*(Aside.)* I left my home dressed like this, with	
	Only my love for company,	3005
	To see if that man, my dearest	
	Enemy, is prowling around.	
	I don't believe I've been deceived.	
	He and Hernando must be those	
	Two men standing on the corner.	3010
	I see I've come at the right time.	
	Is that you, cruel one?	
DORISTEO	Who's there?	
GERARDA	It is I, Lucindo.	
DORISTEO	Who?	
GERARDA	I.	
DORISTEO	My Gerarda?	
GERARDA	No longer yours.	
	My love is Doristeo now.	3015
DORISTEO	Don't you see? I'm Doristeo.	
GERARDA	You? Well, what are *you* doing here?	
DORISTEO	I was looking for you.	
GERARDA	For me?	
FINARDO	It's clear you share the same purpose,	
	Since *you* came to see Fenisa,	3020
	And *you* came to see Lucindo.	
DORISTEO	I confess you're right.	
GERARDA	We've been caught.	
DORISTEO	I'm afraid we're acting like spies.	
	But what's going on in that house?	
	There are three different men inside.	3025
GERARDA	Three men?	
FINARDO	And who knows? Maybe more!	

GERARDA	¡A fe que es Fenisa honesta!	
	Llama con una invención	
	para que quién son sepamos.	
FINARDO	Fuego, que hay fuego digamos.	3030
DORISTEO	Y no con poca razón.	
FINARDO	¡Fuego, fuego!	
DORISTEO	¡Fuego!	
GERARDA	¡Fuego!	

Dentro Belisa.

BELISA	¡Fuego en mi casa! ¡Ah, crïados!	
DORISTEO	¡Fuego!	
BELISA	¡Ah, vecinos honrados!	
	¡Fenisa, levanta luego!	3035

Dentro Fenisa.

FENISA	¡Fuego, madre!	
DORISTEO	Que se abrasa	
	la casa.	

Dentro Lucindo.

LUCINDO	Luces de presto.

Salen el Capitán, Belisa, Lucindo, Hernando, con una hacha encendida.

CAPITÁN	¿Fuego en la casa?	
BELISA	¿Qué es esto?	
LUCINDO	¿Fuego en casa?	
FENISA	[¡Fuego en casa!]	
HERNANDO	¿Dónde, señor, está el fuego?	3040
GERARDA	Entre vosotros está;	
	pero nadie lo verá,	
	estando el honor tan ciego.	
	¡Dentro de una casa honrada	
	de una mujer como vos,	3045
	hay dos hombres!	
DORISTEO	¿Cómo dos?	
	Y aun tres.	
HERNANDO	¡Hermosa empanada!	

GERARDA	But Fenisa's an honest woman!
	We should think of something to yell
	So we'll find out who those men are.
FINARDO	How about "Fire! Fire in the house!" 3030
DORISTEO	I'd say that's quite appropriate.
FINARDO	Hallo! Fire! Fire!
DORISTEO	Help, fire!
GERARDA	Fire! Fire!
BELISA	*(Offstage.)* Servants, wake up! There's a fire here!
DORISTEO	Fire!
BELISA	*(Offstage.)* Neighbors! Everyone! Wake up!
	Get up, Fenisa! Now! At once! 3035
FENISA	*(Offstage.)* Mother! Fire!
DORISTEO	The house is burning
	Down!
LUCINDO	*(Offstage.)* I can't see! Someone bring lights!

Enter the Captain, Belisa, Lucindo, and Fenisa in night dress, and Hernando, carrying a lit torch.

CAPTAIN	Fire in the house?
BELISA	What's happening?
LUCINDO	Fire in the house?
FENISA	Fire in the house?
HERNANDO	You say there's fire. But where is it? 3040
GERARDA	I'd say the fire is in you all;
	But nobody can see it since
	Honor here has turned a blind eye.
	To think that in the house of a
	Respectable woman like you 3045
	There are two men!
DORISTEO	Just two? I count
	Three!
HERNANDO	A triple-decker sandwich!

BELISA	Yo con mi marido estoy.
CAPITÁN	Y yo estoy con mi mujer.
BELISA	Otro pensé yo tener.
CAPITÁN	De otra que aborrezco soy.
BELISA	¿Cómo es aquesto, Fenisa?
FENISA	Con Lucindo me he casado.
BELISA	Pues ¿cómo me has engañado?
	Mas ya lo dice tu risa.
CAPITÁN	Di, Lucindo, ¿a un padre noble
	los buenos hijos engañan?
LUCINDO	Señor, yo adoro a Fenisa,
	y ella, como ves, me paga.
	Cuanto contigo trató
	son enredos que buscaba
	para casarse conmigo;
	los que presentes se hallan
	aunque mis contrarios sean,
	juzguen, señor, nuestra causa.
	¿No es mejor que el padre mío,
	con esta señora honrada,
	que es madre de mi mujer,
	se case, pues que se igualan
	en méritos y en edad,
	y que como nuestras almas,
	los dos juntemos los pechos?
	Habla, y perdona Gerarda.
GERARDA	Aunque celosa venía,
	la razón, Lucindo, es tanta,
	que con los dos asesores
	que a este pleito me acompañan,
	digo que tu padre sea
	de Belisa, y que esta dama
	te goce, amén, muchos años.
DORISTEO	La sentencia está bien dada,
	y yo la confirmo.
FINARDO	Y yo.
LUCINDO	Dame esa mano.
FENISA	Y el alma.

3050

3055

romance a-a

3060

3065

3070

3075

3080

BELISA I tell you, I'm with my husband.
CAPTAIN That's the truth. And I'm with my wife.
BELISA Although he's not the one I chose.
CAPTAIN And she's not the one I'd hoped for.
BELISA Daughter, what's the meaning of this?
FENISA Lucindo and I are married.
BELISA So, you deceived your own mother?
I see from your laughter that's true.
CAPTAIN Lucindo, do devoted sons
Trick their noble fathers like this?
LUCINDO Sir, my only excuse is I
Adore Fenisa, and she, me.
All the things she arranged with you
Were ruses that she devised so
The two of us could be married.
Though they be opponents of mine,
Let us allow those who are here
To judge the rightness of our cause.
(To the others.) Isn't it better that my father
Should marry this honored lady,
The mother of my wife, since the
Two of them are equal in age
And In merit; and that we two,
Who have already joined our souls,
Should now join our bodies as well?
Speak, Gerarda, and please forgive me.
GERARDA Although I came filled with jealous
Thoughts, Lucindo, you have reason
On your side, and thus along with
These other judges of your cause,
I say that your father belongs
To Belisa, and that I wish
You and your lady years of joy.
DORISTEO The judgment is well delivered,
And I confirm it.
FINARDO As do I.
LUCINDO Give me your hand.
FENISA My hand and soul.

CAPITÁN	Dadme vos también la vuestra.	
BELISA	Dais honra y remedio a entrambas.	3085
HERNANDO	Para tan viejo rocín	
	cualquiera silla le basta.	
GERARDA	Los dos me acompañaréis.	
DORISTEO	Llevémoste a tu casa.	
CAPITÁN	Hernando, avisa en la mía	3090
	que allá cenan estas damas.	
HERNANDO	Para en uno sois, ¡por Dios!	
LUCINDO	Si es para muchos la farsa,	
	mi amor lo diga, y dé fin	
	La discreta enamorada.	3095

FIN

CAPTAIN	And I, Belisa, ask for yours.	
BELISA	You do honor to both of us.	3085
HERNANDO	*(Aside.)* (For an ancient war-horse like him	
	Any old saddle will make do.)	
GERARDA	And now I'm off. Please come along.	
DORISTEO	We'll be happy to see you home.	
CAPTAIN	Hernando, give word in my house	3090
	That these two ladies will dine there.	
HERNANDO	Congratulations to you all!	
LUCINDO	And if our play seems but a farce,	
	Blame it on love, and bid farewell	
	To *The Cleverest Girl in Madrid*.	3095

THE END

NOTES

Abbreviations

Cov.   Covarrubias
Dic. Aut.   Diccionario de Autoridades
DLE   *Diccionario de la lengua española*

Act 1

Leonardo su criado. mentioned in the cast of characters, but does not appear in the play.

5.   **bachillera**: know-it-all, impertinent young woman.

32. **liciones**: *lecciones*. Throughout we maintain some archaic usage, especially to respect the rhyme. See Introduction.

34. **trujiste**: trajiste.

34. **Jubileo/**Jubilee: In the strict sense of the term, a period of time proclaimed by the Pope to be a season of rejoicing, marked by a plenary indulgence granted upon repentance and the performance of certain religious acts; by extension, any season or occasion of rejoicing or festivity. [Cf. *Dic. Aut. 1734: Rigurosamente significa la solemnidad y ceremonia Eclesiástica, con que el Papa publica la concessión que hace de gracias y Indulgéncias, a la Iglesia universal... Se llaman por extensión las demás gracias, indulgéncias y perdones, que conceden los sumos Pontífices en qualquier tiempo*].

38. **estremos haces**: (*hacer extremos*) to speak wildly and vehemently. [Cf. *Dic. Aut. 1732: Lamentarse, haciendo con ánsia y despecho varios ademanes, y dando voces y quejas en demonstración de sentimiento*].

40. **me acabes**: (*acabarle a alguien*) to attack verbally, sharply criticize someone.

41. **ojos/**eyes: 'Eyes' and 'looking' constitute a repeated motif in the play. The impression given is that the characters are constantly observing – and judging – each other. See Introduction.

48. **morirse de ojo**: to die from being bewitched by the evil eye. See introduction. [Cf. Burgos: *Ojo equivale aquí a mal de ojo, es decir, a la supuesta influencia maligna que una persona puede ejercer sobre otra al mirarla de un modo concreto.*]

50. **al soslayo**: askance, sidewise, obliquely. [Cf. *Dic. Aut. 1739: obliquamente, al través*].

60. **cazadores/**hunters: 'Hunting' and 'fishing' are another prominent motif in the play. See Introduction.

74. **hacienda**: wealth, accumulation of earthly goods.

79. *lindo*: an effeminate man, vain about his (presumed) attractiveness, and obsessed with his grooming and appearance. [Cf. *Dic. Aut. 1734: Usado como substantivo, se toma por el hombre afeminado, presumido de hermoso, y que cuida demasiado de su compostúra y aseo*].

89. *chacota*: noisy mirth, joking around. [Cf. *Dic. Aut 1729: Bulla y alegria llena de risa, chanzas, voces y carcajadas, con que se celebra algún festejo, o se divierte algúna conversación*].

92. *a[l]galia*: a sticky substance emitted from a gland found near the anus of civets when they are frightened. Highly aromatic, it is used in the making of perfume. [Cf. *Dic. Aut 1726: El sudór que despide de sí el gato llamado de algália: al qual se le fatiga batiendole con unas varas, de suerte que se le hace sudar, y recogiendo el sudór con una cucharilla junto hace como una espécie de mantéca, la qual es sumamente odorífera*].

103–4. ***Vaya a poner esa tienda / a las Indias del Perú***: Go set up that shop in Perú. Gerarda sarcastically refers to the tremendous output of the Spanish colonial silver mines in Peru and Mexico that lowered the value of silver relative to gold from 10.5 to 1 around 1500 to 15.5 to 1 by 1800. See 'Colonial Spanish America'.

108. *argenterías*: silverwork, silver embroidery.

124. *mosquetazo*: a shot from a musket, a 16th-century firearm that is the predecessor of the modern rifle; by extension, any blow or hit.

140. *Prado*: See introduction. Note that after this speech, Gerarda does not, in fact, go to the Prado, but apparently returns home.

142. *martelo*: gallantry, sweet-talk, oftentimes insincere; also jealousy.

146. Cerberus: in classical mythology, a three-headed dog that guarded the gates of the underworld to prevent the dead from leaving; by extension, a watchful guard of fearsome appearance.

146–7. *emprender a Irlanda*: According to Pedraza (1990), the phrase means to undertake something that is destined to fail, with particular reference to efforts on the part of Spain to assist the Irish Catholics in their struggle to gain independence from Protestant England in the time of Elizabeth I.

191. *quedo*: [be] quiet, hush. [*Dic. Aut. 1737: Lo mismo que Quieto; Usado como adverbio, vale tambien con voz mui baxa; Significa algunas veces con tiento*].

209. *randas*: lace adornments, normally crocheted or hand-woven, found on articles of clothing. [*Cf. Dic. Aut. 1737: Adorno que se suele poner en vestidos y ropas: y es una especie de encaxe, labrado con aguja o texido, el qual es más gruesso, y los nudos más apretados que los que se hacen con palillos. Las hai de hilo, lana, o seda*].

213. *v[uestra] m[erced]*: We open up the abbreviation throughout. See Introduction.

234–5. ***la calle de los jardines***: See Introduction.

243. ***porfia***: persistence, insistence, stubbornness, refusal to give up. [Cf. *Dic. Aut. 1737: Contienda o dispúta de palabras, tenaz y obstinada. Significa tambien la continuación o repetición de una cosa muchas veces, con ahinco y tesón. Se llama tambien la instancia y importunación para el logro de alguna cosa*].

287. ***coca***: (*cocar*) to make a noise, to gesticulate or put on a facial expression to frighten, or, alternatively, to capture one's goodwill in order to ask for something. [Cf. *Cov.: Cocar está tomado del sonido que hace la mona para espantar a los muchachos, y ponerles miedo, porque no le hagan mal.* Cf. also *Dic. Aut.1729: Hacer cocos ò gestos, para causar miedo y espanto: como hace la mona para poner miedo à los muchachos, porque no la hagan mal…. Metaphoricamente se toma por agradar, captar la benevoléncia, ò ganar la voluntád à algúno*].

291. ***espúlgale***: (*espulgarle a alguien*) to remove lice from someone, delouse.

294. ***hacen cocos***: See note to line 287.

315. ***estribarte***: (*estribarse*) to rely on someone or something for support. [Cf. *Dic. Aut. 1732: estribar v. n. Hacer fuerza en alguna cosa sólida y segúra, para afirmarse y apoyarse: como las paredes altas o edificios en los estríbos, que para su firmeza y estabilidad se fabrícan pegados a ellos. Metaphoricamente corresponde a fundarse, afianzarse, assegurarse, apoyarse.*]

321–8. ***Lo que aquel sabio decía***: The reference is to the Scythian philosopher Anarchisis who supposedly commented to Solon of Athens that laws are like spider webs that catch weak flies, while the strong and powerful break through.

339. ***dedo del corazón***: middle finger.

334. There is a pun here in the Spanish text involving '***mosca***' ('fly') and '***moscatel***' ('foolish and ignorant young man') that cannot be captured in English.

403. ***estaciones***/stations of the cross: As the translation indicates, the reference is to stations of the cross, a sequence of representations of fourteen incidents from the passion of Christ, normally displayed in a church, before which the faithful can pause to pray and meditate.

419. ***vosotras***: The use of the plural here is surprising. Does it imply that Fenisa has a sister?

427. The use of disdain to spark romantic interest is amusingly illustrated in *El desdén, con el desdén,* a play by Agustín de Moreto, a follower of Lope.

439. ***bostezos***: According to Pedraza (1990), *bostezo* here means anxiety, restlessness, or agitation; however, it could be an error in printing. See textual variants.

466.   *Flandes*/Flanders: A geographic region in northwestern Europe, Flanders is today divided among France, Belgium, and the Netherlands. A sovereign principality in the Middle Ages, in the fifteenth century it passed into the hands of the Burgundian Habsburgs, and in the time of Charles I of Spain it was absorbed into the Spanish empire. It was an important participant in the so-called Dutch Revolt against Spain that commenced in 1568 and was not fully over until 1648, hence the term Eighty Years' War.

501.   *de coro*: from hearsay; or by memory. [*Cf. Dic. Aut. 1729 CORO. Se toma también por memória. Usase regularmente de esta voz con las phrases Saber, decir, o tomar de coro.*]

515.   *Carlos Quinto*/emperor Charles: Crowned king of Spain as Charles I in 1516, and three years later elected Holy Roman Emperor as Charles V, Charles was the founder of the family known as the Spanish Habsburgs that was to rule Spain until the death of Charles II in 1700.

519–20.   *el Duque y la Duquesa*/the Duke and Duchess of Alba: The reference is to the third Duke of Alba, Don Fernando Alvarez de Toledo (1507–82) and his wife María Enríquez de Toledo y Guzmán. The Duke was known both as one of the greatest generals of his day, and as an iron-fisted commander in the Spanish effort to put down the Dutch revolt against Spain that brought about the Eighty Years' War. He was the grandfather of the fifth Duke of Alba, Antonio de Toledo y Beaumonte, who was Lope's patron in the 1590s. [See Introduction.] Note that in Spanish there is a pun here on 'Alba', the family name, which can also mean 'dawn' or 'first light'. See also the note to line 466.

521.   *jornadas*: military expeditions.

531.   *me ha sangrado*: The Captain is saying that he's never been medically bled, a practice that was frequently used in past times to cure a variety of ailments.

532.   *Palermo*: an important city and seaport on the north coast of Sicily which was ruled by the Spanish monarchy from 1479 to 1713.

534.   *bandera*: officer in a company of the Spanish army who carried the flag into battle, equivalent in rank to 2nd Lieutenant. His position was important because if in the heat of attack or defense the soldiers of the company should become confused or disoriented, they could head toward the flag and reorganize.

535.   *hábito*: the uniform worn by the knights belonging to one of the military orders of Spain, including, prominently, Santiago, Calatrava, Alcántara, and Montesa. To be awarded such a uniform was the mark of great social esteem.

545.   There is an extra (4th) line in this final tercet. See Introduction.

557–81.   *soñaba yo que tenía ... Que los sueños, sueños son*: a song that was well-known in the Golden Age, glossed in the following lines. See Introduction.

633. *alcaide*: governor of a castle or fortress; by extension, defender, warden.
636. *barbacana*: protective tower or outwork of a fortified castle or fortress.
650. *¡Pesia tal!*: familiar interjection expressing surprise, astonishment, or anger.
681. *melindres*: caprices, quirks, finicky or petty behavior.
684. *terceras*: women who arrange or facilitate sexual encounters; go-betweens. See Introduction.
738. Stage direction *en el alto*: The reference is to one of the galleries, or upper corridors, located above the stage in Spanish *corrales*, frequently used in balcony scenes. See Introduction.
766: *Prado*: See note to line 140.
775. *tiros*: shots from a firearm; barbs, insults or unpleasant remarks. Burgos suggests that the reference here is to thrusts of a sword.
793. *de palabras corta*: sparing with words, inclined to act quickly, decisively, and oftentimes rashly.
814. **Durandarte**: In the French medieval epic poem, *La chanson de Roland*, Durandarte is the name of the sword of Roland, the hero. In later Spanish ballads, the name is given to a brave knight who fights for King Charlemagne in the Frankish invasion of Spain in the eighth century. During battle he is mortally wounded, and as he dies he asks his friend and cousin, Montesinos, to cut out his heart and bring it to his beloved, Belerma.
817. **Beltenebros**: The reference is to an episode in the Spanish chivalric romance, *Amadís de Gaula*. Wrongly suspected by his lady-love, Oriana, of being unfaithful, Amadís resolves to win back her trust by doing penance, under the name of Beltenebros, on the island of La Peña Pobre.
817. **Sir Lancelot**: In the King Arthur tales, Sir Lancelot is the rival of the King for the love of Queen Guinevere.
827. *agua de azar*: a drink made of water and orange blossom, believed to have medicinal properties, it was used as a sedative and analgesic.
829. *amartelar*: to make love to, caress another person. See note to line 142.
835. *cantaleta*: a burlesque song, accompanied by loud instruments and normally performed at night, the intention of which is to embarass or make fun of somebody. [*Cf. Dic. Aut 1729: El ruido que se forma cantando, y metiendo bulla desordenada con algunos instrumentos desconcertados: lo qual se hace para dar chasco, y burlarse de alguno, haciéndole o dandosele a su puerta, o ventana de noche: y de aquí todo el chasco que uno da a otro zumbándole, se llama Cantaleta.*]
836. *pandorga*: a noisy gathering of people, with shouting, singing, playing of instruments, etc.; comparable to a *charivari*. [*Cf. Cov.: una consonancia medio alocada, y de mucho ruido que resulta de variedad de instrumentos.*] See also note to line 835.

979.   ***arpia***: harpy. The harpies were loathsome bird-like women sent by Zeus to punish King Phineas of Thrace by snatching away his food and leaving their droppings all over his table.

990.   ***Argel***: In the early modern period, soldiers from Spain were frequently captured by pirates from North Africa and carried off to imprisonment in the city of Algiers, where they were typically held for ransom. Hence the name Algiers here stands for the notion of captivity.

1081.   ***desamartelarme***: (*desamartelarse*) to cease loving. See note to line 142.

1082.   ***despicarme***: (*despicarse*) to avenge a grievance, to receive satisfaction, to obtain relief. [Cf. *Dic. Aut. 1732: Satisfacerse, vengarse de la ofensa o pique.*]

1098.   ***ropilla:*** a shirt-like garment normally worn under the doublet. See Introduction.

Act 2

1113.   ***tazas***: the basins into which fountains empty their water.

1122.   ***prima***: the highest in pitch of the strings of a stringed instrument. Normally under great tension when it is tuned, it loosens easily. When that happens the pitch falls.

1125.   ***la de Lope***: Lope was the author of a great number of lyrical poems, quite a few of them in a folkloric style. Many came eventually to be set to music. See Introduction.

1128.   ***tope***: *(topar)* to be appropriate, fit the occasion.

1186.   ***Hero***: In classical mythology, Hero was a priestess of Aphrodite who lived in a tower on the European side of the Hellespont. Her lover, Leander, lived on the Asian side, and every night he swam the strait to be with his beloved. One night a fierce storm arose, and Leander lost his way and drowned. Seeing what had happened, Hero was overcome by grief and threw herself from her tower into the sea below, where she also drowned.

1194.   ***saya***: skirt. See Introduction.

1194.   ***herreruelo***: a long cape with no hood.

1196.   ***te ve***: *vete.*

1203.   ***con la barriga a la boca***: to be on the verge of giving birth. [Cf. *Dic. Aut. 1726: Dícese de las mugéres preñadas que están en dias de parir.*]

1223.   ***bajos***: underclothing worn by women beneath such outerwear as skirts. [Cf. *DLE 1817: La ropa interior que traen las mujeres debajo de las sayas, y también se llama así su calzado.*]

1231.   ***pastilla***: a tablet or lozenge chewed by women to impart a pleasing fragrance to their mouth and breath.

1237.   ***el quinto elemento***: In Classical times it was believed that all earthly matter was composed of various combinations of the four basic elements: earth, air, fire, and water. To these was added in later years a fifth element, known by a number of names, including 'ether' and 'quintessence'. Supposedly this element filled all of space above the terrestrial sphere, and explained such phenomena as the traveling of light and the pull of gravity. Finardo is here jokingly attributing Hernando / Estefanía's sitting down so heavily to the force of gravity.

1284.   *mohína*: aggressiveness, hostility. [Cf. *Dic. Aut. 1734: Enojo o encono contra alguno.*]

1288.   *enfaldarse*: to gather one's skirts about oneself.

1397.   *despicado*: See note for line 1082.

1407.   *cotas ... broqueles*: coats of mail ... shields.

1415.   *Carro*: Ursa Major, a constellation in the northern sky also known as Big Bear. The constellation Ursa Major contains the group of stars commonly called the Big Dipper. The handle of the Dipper is the Great Bear's tail and the Dipper's cup is the Bear's flank.

1432.   *mojicones*: blows to the face with a hand; slap or punch. [Cf. *Dic. Aut. 1734: (mogicón). El golpe dado en la cara con la mano, a puño cerrado, mojándola, de donde algunos trahen la etymología.*]

1435.   *quedo*: See note for line 191.

1440.   *mira no echemos azar*: (*echar azar*) to tempt fortune, make a bad mistake, put oneself in danger.

1442.   *Arias Gonzalo*: An eleventh-century citizen of the city of León in the north of Spain, Arias Gonzalo was an ally of the princess Urraca, ruler of the city. When Urraca's brother, King Sancho II of Castile, attempted to wrest the city from her by creeping up on it with his army in the dead of night, Arias Gonzalo sounded the alarm. An important character in later ballads, his name has come to stand for watchfulness.

1455.   *terceras*: See note for line 684.

1531.   *recaudos*: *recados*.

1670.   *alférez*: See note to lines 534–35.

1793.   *Portugal de amor*: In the early modern period in Spain, the country of Portugal came to be associated with the concepts of romance and erotic love. Tejeiro Fuentes points out in his study 'Portugal en la vida y obra de Cervantes' that the Portuguese character frequently appeared in the writings of Cervantes in two depictions, the first reflecting the political tensions between Spain and Portugal, and the second, highlighting the reputation of the Portuguese as gallant gentlemen, inclined to fall in love (693–94). Among the works of Lope we find *El más galán portugués* (1610–1612).

1806.   *noramala: enhoramala.* an expression of anger or contempt (e.g., damn you, go to blazes).

1896.   *cuartana*: fever.

1917. **_Tántalo_**/Tantalus: in Greek mythology, the son of Zeus and the nymph Plouto. For his crimes against the Olympian gods, he was condemned after his death to the lowest region of the underworld, Tartarus. There he stood for eternity in a pool of water where, when hungry, if he reached for fruit that was hanging from a tree, the branch would pull away, and when thirsty, if he bent for a drink, the water would recede.

1918. *divisa*/emblem: a sign or symbol that represents an object, condition, category of things or beings, etc.

1926. **_mármol indiano_**: marble from India. Available in a variety of colors and patterns, it is prized for its beauty. Fig., to be insensitive, incapable of feelings.

1943. **_bellacón_**: someone who is badly behaved; but also clever, astute.

1945. ***a la sombra de un cabello***: obsession with something that is insubstantial, insignificant.

2074. ***la de Juanes***: The reference is to a sword made by 'Juanes'. As there were many famous sword makers of the name Juan or Juanes in the period, the precise identity of the one mentioned here cannot be established.

Act 3

2123. ***La doncella Teodor***: the heroine of a medieval narrative, composed originally in Arabic. It tells the story of Teodor, a beautiful and clever slave girl who is purchased by a merchant who undertakes to educate her. He falls into penury, however, and is forced to sell her to the king. At the court of the latter, Teodor debates the wisest men of the realm and defeats them all, thus securing her future and that of the merchant as well. The tale has been incorporated into some collections of *The Thousand and One Nights*.

2123. **Scheherazade**: another wise and beautiful character from *The Thousand and One Nights,* and the narrator of the collection. One of the many wives of the sultan, she avoids the death that befell the others by entertaining him night after night with a new and absorbing story.

2147. *embozados*: with faces half-covered.

2164. ***Pesia tal***: See note to line 650.

2166. **_Cicerón_**/Cicero: Roman statesman and writer, famous for his oratorical prowess.

2178. Stage direction: ***al otro lado del teatro***: on the other side of the stage.

2189. ***mongil***: dress worn by a widow in mourning; also a nun's habit. See Introduction.

2195. ***frisón***: a horse of the Friesian breed. Normally all black, such horses are known for their high-stepping action, long manes, and stocky build.

2199. *tocas:* headdresses worn by women. See Introduction.

2200.   *antojos*: blinders (on the side of the head) or eye glasses (in front). The term can also refer to whims or appetites that might appear before Belisa's eyes.

2206.   *tacamaca*: a resin secreted by the tree of the same name, a member of the poplar family. Used in the manufacture of ointment and incense.

2211.   *selvas de varia lición*: books of miscellaneous content, modeled on the *Silva de varia lección* (1540) of Pero Mexía.

2276.   *arcabuz*: harquebus, a matchlock long gun invented in Spain in the 15th century.

2301.   *menudo*: a dish made from the intestines (*tripas*) or other internal parts of animals.

2302.   **tripe**: See note to line 2301.

2506.   *por puntos*: from one moment to the next.

2508–20.   In this passage, impossible to reproduce in English, Lope puns on a number of words including 'alférez' (a military rank) and 'alferecía' (a disease like epilepsy). Pedraza (1990) explains as follows: "*alferecía*: *epilepsia, enfermedad cuyo síntoma más notable son las convulsiones y pérdida del sentido. El personaje [Gerarda] juega equívocamente con los términos militares: la compañía (de su marido), el alférez y la alferecía, la marcha (amorosa). el bando, los tiros, etc.*"

2526   *se baraja: (barajarse)* To make things so intricate and confusing that the truth cannot be known. [Cf. *Dic. Aut. 1726: Metaphoricamente vale confundir, poner tan intricada, enredada y obscúra alguna cosa, que con dificultad se pueda entender y averiguar la verdád.*] The meaning here seems to be that with the help of neighbors, doors, and windows, Gerarda and her lover were able to defeat the gardener's scarecrow.

2624.   *Moncayo*: the highest peak of the Sierra del Moncayo in northern Spain, the summit of which is snow-covered most of the year.

2646.   *fénix*/Phoenix: in ancient folklore, a large and colorful bird said to have a life of 500 or more years. When it sensed that its death was approaching, it set itself on fire and then was reborn from its own ashes. Associated with the sun and the idea of immortality.

2648.   *Proserpina*: in classical mythology, the daughter of Zeus and Demeter. She was abducted by the god Hades, also known as Pluto, and carried off by him to the underworld, over which he ruled. She was allowed, however, to return to earth for a part of every year.

2649.   *Plutón*/Pluto: See note to line 2648.

2653.   *Dulce prenda*: Lucindo's words here recall the opening line of Garcilaso's "Soneto X": "*¡Oh dulces prendas, por mi mal halladas, / dulces y alegres cuando Dios quería!*"

2689.   *dulce la fruta*: another reminiscence of Garcilaso, in this instance Tirreno's speech in praise of his beloved, in 'Egloga III': *"Flérida, para mí dulce y sabrosa / más que la fruta del cercado ajeno ..."* [Cf. Pedraza, p. 721, note to line 2688].

2815.   *divertida*: distracted, not following the conversation.

2890.   *mirlado*: serious, downcast. [Cf. *Dic. Aut. 1734*: *part pass. del verbo Mirlarse. Entonado, grave, y que afecta señorío en el rostro.*]

2961.   *décima musa del Parnaso*/tenth muse of Parnassus: The muses were sister-goddess who were the objects of a cult in Ancient Greece. Originally undifferentiated and varying in number, in time nine were given individual identities. In that guise, each presided over a specific art or science and acted as inspiration to those who were practitioners in those fields. In referring to Fenisa as 'tenth muse', Doristeo conveys the supposed extent of his adoration of her.

2963.   *la dama del Toro ha visto Apolo*: The sense of this line is not clear. Pedraza suggests, plausibly, that the *dama* referred to is Europa, who was beloved by Zeus, and who was abducted by him in the form of a white bull. The reference to Apollo at the end of the line could refer to the sun (Phoebus Apollo), indicating that in his circling of the planet, the god has never seen any beauty to compare to Fenisa's, save that of Europa.

2966.   *prefiere*: exceeds.

TEXTUAL VARIANTS

Base text

1653   Parte tercera de comedias de los meiores ingenios de España
(Madrid: Melchor Sánchez).

Variants

MS1135 Biblioteca Palatina, Parma

MS1851 Biblioteca Nacional de España

1853   *Comedias escogidas de Frey Lope Felix de Vega Carpio*. BAE
vol. 24 (Hartzenbusch).

1876, 1899 Biblioteca Universal. vol. XXV (Hernando).

1910   *Lope de Vega. Comedias* (Valencia: Prometeo).

1913   *Obras de Lope de Vega* RAE, vol. XIV (Marcelino Menéndez
Pelayo).

1928   Ibero-Americana de Publicaciones (Tenreiro).

1928EC Espasa-Calpe. Colección Universal.

1940   Buenos Aires: Sopena.

1948   Buenos Aires: Espasa-Calpe

1955   Editorial Iberia. Colección Obras Maestras. (Guarner).

1971   BAE vol. 247 (see 1913).

1990   *Lope de Vega esencial* (Pedraza).

1998   *Obras completas de Lope de Vega*, vol. 15. Turner (Gómez).

2012   Linkgua

Act 1

35	más **cumplieras** tu deseo	1928EC, 1940: **cumplirás.**
72	mucho la hermosura **[llama]**	1653, MS1851,1928, 1955: **falta.**
90	**por** vida del gusto mío.	1653: **dor**, clearly an error.
92	¡Qué gato de **a[l]galia** azota!	1653. 1990: **argalia.**
106	**[de]** cuentas y de espejuelos;	1653, MS1735, MS1851: **me.**
121	Cuanto **[te]** dije es fingido;	1653, 1735, MS1851, 1928, 1955,1990, 1998: **le.**
122	cuanto **[te]** quise es burlando.	1653, MS1735, MS1851, 1928, 1955, 1990, 1998: **le.**
129	¡Que nadie merezca **[amor]**	1653: **amar**, which breaks the rhyme.
138–	Ven**[te]** conmigo. **[Que voy.]**	A defective *redondilla* in 1653. The
140	[...]	missing words in lines 139 and 140 have
	[Hacia e]l Prado.	been reconstructed/supplied to complete

the sense and the rhyme scheme. We
amend the 1635 to reflect the version in
MSMS1735.

1853, 1876, 1913, 1928EC, 1971 have a
note: "Falta un verso para la redondilla."
1928 has periods to indicate missing line.
1910, 1990, 1998 say nothing.
1955 has in parentheses **[y donde vayas
yo voy.]**
1940, 1948: *(1) Falta un verso para
completar la redondilla.
2012 suggests "**Que me mandas hacer
hoy?**"

144	que **[es la]** vecina Fenisa;	MS1735, 1910, 1913, 1940, 2012: **es la**; 1653, MS1851, 1853, 1928EC, 1948, 1998: **esta**; 1928, 1955, 1971: **está**; 1990: **es tu.**
199	El lienzo me **[da]**.	1653, MS1851, 1998: **dad.**
205	Miraré las **faldriqueras.**	1928, 1928EC, 1940: **faltriqueras.**
215	Señora, de vos **le** fío.	MS1735: **lo**; 1955: **me.**

220	**Sospecho que de vos ha sido.**	One syllable too many. 1653, MS1851, 1998: as written here; MS1735: **Juzgo** 2012, 1853, 1876, 1910, 1913, 1928EC, 1940, 1948, 1971, 1990, 2012: **De vos sospecho que ha sido.** 1928, 1955: **Sospecho de vos que ha sido.**
221	Señor, **deja[d]nos** pasar.	1653, MS1851, 1928, 1955, 1998: **dejanos**. Given that in the next line Belisa uses the *vosotros* form, we use it in this line as well, as it appears in MS1735.
250	resbaladizo de **[suerte]**	1653, MS1735, MS1851: **fuente**, which does not obey the rhyme scheme.
260	**bastaba** [a] volverme loco.	MS1753: **basta**.
285	Har[t]as causas me retiran.	1653: **harras**, obviously an error.
288	a los niños que la **miran**;	MS1735: **tiran**.
293	A los mozos sin **consejo**	1653, MS1851: **consejos**; "consejo" is necessary to keep the rhyme.
295	**porque son niños y locos;**	This line is missing in MS1735.
301	**Buscar, señor,**	MS1735: **Señor, buscar.**
302	**una bella [contra]cifra.**	1653, MS1735, MS1851, 1998: **cifra**. Needs to be "contracifra" for syllable count.
310	cañas de pescar **[los]** llama!	1653, MS1735, MS1851, 1853, 1876, 1910, 1913, 1928, 1928EC, 1940, 1948, 1955, 1971, 1990, 1998: **las**; however, the antecedent seems to be "celos, so we agree with 2012 and change to **los**.
315	para **estribarte** sea	1853, 1876, 1910, 1913, 1928EC, 1940, 1948, 1971, 2012: **derribarte**; 1928, 1955: **destribarte**.
318	de celos hace seda[l];	1653: **sedas**; MS1735 corrects to **sedal**, which is necessary for the rhyme.
319	pues ¿ **cómo** que en hilo igual	1853, 1876, 1910, 1913, 1928EC, 1940, 1948, 1971, 2012: **cabe**.

323	por la mujer **de amor**	MS1735: **sin amor**; 1853, 1876, 1910, 1913, 1928, 1928EC, 1940, 1948, 1955, 1971: **y el amor**; 1990: **la[s] mujer[es] de amor.**
353	Si yo te **cerrase** en casa,	MS1735, 1876: **encerrase.**
354	pocas veces me **[darías]**	1653, MS1851: **dareis.** MS1735 corrects to **darías** and all others follow.
367	¿Qué **[guijas]** desde la calle	1635, MS1735, MS1851, 1928, 1955: **ojos.**
383	Pues ¿qué es esto? ¿Prevención?	1853,1876, 1910, 1913, 1928, 1928EC, 1940, 1948, 1955, 1971, 2012 attribute the word to Belisa, as a declarative.
384	Mi honor **[el]** tuyo desea.	1653, MS1851, 1928, 1955: **es**; MS1735: **ser.**
425	Ya **[ha]** días que da en mirarme.	1653, MS1735, MS1851, 1928: **Ya**; 1990: **Ya [ha].**
439	¿esos **bostezos** te dan?	1853, 1876, 1910, 1913, 1928EC, 1940, 1948, 1971, 1998, 2012: **barruntos.**
470	si v[uestra] m[erced] no entrara,	1653: **v.m.** We amplify this abbreviation throughout.
475	**[*Vanse los criados.*]**	Om 1653, MS1735, 1913, 1928,1940, 1955, 1971; 1853, 1876, 1913, 1940, 1948, 1955, 1928, 1928EC, 1971: *(A sus criados que se van.)* at end of line. 2012: ***Vanse los criados.***
489	Hoy me descuidé en **prenderme**	1653, 1928, 1955, 1990: **prenderme**; all others: **ponerme.**
497	Belisa, el ser vecino, que en **efeto,**	MS1735, MS1851, 1876, 1940: **efecto.**
499	de su virtud me ha dado buen **[conceto].**	1653,MS1735, MS1851, 1940, 1998: **concepto**; 1853, 1876, 1910,1913, 1928, 1928EC, 1948, 1955, 1971, 1990, 2012: **conceto**, to rhyme with **efeto.**
508	de los que **habéis**, de verme, conocido;	1853, 1876, 1899, 1913, 1918EC, 1940, 1948, 1971, 1998, 2012: **habréis.**
522	que si **fueran** de bronce me acabaran.	1853, 1876, 1899, 1910, 1913, 1928EC, 1940, 1948, 1955, 1971, 1990, 1998, 2012: **fuera.**

543	no poca hacienda que ganó mi espada,	1853,1876, 1910, 1913, 1928EC, 1940, 1948, 1971, 1990, 2012: **la**.
544	**si no** es que mi cansada edad la aflija;	1653, MS1735, MS1851: **sino**; 1853 corrects to **si no**.
570	fe de un sueño que [**dormía**];	1653, MS1735, MS1851: **dormida**.
607	que este casamiento [**aceto**],	1653, MS1735, MS1851, 1940, 1998: **acepto**, which breaks the rhyme.
608	pues de mi amor el [**efeto**]	1653, MS1735, MS1851, 1940, 1998: **efecto**.
609	[**puedo**] por él conseguir;	1653, MS1851, 1955, 1990: **pudo**. MS1735 corrects to **puedo**.
620	Pero déjam**ele** hablar.	MS1851, 1853, 1876, 1913, 1928EC, 1940, 1948, 1971, 2012: **la**; 1928, 1955: **dejádmele**.
630	**Haré** de hoy más, pues me [**honra**]	1853, 1876, 1899, 1910, 1913, 1928EC, 1940, 1948, 1971, 1990, 1998, 2012: **Seré**; 1653, MS1735: **honras**.
635	esta misma barba **anciana**	MS1735: **cana**.
640	[**juntando a tus hebras de oro**]	The entire line is missing in 1653, MS1735, MS1851, 1998; 1853, 1876, 1910, 1913, 1928, 1928EC, 1940, 1948, 1955, 1971, 1990: **juntando**; 2012: **juntado**.
644	[**FENISA**] Con tu honor y calidad,	In 1653, MS1735, MS1851 this is the last line of the Capitan's speech; Fenisa's speech begins next line (**Señor**). We have accepted 1853's correction.
660	Haré lo que me [**mandéis**],	1653, MS1851: **mandáis**, which breaks the rhyme. We accept the MS1735 correction.
675	la nieve de las canas me **derrit[e]**.	1653, MS1735, MS1851, 1998: **derrito**.
676	Digo, señor, que importará **atajar[l]e**	1653, MS1851: **atarjarte**; MS1735 emends.
684	por manos de **terceras**, que a mi casa	1853, 1876, 1910, 1913, 1828EC, 1940, 1948, 1971, 1998, 2012: **terceros**.

685	[vienen] con mil achaques [e] invenciones,	1653, MS1735: **viene/y**; 1853, 1876, 1928EC, 1948, 1990: **vienen/y**; 1928, 1955: **viene/e**; 1940: **vienen/e**.
686	echando **mil** amigas por terceras;	1853, 1876, 1910, 19113, 1928E, 1940, 1948, 1971, 1990, 2012: **mis**.
689	Es loco el mozo; **perdonalde**, os ruego;	MS1735, MS1851, 1876, 1910, 1940, 1955, 1998, 2012: **perdonadle**.
695	**Deja[d]me** ese cuidado.	1653, MS1851, 1928, 1955, 1998: **dexame**.
706	**Malicia tuya**. Ven.	MS1735: **Malicia es tuya**. Ven.
730	y con [un] alma de acero.	1653, MS1735, 1853, 1990, 2012: **una**.
758	¿Y a **mí**, señora?	MS1735: **vos**.
787	**Hallarla** será imposible.	MS1735: **hablarla**.
800	celos **serán** menester.	MS1735: **serás**, clearly an error.
822	si está, de **verme**, temblando?	MS1735: **miedo**.
827	dos tragos de agua de **azar**.	1928, 1955, 2012: **azahar**.
843	**Quítate delante**.	1853, 1876, 1910, 1913, 1928EC, 1940, 1948, 1971, 1990, 1998, 2012: ¿Quítaste delante?
859	antes señal de **tener**	1913, 1971, 1998: **querer**.
876	Pésame que **hables** con ella;	MS1735: **halles**.
896	Mas quiero **volverle** [a] hablar,	MS1735, 1853, 1876, 1910, 1913, 1928EC, 1940, 1948, 1971, 1990, 1998, 2012: **volverla**.
899	**[Por ésta]**	Om 1653, creating a defective quintilla. MS1735: **de aquesta**.
900	**hoy me tengo de matar**.	1853, 1876, 1899, 1910, 1913, 1928EC, 1940, 1948, 1971, 2012: **mujer hoy me he de matar**.
901	Rompe [esas] puertas.	1653, MS1735, 1851, 1998: **aquestas**, which gives the line one syllable too many, as does **aquesas**: MS1851, 1998; 1853 corrects to **esas**; 1990: **aquesa puerta**.
904	¡Golpes en mi casa, loco!	1653, MS1753 erroneously attributes this line to Hernando. The stage direction *Sale Gerarda* appears after the line. We accept 1853 correction.

913	esto ¿en qué razón está?	1853, 1876, 1910, 1913, 1928EC, 1940, 1948, 1971, 2012: **ese**; 1998: **eso**.
915	¿Por qué no te mato [ya]?	1653, MS1735, MS1851, 1998: **yo** (which breaks the rhyme).
917	Pues él me ha dicho, [crüel],	1653, MS1735, MS1851, 1998: **como él**. We accept the 1853 correction.
932	¿**Dónde** te habló?	MS1735: **Cuándo**.
959	¡Qué **gentil** hielo en invierno,	MS1735: **es gentil**.
990	dulce Argel de [mi sentido]?	1653, MS1851, 1998: **mis sentidos**.
991	¿Estaste aquí todavía?	1653, MS1735: This line is erroneously attributed to Lucindo. The stage direction (*Sale el Capitán*) appears after the line.
1016	en **aquesta** calle estaba	MS1735: **aquella**.
1017	cuando **me** reprehendiste	MS1735: **tú me**.
1032	muy **tiern[o]** llegaste a hablarla.	1653, MS1735, MS1851: **tierna**.
1047	Que **la** digas	1853, 1876, 1910, 1913, 1928EC, 1940, 1948, 1971, 2012: **le**.
1051	a hacer**me** tan malas obras.	MS1735: omitted
1095	que con **su madre Belisa**,	1853, 1876, 1910, 1913, 1928EC, 1940, 1948, 1971, 2012: **Belisa, su madre**.

Act 2

1124	**Comenzar [puedes]**.	1653, MS1851, 1998: **Comenzar podeis**. MS1735: changes to **puedes**,which rhymes with "mercedes" (line 1121). 1853, 1876, 1910, 1913, 1928EC, 1940, 1948, 1971: **Empezar podéis**; 2012: **Empezar puedes**; 1928, 1955, 1990: **Empezar podedes**.
1139	**suspiro por mi deseo**.	1853,1876, 1910, 1913, 1928EC, 1940, 1948, 1971, 2012: **suspira por mí el deseo**.
1157	**que de casa se le fue**.	MS1735 erroneously copies: **que debe de bus casa se le fue**.
1161	Luego ¿es [**Gerarda**]?	1653 MS1851: **guarda**. MS1735 corrects to **Gerarda**.
1170	**ya** el alma comienza a arder.	1853, 1876, 1910, 1913, 1928EC, 1940, 1948, 1971, 2012: **Y**.

1191	har[a]me el alma pedazos.	1653, MS1735, MS1851, 1928, 1955: **hareme.**
1200	mas defenderme **[te]** toca,	1653, MS1735, MS1851 **me.**
1204	*Éntrase.*	MS1735, 1853, 1876, 1913, 1928EC, 1940, 1948, 1971: **Vase;** 2012: **Vase Hernando.**
1206	si en las muertas cenizas **[escondida]**,	1653, MS1735, MS1851, 1928, 1955: **escondidas.** The referent of "escondida", which needs to rhyme with "herida", seems to be "lumbre".
1214	el **vivo** de su fuego os ha **engañado.**	1853, 1876, 1910, 1913, 1928EC, 1940, 1948, 1971, 2012: **humo/engendrado.**
1223	¿**Cómo?**	1853, 1876, 1910, 1913, 1928EC, 1940, 1948, 1971, 2012: **Vamos.**
1246	**[GERARDA]**	1653, MS1735: **LUCINDO.**
1257	Ya se altera **[e]** inquïeta.	1653, MS1735, MS1851, 1928EC: **y.**
1277	Lindamente **[nos echó.]**	1653, MS1851, 1998: **lo has hecho;** MS1735: **hecho lo habemos;** 1853, 1876, 1910, 1913, 1928EC, 1940, 1948, 1955, 1971, 1990: **los echó;** 2012: **nos echó.**
1334	*[Húyase Hernando.]*	In 1653, this comes before the previous line. MS1735: *Vase,* before the previous line. MS1851: *Huyase Hernando,* before the previous line. 1853, 1876, 1913, 1928EC, 1948, 1971: *Vase.* 2012: *Vase Hernando huyendo.*
1347	¿**Tu bien soy?**	MS1735: **Yo tu bien;** 1990: ¿**Tu bien yo?**
1349	y **cuanto** hablaba también.	1910, 1913, 1971, 1998: **cuando.**
1354	En **prenda** de que tú eres	MS1735: **prueba.**
1355	mi **verdad,** vente conmigo.	MS1735: **prenda.**
1359	yo adoro **en** Estefanía.	1948, 2012: **a.**
1366	**[GERARDA]**	1653: Lucindo continues, not Gerarda.
1371	No seas **villano,** ven;	1853, 1876, 1910, 1913, 1928EC, 1940, 1948, 1971, 1998, 2012: **tirano.**

1376	*Sale Hernando, ya* **desnudo.**	1853, 1876, 1910, 1913, 1928EC, 1940, 1948, 1971, 2012: *en su traje*; 1955: *sin disfraz.*
1387	a **esta** dama.	1998: **esa.**
1405	¡**Si** en el verano se alaba	1853, 1876, 1910, 1913, 1928EC, 1940, 1948, 1971, 2012: **Y.**
1410	Tarde **llegará** el favor;	1853, 1910, 1928, 1928EC, 1940, 1955, 1990, 1998, 2012: **llegara.**
1416	**Ansí,**	1853, 1876, 1910, 1913, 1928EC, 1940, 1948, 1971, 1998, 2012: **Ah, Si.**
1424	¿Quién **te ha** hecho	1910, 1998: **ha.**
1425	milagro tan notable en **su** sentido?	1853, 1876, 1899, 1910, 1913, 1928EC, 1940, 1948, 1971, 1998, 2012: **tu.**
1437	que habrá [**dejado**] la cama.	1653, MS1735, MS1851: **ajado.**
1483	puesto que más [**merecéis**],	1653, MS1851: **merezcais**, which does not rhyme with "echéis".
1486	Sembrarla **en** almas quisiera	1853, 1910, 1913, 1928, 1928EC, 1940, 1948, 1955, 1971, 1998, 2012: **de.**
1496	[**despertasteis**] el deseo;	1653, MS1735, MS1851, 1853, 1876, 1910, 1913, 1928, 1928EC, 1948, 1971, 1990, 1998: **despertastes**; 1955: **despertaste.**
1551	o [**desengañadme**] aquí.	1653, MS1735, MS1851: **desengáñame.**
1554	**Preguntadla** allá si os quiero.	1853, 1876, 1910, 1913, 1928, 1928EC, 1940, 1948, 1955, 1971, 1990, 2012: **Preguntadle.**
1620	si porque he entrado en **su** casa,	1853, 1876, 1910, 1913, 1928EC, 1940, 1948, 1971, 1998, 2012: **tu.**
1682	mejor, y que le [**dé pena**]	1653, MS1735, MS1851, 1928, 1955: **despena.**
1683	ver que a mi edad **le** condena	1853, 1876, 1899, 1910, 1913, 1928EC, 1940, 1948, 1971, 1990, 1998, 2012: **se.**
1684	donde sin gusto [**padezca**]?	1653, MS1735, MS1851, 1928: **parezca.**
1712	que beses con **epitetos.**	1928EC, 1971, 1955, 2012: **epítetos**, which breaks the rhyme with **discretos.**
1760	Celos [**tiene**].	1653, MS1735, MS1851: **tienes.**
1774	[**Escuchadme**] a esta parte dos palabras.	1653, MS1735, MS1851, 1928, 1955, 1990: **Escúchame.** We change to the formal usage to maintain consistency in Belisa's address.

1801   *Cayga.*   MS1735, 1853, 1876, 1910, 1913, 1928EC, 1940, 1948, 1971, 2012: *Cae.*

1821   ¿Quieres verle? ¡**Hola, Beatriz,**   1853, 1876, 1910, 1913, 1948, 1971,
       de presto!   1990, 2012: **Beatriz, ¡hola, ven**;
                                      1928EC, 1940: **Beatriz, ¡hola, ves**.

1827   **Que** os prometo que es gentil   1653: **ques**; MS1735, 1928, 1955: **pues**.
       mancebo,

1834   ¡Todo es **escusa**!   1853, 1876, 1910, 1913, 1928EC, 1940,
                                      1948, 1971, 2012: **escucha**;
                                      1928: **Todo excusa**.

1859   Si esto pasa, ¿qué hará quien   1853, 1876, 1899, 1910, 1913, 1928EC,
       andar puede?   1940, 1948, 1971, 1998, 2012 **mandar**.

1885   que me privó **del** sentido.   1853, 1876, 1899, 1910, 1913, 1928EC,
                                      1940, 1948, 1971, 1990: **de**.

1890   ¿De qué **estás** tan inquïeto?   MS1735, 1853, 1876, 1910, 1913, 1928,
                                      1928EC, 1940, 1948, 1955, 1971, 1998:
                                      estáis.

1928   ¿No basta, si es imagen, que **le**   1853, 1876, 1910, 1913, 1928, 1928EC,
       bese?   1940, 1948, 1955, 1971, 2012: **la**.

1929–   ....   The first three lines of the *octava* that
31   ....   begins here are missing. From the rhyme
           ....   scheme, the first line would end in
                                        [*-ones*], the second in [*-ase*], the third in
                                       [*-ones*].

1939   ¿No me mandaste tú que **la**   1853, 1876, 1899, 1910, 1913, 1928EC,
       besase   1940, 1948, 1955, 1971, 1998, 2012: **le**.

1940   la [**mano**] como a madre? ¿Es,   1653, MS1735, MS1851: **madre**.
       por ventura,

1958   que pasa alguna gente, y no   MS1735: **intento**.
       querría

1967   de responderos a [**solas**].   1653, MS1851, 1998: **todo**; MS1735:
                                         ella. Both break the o-a rhyme; 1990:
                                         toda.

1981   que sólo el [**ver me**] reporta   1653, MS1735, NS1851: **verme**.
1997   ¿Cómo engañado, si **nombra**   1653, MS1735, MS1851: **me nombra**,
                                         which makes the line too long.

2049   ¿**Mandaisnos** otra cosa?   1955: **Mándasnos**.
2064   De noche por las rejas **la**   MS1735: **me la**; 1955: **le**.
       inquïeta;

Act 3

2076	*capa con oro y plumas.*	MS1735: **capa de galón de oro y sombrero de plumas.**
2159	después que [**vivís**] en mí;	1653, MS1851, 1990: **vives.**
2165	que **hablas** con gran discreción!	MS1735: **habláis.**
2173	llegado a que me [**queráis**],	1653, MS1851, 1998: **queréis**, which breaks the rhyme.
2253	joyas y **vestidos** coge,	MS1735: **dineros.**
2313	ponerse [**ese**] gusto en [**duda**],	1653, MS1851, 1998: **el** gusto en **dudar**; MS1735: ponserse**me el** gusto en **duda**; 1853, 1876, 1910, 1913, 1928, 1928EC; 1955: **este** gusto en **duda**; 1990: poner**me ese** gusto en **duda**.
2366	....	Last line of this quintilla is missing. Presumably, it ends in accented "*í.*"
2390	Si [**yo**] estuviera avisado	1653: **ya**. MS1735 changes to **yo**, and all other editions adopt this change.
2426	No me acordé que le [**amáis**].	1653, MS1735, MS1851, 1998: **amabais**, which breaks the rhyme.
2442	Gente se nos entra [**acá.**]	1635, MS1851: en **casa;** 1925, 1955: **en ca.**
2481	Criáronme **en su** regalo,	1853, 1876, 1910, 1913, 1928EC, 1940, 1948, 1971, 2012: **con;** 1928: **en un.**
2502	fue en **este** medio templada	2012: **esto.**
2512	[**pudiera**] sufrir las faltas.	1653, MS1735, MS1851, 1990: **pudieran.**
2523	para que el pájaro **viese**	1853, 1876, 1899,1910, 1913, 1928EC, 1940, 1948, 1971, 1998, 2012: **huyese.**
2524	que **el** hortelano **velaba.**	1853, 1876, 1899,1910, 1913, 1928EC, 1940, 1948, 1971, 1998, 2012: **al / burlaba.**
2602	[**Perded**] el miedo.	1653, MS1735, MS1851, 1928, 1998: **Pierde.**
2620	que he **de** matarle en la calle.	MS1735: omitted.
2626	**hielo** derribó su lozanía;	1913, 1971: **cielo.**
2627	que [**cuando**] muda el tiempo, basta un día	1653, MS1851: **quanto;** 1955: **cuanto.**
2629	No más gustos de amor, que **sois** engaños,	1853, 1876, 1910, 1913, 1928EC, 1940, 1948, 1971, 1998, 2012: **son.**

2634	si **dice[n]** que se aumenta amor con ellos?	1653, MS1735, MS1851, 1998: **si dice.**
2718	Eso sí, da voces **falsas,**	MS1735: da voces, **da;** 1853; 1876, 1910, 1913, 1928EC, 1940, 1948, 1971; 1990, 2012: **salta,** which rhymes with "falta"; 1928, 1955: **falso.**
2740	Goza **a** mi padre, que es padre,	MS1735: omitted
2751	**[aguarda mi lindo amor,**	1653 does not include this line or the next, which results in a defective quintilla.. MS1735 adds them.
2752	**suspende, querido esposo.]**	1653 does not include this line or the previous. MS1735 adds them.
2758–59	....	Two lines – presumably the last two – are missing in this quintilla.
2807	Y a mí me los **dan** también	MS1735: **da.**
2808	Pusieron en paz los **celos**	MS1735: **cielos.**
2821	y me ha dicho que **[te]** adora.	1653, MS1735, MS1851: **la.**
2827	y que es forzoso, en **[efeto],**	1653, MS1735: **efecto,** which breaks the rhyme.
2828	el **[casaros]** de secreto.	1653, MS1735, 1990: **sacaros.**
2832	**donde m[u]rmurar** podrán	1653, MS1735, MS1851: **donde mormurar;** **porque mormurar:** 1853, 1876, 1910, 1913, 1928, 1928EC, 1940, 1948, 1955, 1971, 1990, 1998, 2012; 1990: **mormurar.**
2844	no digo lo que **me [ofrece].**	1653, MS1851, 1928, 1955, 1990: **me crece;** MS1735: **merece.**
2897	se volvieron **[a su casa].**	Om 1653, MS1851; MS1735, 1853, 1876, 1910, 1913, 1928, 1928EC, 1940, 1948, 1955, 1971, 1990, 1998, 2012 supply the last three words.
2898	**[Pues ella]** toda se abrasa,	Om 1653, MS1851, 1998.
2916	y aún es grande amigo **[tuyo.]**	1653, MS1735, MS1851: **suyo.**
2930	**[Señor, sí;]**	1653, MS1851: **Sí señor,** which breaks the rhyme.
2940	Mas los celos **le** han picado;	1853, 1876, 1899, 1913, 1928EC, 1940, 1948, 1971, 1990, 2012: **la.**

2947	pero allá la pienso **hablar**.	1853, 1876, 1899, 1910, 1913, 1928EC, 1940, 1948, 1971, 1998, 2012: **hallar**.
2958	pedile a Fenisa **[en]** casamiento.	1653, MS1851: **el**.
2963	que en la **dama del Toro** ha visto Apolo!	1853, 1876, 1913, 1928EC, 1940, 1948, 1971, 2012: **su giro veloz**.
2972	*[Salen]* el Capitán, con barba diferente, muy hecha, en hábito de noche; y Fulminato.	1653, MS1851: *Entre*; 1853, 1913, 1955: omitted; 1928: *Entra;* 1990: *Entran*.
2980	**[Entro]**, vuélvete.	1653, MS1735, MS1851: **entró**; *Vase* at end of line.
2981	*[Vase el Capitán.]*	1653, MS1735, MS1851: *Vase* at the end of line 2980.
2992	Pies, en mi amor os tened. /	1853, 1913, 1917, 1928EC, 1948
2993	**[por la escala se llegará]** /	presume that 2992 and 2994 constitute
2994	¿Echó escala?	the beginning of a series of *versos*
	¡Y suben ya. /	*sueltos*. For the missing line 2993,
2995	**[traspasando la pared]**	2012 hypothesizes: **por la escala se llegará**; for the missing line 2995. 2012 hypothesizes: **traspasando la pared**. While they are conjectures, they complete the stanza well.
3009	él y su **Hernando** serán	MS1735: **hermano**.
3014	¿**[Mi]** Gerarda?	1653, MS1735, MS1851, 1853, 1876, 1910, 1913, 1928, 1928EC, 1948, 1955, 1971, 1990, 1998: **Es**; 1940, 2012: **Mi**, which makes more sense, given the line that follows.
3039	**LUCINDO: ¿Fuego en casa? FENISA:** **[¡Fuego en casa!]**	1635: **Fuego en casa / En casa fuego**; MS1735: **En casa fuego / Fuego en casa**, which respects the rhyme. We change only Fenisa's line.
3042	pero nadie **lo** verá,	MS1735: **le**.

WORKS CITED

Alín, José María, and María Begoña Barrio Alonso. *Cancionero teatral de Lope de Vega*. Tamesis, 1997.

Appiah, Kwame Anthony. *The Honor Code: How Moral Revolutions Happen*. Norton, 2010.

Arellano, Ignacio. 'Convenciones y rasgos genéricos en la comedia de capa y espada'. *Cuadernos de Teatro Clásico, no. 1, La comedia de capa y espada*, Ministerio de Cultura, 1988, pp. 27–49.

Arellano, Ignacio. *Convención y recepción: Estudios sobre el teatro del siglo de oro*. Gredos, 1999.

Arellano, Ignacio. 'La generalización del agente cómico en la comedia de capa y espada'. *Criticón*, vol. 60, 1994, pp. 103–28.

Arellano, Ignacio. 'El modelo temprano de la comedia urbana de Lope de Vega'. *Lope de Vega: comedia urbana y comedia palatina. Actas de las XVIII jornadas de teatro clásico, Almagro, 11, 12, y 13 de julio de 1995*, edited by Felipe B. Pedraza Jiménez and Rafael González Cañal, Universidad de Castilla-La Mancha, 1996, pp. 37–60.

Arellano, Ignacio. 'El vestuario en los autos sacramentales (el ejemplo de Calderón)'. *El vestuario en el teatro del Siglo de Oro*, edited by Mercedes de los Reyes Peña. *Cuadernos de Teatro Clásico* 13–14. CNTC, 2000.

Arróniz, Othón. *La influencia italiana en el nacimiento de la comedia española*. Gredos, 1969.

Bakhtin, Mikhail. 'Carnival and Carnivalesque'. *Cultural Theory and Popular Culture*, edited by John Storey, U of Georgia P, 1998, pp. 250–60.

Bakhtin, Mikhail. *Rabelais and His World*. Translated by Héllène Iswolsky, Indiana UP, 1984, pp. 145–277.

Bances Candamo, Francisco. *Theatro de los theatros de los passados y presentes siglos*, edited by Duncan W. Moir, Tamesis, 1970.

Barber, Cesar Lombardi. *Shakespeare's Festive Comedy: a Study of Dramatic Form and its Relation to Social Custom*. Princeton UP, 1959.

Barrionuevo, Gabriel de. 'Entremés famoso del Triunfo de los coches'. *Madrid en el teatro I: Siglos de Oro*, estudio y selección de Ángel Berenguer, Comunidad de Madrid, 1994, pp. 43–68.

Bass, Laura R. 'Visual Literacy and Urban Comedy'. *The Drama of the*

Portrait: Theater and Visual Culture in Early Modern Spain. Pennsylvania State UP, 2008, pp. 13–42.

Bass, Laura R. and Amanda Wunder. 'Veiled Ladies of the Early Modern Spanish World: Seduction and Scandal in Seville, Madrid, and Lima', *The Hispanic Review*, vol. 77, no. 1, 2009, pp. 97–146.

Bates, Margaret J. *'Discreción' in the Works of Cervantes. A Semantic Study*. Catholic U of America, Department of Romance Languages and Literature Publications, no. 31, 1945.

Bennassar, Bartolomé. *La España del Siglo de Oro*. Crítica, 1983.

Bennassar, Bartolomé. 'Honor and Violence'. *The Spanish Character: Attitudes and Mentalities from the Sixteenth to the Nineteenth Century.* Translated by Benjamin Keen, U. of California P, 1979, pp. 213–36.

Bennett, Susan. *Theater Audiences: A Theory of Production and Reception*. Routledge, 1990.

Bergson, Henri. 'Laughter'. *Comedy*. Anchor-Doubleday, 1956, pp. 61–190.

Blue, William R. 'The Diverse Economy of *Entre bobos anda el juego* '. *The Golden Age Comedia: Text, Theory and Performance*, edited by Charles Ganelin and Howard Mancing, Purdue UP, 1994, pp. 76–86.

Blue, William R. *Spanish Comedy and Historical Contexts in the 1620s*. Pennsylvania State UP, 1996.

Boix, Felipe. *Exposición del antiguo Madrid. Catálogo general ilustrado*. Sociedad Española de Amigos del Arte. Gráficas Reunidas, 1926.

Bowman, James. *Honor: A History*. Encounter, 2006.

Brewster, William T., translator. *The New Art of Writing Plays*. By Lope de Vega, Dramatic Museum of Columbia U, 1914.

Bristol, Michael D. *Carnival and Theater: Plebeian Culture and the Structure of Authority in Renaissance England*. Methuen, 1985.

Brook, Peter. *The Empty Space*. Atheneum, 1982.

Brown, Jonathan and J. H. Elliott. *A Palace for a King: The Buen Retiro and the Court of Philip IV*. Yale UP, 1980.

Burgos Segarra, Gemma, editor. *La discreta enamorada*. By Lope de Vega, Artelope. <https://emothe.uv.es/biblioteca/textosEMOTHE/EMOTHE0560_LaDiscretaEnamorada.php>.

Burke, Peter. 'The World of Carnival'. *Popular Culture in Early Modern Europe*. 1978. Ashgate, 1994, pp. 178–204.

Caballero, Judith Griselda. *De las bambalinas al tablado: La presencia de las madres en las comedias del Siglo de Oro*. 2011. U of Arizona, PhD dissertation.

Canseco, Manuel. *El Corral del Príncipe*. <http://aix1.uottawa.ca/~jmruano/Corral.html>.

Cañas, Jesús. 'Diez calas sobre el amor en el teatro del primer Lope de Vega: La configuración del tema en las comedias del destierro'. *Amor y erotismo en el teatro de Lope de Vega: Actas de las XXV jornadas de teatro clásico de Almagro*, edited by Felipe B. Pedraza Jiménez et al., U de Castilla-La Mancha, 2003, pp. 235–50.

Capmany y Montpalau, Antonio. *Orígen histórico y etimológico de las calles de Madrid*. Manuel de Quirós, 1863.

Carlson, Marvin. *Performance: A Critical Introduction*. Routledge, 1996.

Carlson, Marvin. *Places of Performance: the Semiotics of Theatre Architecture*. Cornell UP, 1989.

Caro Baroja, Julio. *El carnaval: análisis histórico-cultural*. Taurus, 1965.

Casey, James. *Early Modern Spain: A Social History*. Routledge, 1999.

Castro, Américo and Hugo R. Rennert. *Vida de Lope de Vega (1562–1635)*. Anaya, 1968.

'Colonial Spanish America'. *Encyclopedia of Latin American History and Culture. Encyclopedia.com*. <https://www.encyclopedia.com>.

Corman, Brian. *Genre and Generic Change in English Comedy, 1660–1710*. U. of Toronto P, 1993.

Cornford, Francis Macdonald. *The Origin of Attic Comedy*, edited by Theodore H. Gaster, Anchor, 1961.

Correa, Gustavo. 'El doble aspecto de la honra en el teatro del siglo XVII'. *Hispanic Review*, vol. 26, no. 2, 1958, pp. 99–107.

Corrigan, Robert W., editor. *Comedy: Meaning and Form*. Chandler, 1965.

Covarrubias Orozco, Sebastián de. *Tesoro de la lengua castellana o española*, edited by Felipe C. R. Maldonado, revised by Manuel Camarero, Castalia, 1994.

Cruickshank, Don W. 'The Editing of Spanish Golden-Age Plays from Early Printed Versions'. *Editing the Comedia*, edited by Frank P. Casa and Michael D. McGaha, Michigan Romance Studies, vol. 5, 1985, pp. 52–103.

Curtius, Ernst Robert. *European Literature and the Latin Middle Ag*es. Translated by Willard.

R. Trask, Bolligen-Pantheon, 1953.

D'Antuono, Nancy L. 'The *Comedia* in Italy: Lope's *La discreta enamorada* and its Commedia dell'arte Counterpart'. *LA CHiSPA '81, Selected Proceedings, February 26–28, 1981: The Second Louisiana Conference* on *Hispanic Languages and Literatures*, *Tulane University, New Orleans, 1981*, edited by Gilberto Paolini, The University, 1981, pp. 69–81.

D'Antuono, Nancy L. '*Discreción* as a Remedy Against Adverse Fortune: Boccaccio's Third Story of the Third Day and Lope's *La discreta enamorada*'. *Bulletin of the Comediantes*, vol. 27, no. 1, 1975, pp. 26–35.

D'Antuono, Nancy L. 'Lope de Vega y la *Commedia dell'Arte*: temas y figuras'. *Lope de Vega y los orígenes del teatro español: Actas del 1 congreso internacional sobre Lope de Vega,* edited by Manuel Criado de Val, EDI-6, 1981, pp. 217–28.

D'Antuono, Nancy L. 'The Spanish Golden Age Theatre'. *The Routledge Companion to Commedia dell'Arte*, edited by Judith Chaffee and Olly Crick, Routledge, 2015, pp. 238–45. Originally published as '*Commedia dell'Arte* and the Spanish Golden Age Theatre' in *Theatre Symposium*, vol.1, 1993, pp. 28–35.

Davis, Charles. 'Cruz, Corral de la'. *The Oxford Encyclopedia of Theatre and Performance*. Oxford UP, 2005. *Oxford Reference*. <https://www-oxfordreference-com>.

Davis, Charles. 'Príncipe, Corral del'. *The Oxford Encyclopedia of Theatre and Performance*. Oxford U P, 2005. *Oxford Reference*. <https://www-oxfordreference-com>.

Davis, Charles and J. E. Varey. *Los corrales de comedias y los hospitales de Madrid, 1574–1615: estudio y documentos*. Tamesis, 1997.

Defourneaux, Marcelin. *Daily Life in Spain in the Golden Age*. Translated by Newton Branch, Stanford UP, 1979.

Deleito y Pinuela, José. *Sólo Madrid es Corte*. Espasa-Calpe, 1942.

Deleito y Pinuela, José and Julián San Valero Aparisi. *La mala vida en la España de Felipe IV.* Alianza, 2005.

Diccionario de Autoridades. Real Academia Española, 1726–1739. <https://webfrl.rae.es/DA.html>.

Diccionario de la lengua española. 23rd ed. Real Academia Española. <https://dle.rae.es/>.

Díez Borque, José María. 'Aproximación semiológica a la 'escena' del teatro del Siglo de Oro español'. *Semiología del teatro*, edited by José María Diez Borque and Luciano Garcia Lorenzo, Planeta, 1975, pp. 49–92. Rpt. in *Lope de Vega: el teatro,* I, edited by A. Sánchez Romeralo, Taurus, 1989, pp. 249–90.

Díez Borque, José María. *Sociedad y teatro en la España de Lope de Vega*. Bosch, 1978.

Díez Borque, José María, editor. *Teatros del Siglo de Oro: corrales y coliseos en la Península Ibérica.* Cuadernos de Teatro Clásico, no. 6, Ministerio de Cultura, Instituto Nacional de las Artes Escénicas y de la Música, 1991.

Diez de Revenga, Francisco Javier. *Teatro de Lope de Vega y lírica tradicional, 2a parte.* U de Murcia, 1983.

Dixon, Victor. 'Lope de Vega no conocía el *Decamerón* de Boccaccio'. *El mundo del teatro español en su siglo de oro: ensayos dedicados a John E. Varey,* edited by José María Ruano de la Haza, Ottawa Hispanic Studies, 1989, pp. 185–96.

Domínguez Búrdalo, José. 'La inauguración del corral de comedias de Salamanca: una crónica sobre el auge escénico en la Castilla la Vieja de Felipe III (1603–1607)'. *Bulletin of the Comediantes,* vol. 52, no. 1, 2000, pp. 171–219.

Elliott, John Huxtable. *Spain and Its World: 1500–1700.* Yale UP, 1989.

Fernández Luzón, Antonio. 'Ligar en la iglesia: La misa, un evento social en el Siglo de Oro'. *Historia. National Geographic,* 15 Octubre 2018. <https://historia.nationalgeographic.com.es/a/ligar-iglesia-misa-evento-social-siglo-oro_13191>.

Feros, Antonio and Juan Gelabert, editors. *España en tiempos del Quijote,* Taurus, 2004.

Ferrer Valls, Teresa et al. *Base de datos de comedias mencionadas en la documentación teatral (1540–1700). CATCOM.* <http://catcom.uv.es>.

Fischer-Lichte, Erika. *History of European Drama and Theatre.* Translated by Jo Riley, Routledge, 2002.

Frazer, James George. *The Golden Bough: A Study in Magic and Religion.* Vol. 1, abridged ed., Macmillan, 1958.

Frenk, Margit. *Corpus de la antigua lírica popular hispánica.* Castalia, 1987.

Freud, Sigmund. *Jokes and their Relation to the Unconscious.* Norton, 1960.

Froldi, Rinaldo. *Lope de Vega y la formación de la comedia.* Anaya, 2nd edn, 1973.

Frye, Northrop. '"The Mythos of Spring: Comedy'. *Anatomy of Criticism: Four Essays.* Princeton UP, 1957, pp. 163–86.

Frye, Northrop. 'The Triumph of Time'. *A Natural Perspective. The Development of Shakespearean Comedy and Romance.* Columbia UP, 1965, pp. 72–117.

Gal, Susan. 'A Semiotics of the Public/Private Distinction'. *Differences: A Journal of Feminist Cultural Studies,* vol. 13, no. 1, 2002, pp. 77–95.

García de León Álvarez, María Concepción. 'Corrales de comedias en Castilla-La Mancha: El hospital del Corpus Christi, (Alcázar de San Juan), El hospital de Nuestra Señora de la Piedad (Ocaña), El patio de comedias de Nuestra Señora de la Concepción (Torralba de Calatrava)'. *Amor y erotismo en el teatro de Lope de Vega*, edited by Felipe B. Pedraza Jiménez et al., U de Castilla-La Mancha, 2003, pp. 17–40.

García Lorenzo, Luciano. 'Cuando el gracioso se impone en la comedia: *La discreta enamorada*, de Lope de Vega'. *La construcción de un personaje: El gracioso,* edited by Luciano García Lorenzo. Fundamentos. Colección Arte. Monografías RESAD, 2005, pp. 123–40.

García Santo-Tomás, Enrique, editor. *Arte nuevo de hacer comedias.* By Lope de Vega. Cátedra, 2006.

Gelabert Juan E. 'La restauración de la república'. *España en tiempos del Quijote*, edited by Antonio Feros and Juan Gelabert, Taurus, 2004, pp. 197–234.

Gilmore, David D. *Carnival and Culture: Sex, Symbol, and Status in Spain.* Yale UP, 1998.

Gitlitz, David. 'How to Read a *Comedia*: Branching Points in the Script of Lope's *La discreta enamorada*'. *Bulletin of the Comediantes*, vol. 40, no. 1, 1988, pp. 53–65.

Goffman, Erving. *Frame Analysis: an Essay on the Organization of Experience.* Harvard UP, 1974.

Gomez, Jesús. 'Primeros ecos de Celestina en las comedias de Lope'. *Celestinesca,* vol. 22, no.1, 1998, pp. 3–42.

Greer, Margaret. 'The (Self) Representation of Control in *La dama duende*'. *The Golden Age Comedia: Text, Theory and Performance*, edited by Charles Ganelin and Howard Mancing, Purdue UP, 1994, pp. 87–106.

Greer, Margaret. 'A Tale of Three Cities: the Place of the Theatre in Early Modern Madrid, Paris and London'. *Bulletin of Hispanic Studies*, vol. 77, no. 1, 2000, pp. 391–419.

Hesse, Everett. 'Lope's *La discreta enamorada* and the Generation Gap', *Hispanófila*, vol. 44, 1972, pp. 1–12.

Hollander, Anne. *Seeing Through Clothes.* 1978. U of California P, 1993.

Hsu, Carmen. *Courtesans in the Literature of Spanish Golden Age.* Estudios de Literatura 71. Reichenberger, 2002.

Jekels, Ludwig. 'On the Psychology of Comedy'. *Selected Papers of Ludwig Jekels.* Translated by I. Jarosy, International UP. Rpt. in *Comedy: Meaning and Form*, edited by Robert W. Corrigan, Chandler, 1965, pp. 263–69.

Julià Díez, Santos, *et al. Madrid: historia de una capital.* Alianza, 1994.

Kamen, Henry. *Cambio cultural en la sociedad del Siglo de Oro.* Siglo XXI, 1998.

Kamen, Henry. *Golden Age Spain.* Palgrave Macmillan, 2004.

Kamen, Henry. *Spain: 1469–1714. A Society of Conflict.* 3rd edn, Pearson, 2005.

Kerber, Linda K. 'Separate Spheres, Female Worlds, Woman's Place: The Rhetoric of Women's History'. *Journal of American History,* vol. 75, no. 1, 1988, pp. 9–39.

King. Margaret L. and Albert Rabil, Jr. 'The Other Voice In Early Modern Europe: Introduction To The Series'. *The Education of a Christian Woman: A Sixteenth-Century Manual,* by Juan Luis Vives, edited and translated by Charles Fantazzi. The Other Voice in Early Modern Europe. U of Chicago P, 2000, pp. ix–xxviii.

Kris, Ernst. *Psychoanalytic Exploration in Art.* International UP, 1952.

Landes, Joan B, editor. *Feminism, the Public and the Private.* Oxford UP, 1998.

Larson, Donald R. 'Clothes Encounters: Revealing and Concealing The Body in Lope's *La discreta enamorada'. Bulletin of the Comediantes,* vol. 57, no. 1, 2005, pp. 11–44.

Larson, Donald R. *The Honor Plays of Lope de Vega.* Harvard UP, 1977.

Leggatt, Alexander. *English Stage Comedy, 1490–1990: Five Centuries of a Genre.* Routledge, 1998.

León Pinelo, Antonio de. *Velos antiguos y modernos en los rostros de las Mujeres.* 2 vols. Centro de Investigaciones de Historia Americana, 1966.

Loftis, John Clyde. *Renaissance Drama in England and Spain: Topical Allusion and History Plays.* Princeton UP, 1987.

Lucas Domingo, Javier. 'Asomados a la esperanza'. *Revive Madrid.* <https://www.revivemadrid.com/espacios-emblematicos/balcones-casa-cisneros>.

Lynch, John. *The Hispanic World in Crisis and Change: 1598–1700.* Blackwell, 1994.

Madripedia. 'Calle Marqués de Cubas'. <https://madripedia.wikis.cc/wiki/Calle_Marques_de_Cubas>.

Madroñal, Abraham, 'Glosario de voces comentadas relacionadas con el vestido, el tocado y calzado en el teatro español del Siglo de Oro'. *El vestuario en el teatro clásico español del Siglo de Oro.* Cuadernos de Teatro Clásico, 13–14, 2000, pp. 236–301.

Works Cited

Martínez Aguilar, Miguel. 'Un estudiante florentino, un patio de comedias, y un drama de Mira de Amescua. Reconstrucción de una posible escenificación de *El primer conde de Flandes* en la Salamanca de 1605'. *Escenografía y escenificación en el teatro español del Siglo de Oro: actas del II Curso sobre Teoría y Práctica del Teatro*, edited by Miguel González Dengra and Roberto Castilla Pérez, U de Granada, 2005, pp. 347–82.

McAuley, Gay. *Space in Performance: Making Meaning in the Theatre*. U of Michigan P, 2000.

Menéndez Pelayo, Marcelino. *Calderón y su teatro: conferencias dadas en el Círculo de la Unión Católica*. 3rd edn. Madrid, A. Pérez Dubrull, 1884.

Miaja de la Peña, María Teresa. '*Ex visu* in *La Celestina*. Los personajes como reflejo de la mirada de los otros'. *eHumanista. Journal of Iberian Studies*, vol. 35, 2017, pp. 369–76.

Montesinos, José F. 'La paradoja del "Arte nuevo"'. *Estudios sobre Lope de Vega*. Anaya, 1967, pp. 1–20.

Morley, S. Griswold and Courtney Bruerton. *Cronología de las comedias de Lope de Vega*. Translated by María Rosa Cartes, Gredos, 1968.

Muñoz Sánchez, Juan Ramón. 'Yo he pensado que tienen las novelas los mismos preceptos que las comedias': De Boccaccio a Lope de Vega. *Estelas del Decamerón en Cervantes y la literatura del Siglo de Oro*, edited by Isabel Colón Calderón and David González, U de Málaga, 2013, pp. 163–88.

Olmedo, Félix G. *Las fuentes de 'La vida es sueño'*. Voluntad, 1928.

Orozco Díaz, Emilio. *El teatro y la teatralidad del barroco (ensayo de introducción al tema)*. Planeta, 1969.

Pedraza Jiménez, Felipe. 'Fedra cómica, Fedra trágica: variaciones del mito en Lope'. *Reescrituras de los mitos en la literatura: estudios de mitocrítica y de literatura comparada*, edited by Juan Herrero Cecilia, U de Castilla-La Mancha, 2008, pp. 117–30.

Pedraza Jiménez, Felipe, editor. *Lope de Vega esencial*. Madrid: Taurus, 1990.

Pedraza Jiménez, Felipe. *Lope de Vega: Pasiones, obra y fortuna del 'monstruo de la naturaleza'*. Edaf, 2009.

Peristiany, J. G. and Julian Pitt-Rivers, editors. *Honor and Grace in Anthropology*. Cambridge UP, 1992.

Peyton, Myron. '*La discreta enamorada* as an Example of Dimensional Development in the Comedia'. *Hispania*, vol. 40, no. 2, 1957, pp. 154–62.

Pfister, Manfred. *The Theory and Analysis of Drama*. Translated by John Halliday, Cambridge UP, 1988.

Pitt-Rivers, Julian. 'Honour and Social Status'. *Honour and Shame: the Values of Mediterranean Society*, edited by J. G. Peristiany, U of Chicago P, 1977, pp.19–77.

Regimiento de Infantería 'Tercio Viejo de Sicilia' N° 67. <https://ejercito. defensa.gob.es/unidades/Guipuzcoa/ril67/Historial/HistorialRIL.html>.

Rico, Francisco. Introduction. *El caballero de Olmedo,* by Lope de Vega, Cátedra, 2008, pp. 13–101.

Rico, Francisco. *El pequeño mundo del hombre: varia fortuna de una idea en las letras españolas*. Castalia, 1970.

Ringrose, David. 'Madrid, capital imperial (1561–1833)'. *Madrid: historia de una capital,* edited by Santos Juliá et al., Alianza, 1994, pp. 120–251.

Roca de Togores, Mariano, marqués de Molíns. *Obras*. Vol. VI. *Discursos Académicos*. Madrid, M. Tello, 1881–1890.

Rodríguez G. de Ceballos, Alfonso and José Ramón Nieto González. 'Patios de comedias en Salamanca, Zamora, y Ciudad Rodrigo'. *Calderón: Actas del Congreso Internacional sobre Calderón y el teatro español del siglo de oro,* edited by Luciano García Lorenzo, vol. 3, Consejo Superior de Investigaciones Científicas, 1983, pp. 1673–83.

Roso Díaz, José. *Tipología de engaños en la obra dramática de Lope de Vega*. U de Extremadura, 2002.

Rothberg, Irving P. 'Algo más sobre Plauto, Terencio y Lope'. *Lope de Vega y los orígenes del teatro español: Actas del 1 congreso internacional sobre Lope de Vega,* edited by Manuel Criado de Val. EDI-6, 1981, pp. 61–65.

Rothberg, Irving P. 'El agente cómico de Lope de Vega'. *Hispanófila,* no. 16, Número especial dedicado a Lope de Vega, 1962, pp. 69–90.

Rozas, Juan Manuel. *Significado y doctrina del 'Arte nuevo' de Lope de Vega*. Sociedad General Española de Librería, 1976.

Ruano de la Haza, José María and John J. Allen. *Los teatros comerciales del siglo XVII y la escenificación de la comedia*. Castalia, 1994.

Ruiz, Teófilo F. *Spanish Society: 1400–1600*. Longman, 2001.

Samson, Alexander and Jonathan Thacker, editors. *A Companion to Lope de Vega*. Tamesis, 2008.

Schevill, Rudolph. *The Dramatic Art of Lope de Vega: Together with* La Dama Boba. U of California P, 1918.

Segal, Erich. *The Death of Comedy*. Harvard UP, 2001.

Segal, Erich. *Roman Laughter: The Comedy of Plautus*. Harper, 1968.

Serrano Poncela, Segundo. 'Amor y apetito en el teatro clásico español'. *Asomante,* no. 4, 1953, pp. 46–62.

Shergold, N. D. 'Ganassa and the *Commedia dell'Arte* in Sixteenth-Century Spain'. *Modern Language Review,* vol. 51, 1956, pp. 359–68.

Skrine, Peter N. *The Baroque: Literature and Culture in Seventeenth-Century Europe*. Methuen, 1978, pp. 1–24.

Sommaia, Girolamo da. *Diario de un estudiante de Salamanca,* edited by George Haley, U de Salamanca, 1977.

Stewart, Frank Henderson. *Honor*. U of Chicago P, 1994.

Stroud, Matthew D. 'Gender and the Gaze: Sor Juana, Lacan, and Spanish Baroque Poetry'. *Calíope,* vol. 9, no. 2, 2003, pp. 61–74.

Taylor, Scott K. *Honor and Violence in Golden Age Spain*. Yale UP, 2008.

Tejeiro Fuentes, Miguel Angel. 'Portugal en la vida y obra de Cervantes'. *Revista de estudios extremeños,* vol. 72, no. 2, 2006, pp. 683–700.

Templin, Ernest. *The Exculpation of* Yerros por Amores *in the Spanish Comedia*. Publications of the University of California at Los Angeles in Languages and Literature, vol. 1, no. 1, U of California P, 1933, pp. 1–50.

Templin, Ernest. 'The Mother in the Comedia of Lope de Vega'. *Hispanic Review,* vol. 3, no. 3, Lope de Vega Number, 1935, pp. 219–44.

Thacker, Jonathan. *A Companion to Golden Age Theater*. Tamesis, 2007.

Thacker, Jonathan. *Role-Play and the World as Stage in the* Comedia. Liverpool UP, 2002.

Thomas, Keith. *Ends of Life. Roads to Fulfillment in Early Modern England*. Oxford UP, 2009.

Thomson, James K. J. *Decline in History: The European Experience*. Polity, 1998.

Thurston, Herbert. 'Holy Year of Jubilee'. *The Catholic Encyclopedia,* vol. 8. Appleton, 1910. <http://www.newadvent.org/cathen/08531c.htm>.

Umpierre, Gustavo. *Songs in the Plays of Lope de Vega: A Study of Their Dramatic Function*. Tamesis, 1975.

Uriarte, José Angel. *Edición crítica de* La discreta enamorada *de Lope Félix de Vega Carpio*. 1971. Universidad de Deusto, Memoria de Licenciatura.

Vega Carpio, Lope Félix de. *Arte nuevo de hacer comedias*. Biblioteca Virtual Cervantes. <http://www.cervantesvirtual.com/obra-visor/arte-nuevo-de-hacer-comedias-en-este-tiempo--0/html/ffb1e6c0-82b1-11df-acc7-002185ce6064_4.html>.

Vickery, Amanda. 'Golden Age to Separate Spheres? A Review of the Categories and Chronology of English Women's History', *The Historical Journal,* vol. 36, no. 2, 1993, pp. 383–414.

Vilanova, Antonio. 'El tema del gran teatro del mundo'. *Biblioteca de la Real Academia de Buenas Letras de Barcelona,* vol. 23, 1950, pp. 153–88.

Vives, Juan Luis. *The Education of a Christian Woman: A Sixteenth-Century Manual,* edited and translated by Charles Fantazzi. The Other Voice in Early Modern Europe. U of Chicago P, 2000.

Vossler, Karl. *Lope de Vega y su tiempo.* 2nd edn, Revista de Occidente, 1940.

Wagschal, Steven. *The Literature of Jealousy in the Age of Cervantes.* U of Missouri P, 2007, pp. 76–91.

Wardropper, Bruce W. 'La comedia española del Siglo de Oro'. *Teoría de la comedia,* edited by Elder Olson, Ariel, 1978, pp, 183–242.

Wardropper, Bruce W. 'Lope de Vega's Urban Comedy'. *Hispanófila.* Número especial dedicado a la comedia, vol. 1, 1974, pp. 47–61.

Warnke, Frank J. 'The World as Theatre: Baroque Variations on a Traditional Topos'. *Festschrift für Edgar Mertner,* edited by Bernhard Fabian *et al.* Fink, 1969, pp. 185–200.

Weiger, John G. *The Valencian Dramatists of Spain's Golden Age.* Twayne, 1976.

Williamsen, Amy. 'The Comic Function of Two Mothers: Belisa and Angela'. *Bulletin of the Comediantes,* vol. 36, no. 2, 1984, pp. 167–74.

Williamsen, Vern G. 'The Woman Characters in Lope de Vega's *La discreta enamorada'. Proceedings of the Second Annual Golden Age Spanish Drama Symposium: Texto y Espectáculo,* edited by Richard Ford, UTEP, 1982, pp. 127–43.

Ziomek, Henry K. *A History of Spanish Golden Age Drama.* UP of Kentucky, 2015.